PUBLIC ADMINISTRATION AND INFORMATION TECHNOLOGY

Christopher G. Reddick, PhD

Associate Professor and Department Chair
Department of Public Administration
The University of Texas at San Antonio

JONES & BARTLETT
LEARNING

World Headquarters

Jones & Bartlett Learning	Jones & Bartlett Learning	Jones & Bartlett Learning
5 Wall Street	Canada	International
Burlington, MA 01803	6339 Ormindale Way	Barb House, Barb Mews
978-443-5000	Mississauga, Ontario L5V 1J2	London W6 7PA
info@jblearning.com	Canada	United Kingdom
www.jblearning.com		

Jones & Bartlett Learning books and products are available through most bookstores and online booksellers. To contact Jones & Bartlett Learning directly, call 800-832-0034, fax 978-443-8000, or visit our website, www.jblearning.com.

Substantial discounts on bulk quantities of Jones & Bartlett Learning publications are available to corporations, professional associations, and other qualified organizations. For details and specific discount information, contact the special sales department at Jones & Bartlett Learning via the above contact information or send an email to specialsales@jblearning.com.

This publication is designed to provide accurate and authoritative information in regard to the Subject Matter covered. It is sold with the understanding that the publisher is not engaged in rendering legal, accounting, or other professional service. If legal advice or other expert assistance is required, the service of a competent professional person should be sought.

Production Credits
Publisher: Michael Brown
Editorial Assistant: Teresa Reilly
Editorial Assistant: Chloe Falivene
Production Manager: Tracey McCrea
Associate Editor: Maro Gartside
Marketing Manager: Grace Richards
Associate Marketing Manager: Jody Sullivan
Manufacturing and Inventory Control Supervisor: Amy Bacus
Composition: Cenveo Publisher Services
Cover Design: Kristin E. Parker
Cover Image: © Neo Edmund/ShutterStock, Inc.
Printing and Binding: Malloy, Inc.
Cover Printing: Malloy, Inc.

Library of Congress Cataloging-in-Publication Data
Reddick, Christopher G.
  Public administration and information technology / by Christopher G. Reddick.
    p. cm.
  Includes bibliographical references and index.
  ISBN-13: 978-0-7637-8460-7 (pbk.)
  ISBN-10: 0-7637-8460-5 (pbk.)
  1. Public administration—Data processing. 2. Information technology—Political aspects. 3. Internet in public administration. 4. Electronic government information. 5. Government Web sites. I. Title.
  JF1525.A8R37 2012
  352.3'80285—dc23
                              2011014856

6048

Printed in the United States of America
15 14 13 12 11   10 9 8 7 6 5 4 3 2 1

This book is dedicated to Cathy Obien.

Contents

Public Administration and Information Technology explores the important influence of information technology (IT) on public sector organizations as well as the major issues that public administrators need to know concerning the impact of IT on their organizations. Specifically, there is an examination of the external environment that influences IT and public administration such as e-democracy, e-participation, and e-governance. There is also a discussion of the internal environmental issues of IT and public administration such as leadership, organizational change, and enterprise architecture. Finally, some of the most important issues in the domain of IT and public administration are examined: e-procurement, e-commerce, human resources, privacy, and information security. This book takes a sociotechnical perspective, arguing that an understanding of both the external and internal environments, and the technology used, is needed to grasp the most important issues in the realm of IT and public administration.

Public Administration and Information Technology is essential reading for those teaching courses in IT and public administration. It can also be used as a supplementary textbook for courses that explore innovation in public sector reform through the use of IT. This book could be used in a management information systems class where the importance of public sector IT is stressed. Finally, this book is ideal for practitioners who want the latest research on IT and public administration. Chapter objectives and discussion questions are included in each chapter. Additionally, the main points of each chapter are demonstrated within opening and closing case studies. Particularly innovative in this textbook is the use of survey research infused in each chapter that delves into the important issues of IT and public administration. Survey research provides real-world relevance to many of the issues discussed in the chapters. Finally, *Public Administration and Information Technology* examines both the external and internal environment, bridging the research on IT and politics with the study of the bureaucracy, which are both essential to the field of public administration.

Christopher G. Reddick
San Antonio, Texas

Christopher G. Reddick is an associate professor and Chair of the Department of Public Administration at the University of Texas at San Antonio, USA. Dr. Reddick's research and teaching interests are in information technology and public sector organizations. Some of his publications can be found in *Government Information Quarterly*, *Electronic Government*, and the *International Journal of Electronic Government Research*. Dr. Reddick recently edited the two-volume book entitled *Handbook of Research on Strategies for Local E-Government Adoption and Implementation: Comparative Studies*. He is also author of the book *Homeland Security Preparedness and Information Systems*.

Public Administration and Information Technology

Opening Case Study

President Obama's Vision for IT and the Federal Government

Some have argued that President Barack Obama's technology agenda is game changing (McClure and Dorris, 2010). The agenda brings together collaboration, participation, and transparency to government through information technology (IT). Collaboration can be seen through free tools and technologies that provide fast, cheap, and effective support to increase citizen interaction with the federal government. In addition, social media networks such as Twitter, Facebook, MySpace, and YouTube are now used by many federal agencies. Finally, through increased participation there has been a deluge of data provided to the public, which provides more opportunities for citizens to interact with their governments. However, with this increase in collaboration, participation, and transparency there are some opportunities and challenges.

Disclosure Management

Federal government databases have publicly available data intertwined with personally indefinable information and other protected data. The time period for releasing this information is shortened, and this information can be mashed-up with other information. As a result there is a risk of not having the proper safeguards in place before posting information.

Data Sharing

Data sharing is increasing in the Government 2.0 environment through websites such as www.data.gov. There also is a need for government to package the data, which creates challenges between information ownership and control.

Data Quality

The accuracy, integrity, timeliness, and reliability of federal government data and information are a recurring problem, and this becomes an increasingly challenging problem as more data are placed on the Web. These data may have errors and also could be dated and irrelevant.

Multichannel Information

Government must increasingly be able to interact with the public in different delivery channels such as Internet, phone, face-to-face, and printed materials. Governments must find ways to connect with the public in these different contact channels.

Data Analysis

Because of the large volume of data and the movement for greater performance and accountability in government, there will be an emergence of knowledge management technology, or technology that is able to analyze data to produce usable results for decision making. This will include search queries, which will enable citizens to get the right information faster with their government.

Disruption

These innovative technologies can disrupt the status quo, thereby requiring organizations to be more agile and flexible in this changing environment.

As part of introducing his agenda, President Obama also gathered leading chief executives from many high profile companies to get lessons from them on what they should do to harness the full power of technology to increase efficiency and to improve customer service (Holleyman, 2010). Those executives listed the following as important for Obama's IT agenda:

1. To try not to resolve everything at once and to focus on smaller projects that can have an impact
2. To maintain interoperability, which is also critical for the advancement of Obama's agenda, in which systems are able to communicate and work together
3. To look at the advantages of existing technology rather than creating new systems from scratch
4. To ensure that any system implemented focuses on privacy and security of federal government data

Chapter Objectives

There are five primary objectives to this introductory chapter showing the importance of information technology (IT) and public administration:

1. To introduce the importance of IT to modern public administration
2. To introduce the external environment of IT and public administration
3. To introduce the internal environmental influence of IT on public administration
4. To examine the differences between the public and private sectors
5. To introduce the major issues that public organizations face in IT and public administration

Introduction

This book deals with the important subject of IT and its influence on public administration. IT influences every aspect of our daily lives from simply checking bus schedules online to banking over the Internet. IT influences our work lives as well through checking e-mail or preparing an important presentation. Much of our lives have become easier as a result of IT and its impact on society, but we also face numerous challenges, such as the disparity in access to IT between different socio-economic groups, the different skill levels of individuals that use IT, and issues of privacy of our personal information.

This book examines IT and its influence on public sector organizations. The U.S. government is composed of 50 state governments, numerous local governments, and the federal government with is multitude of departments and agencies. All these governments have incorporated IT into their operations. Some of them use simple systems such as spreadsheets, word processors, and e-mail, whereas other public organizations use complicated database systems and advanced information systems. The diversity in the needs of all these governments and their use of IT is enormous. As an example, the U.S. federal government is introducing a tremendous amount of change through the use of IT to create more efficient and transparent government, as seen in the opening case study.

There is a great need to study IT and public administration, given that most of the textbooks on the market examine IT and its influence on private sector organizations. As this book argues, the public sector is much different from private sector entities; therefore, it deserves to have a book that focuses exclusively on this sector. As discussed, the goals of private sector organizations are usually well known, to sell a good or generate a profit, whereas in the public sector, given the diverse interests it must serve, generating a profit is not feasible or even desirable. In addition, the outside environment influences public sector agencies more so than private sector entities, and this provides a unique constraint on what can be accomplished.

In addition, there is a great need to study IT and its impact on public administration given the rise of the Internet and its use in modern public organizations. The Internet has made it possible for organizations and people to be connected together, creating a virtual government. This was not possible until around the mid-1990s with the rapid rise of the Internet through commercialization, creating broad use by the general population. This networked organization has changed many functions of the workplace and makes it worthy to study the influence of IT on public administration in this new and important environment.

What Is Public Administration and IT?

Public administration is concerned with the goal of advancing management and policies of government. Public administration is what takes place after the election, in which the day-to-day business of governing actually occurs. Public administration also deals with management of public programs and is the study of government decision making, the analysis of the policies themselves, the various inputs that have produced them, and the inputs necessary to produce alternative policies (Henry, 2007).

IT is the study, design, development, application, implementation, support, or management of computer-based information systems, particularly software applications and computer hardware (Laudon and Laudon, 2009). IT deals with the use of computers and computer software to securely convert, store, protect, process, transmit, input, output, and retrieve information. IT can contribute toward the operational and strategic activities of the public sector organization (Boynton et al., 1994). Moreover, IT can provide cost reduction, management support, strategic planning, cost-reduction applications, management support, and, most importantly, outreach to constituencies such as citizens, policymakers, employees, and contracts.

Essentially, public administration and IT deal with the use of information systems to shape organizational change in government. Much of the literature on public administration and IT argues for the transformation of government through IT. This book focuses on how IT has influenced almost every functional area of public administration, with a specific focus on organizational change.

Theories of IT and Public Administration

Here we review the three common theories of public administration and IT. Each theory examines the impact of technology on social and organizational change.

Technological Determinism

One important driver of change in information systems is the theory of technology determinism (Volti, 1992; Smith and Marx, 1994). This implies that when a new technology appears it creates change and will be adopted by public administration.

For example, the automobile created suburbia, and the birth control pill produced a sexual revolution. Therefore, inventions sometimes are viewed as taking on a life of their own, causing dramatic social and economic change. For example, technology determinisms can be seen through the implementation of enterprise resource planning systems in government; these systems connect business functions such as human resources and purchasing. Many vendors and consultants stress the benefits of enterprise resource planning systems regardless of the organizational context (Grant et al., 2006). This is most exemplified in the statistics that vendors often quote, explaining the reduction in costs and increases in performance of the public sector organization as a result of enterprise resource planning implementation. This type of "selling" of the technology for the sake of changing the organization is known as the technology determinism theory.

Reinforcement Theory

Another theory of technology and social change is the reinforcement theory. This theory argues that administrators implement IT if it supports their view of the organization change (Sherrod, 1971). This theory comes from the political science literature that examines why voters seek out candidates with which they agree. Therefore, citizens choose candidates that have a similar position to them on the issues. The theory applies for the adoption of IT in the public sector; technology is adopted if it agrees with the view of the public manager on the future direction of the organization. For example, if the chief information office, the highest IT executive in an organization, does not believe a new information system will work in the organization, he or she most likely will not adopt the system.

Sociotechnical Theory

The third and most important perspective from the point of this book is the sociotechnical perspective. This sociotechnical perspective argues that organizations are made up of people in the social system that use tools, techniques, and knowledge to shape the organizational change (Pasmore, 1988). The sociotechnical system states that technical change is influenced by the demands of the external environment that impacts information systems change in an organization. The sociotechnical perspective is the most commonly used theory in public administration to demonstrate the impact of technology on organizational change (Perry and Danziger, 1980; Norris and Moon, 2005). This perspective is unique and important for this book because it implies public managers need to know IT from both the technical perspective, understanding the technology that is being implemented, and the social perspective. The closing case study at the end of this chapter shows the impact of the change in baby boomer population and IT use as seen through the Social Security Administration.

Why Study IT in Public Administration?

We study public administration and IT for four important reasons: how it impacts trust in government, the sheer money spent on IT, the lack of performance of existing systems, and the increased demands on public managers.

Trust in Government

According to the Gallup Poll, we know that trust in all levels of government has fallen in recent years. This is even more pronounced as a result of the recession in the late 2000s in the United States, as Gallup has examined the trends in trust in federal and state government overtime (Jones, 2009). In 2009 trust in state government was at an all time low. The Gallup Poll asked the question, "How much trust and confidence do you have in the government of the state where you live when it comes to handling state problems." The ratings for a great deal/fair amount of trust indicate that trust was down from 67% in 2004 to 51% in 2009. This decline in trust is due to the economic downturn during this time, which means there were budget cuts to state programs. This lack of trust influences citizens and their confidence in their government. It is important for elected officials to increase trust in government to provide confidence in governing institutions. IT is one way to make the public sector more responsive to citizens, by being able to deliver services faster and more efficiently. In addition, IT can be used to create more open and transparent government because information on governments can be made freely available and easily posted online.

Money Spent on IT and Public Administration

Another reason we study IT and public administration is the sheer amount of money spent on IT projects. President Barack Obama's budget for fiscal year 2011 requested $79.4 billion in spending on IT projects, which is a 1.2% increase from what was proposed in the fiscal 2010 budget (Bain et al., 2010). The Obama Administration proposed an increase in the number of IT projects in this budget. For example, for fiscal year 2010, 781 IT projects worth $40.3 billion were proposed. For fiscal year 2011 the Obama Administration proposed 809 major IT projects worth $40.4 billion. With this modest increase, Obama plans on increasing money to IT efforts that promote more open government and technology modernization for fiscal year 2011. For example, one budget request calls for launching a new tracking tool with daily updates that would allow the public to see aggregate spending by agency and geographical area. The hope of this is to allow the public greater understanding of how government works and make more responsible spending decisions. In addition, the Obama Administration proposed a new outcome-focused metric for information security performance for agencies to be in compliance with the Federal Information Security Management Act.

Historically, a number of IT projects and their associated budgets appear on the Office of Management and Budget's Management Watch List (U.S. Government Accountability Office, 2010). The number of projects on the Management Watch List increased by 239 projects and was $13 billion for fiscal year 2009; this represents a significant portion of the budget. To improve transparency into the oversight of IT investment in June 2009, the Office of Management and Budget deployed a website known as the IT Dashboard (http://it.usaspending.gov), which replaced the Management Watch List. The data displayed in the IT Dashboard are intended to provide a real-time perspective on the performance of these investments, as well as a historical perspective. Therefore, given the magnitude of spending on IT projects and the scope of its impact on government, it is essential to study public administration and IT.

Lack of Performance of Systems

There has been tremendous growth in spending on IT investments in public sector organizations, but what is the impact of this growth in spending on the relative performance of public sector organizations (Lee and Perry, 2002)? Investing in IT can help the public sector improve the efficiency of internal operations through automation. IT can also improve the quality of existing public services, creating new types of services that were not previously available. The improvement in government performance overall is one of the perceived net benefits of IT spending. Empirical results indicate a connection, at the state government level, between IT investment of the state and an increase in its economic performance. With American society increasingly focused on performance of its government, IT is one method of enhancing overall public sector performance.

Increased Demands by Public Sector Managers for IT

The final reason to study public administration and IT is the increased demands placed on public sector workers for results. To meet these demands, government needs to use IT to translate goals into outcomes. Therefore, public managers must be cognizant of the impact of IT on their organization. For example, the National Association of Schools of Public Affairs and Administration recognizes the need of public affairs programs to provide knowledge of IT to master's students. There is no doubt that knowledge of IT is important to be an effective manager, and this book discusses its importance for public sector organizations.

Differences Between Public and Private Sectors

There are unique differences between the public and private sectors, as noted in the literature, and this explains why it is important to study public administration and IT (Rainey and Bozeman, 2000). First, public sector agencies typically have more concerns and issues than their private sector counterparts. Therefore, their goals are usually more complex and ambiguous than business firms. Public sector agencies typically have vague, hard-to-measure, multiple, and even conflicting goals with which they must contend. This is usually a product of the lack of profit indicators and incentives for the public sector due to political oversight and multiple interests that need to authorize programs. Second, public sector agencies typically have more formalization, such as excessive rules and procedures that need to be enforced, which is called "red tape." Public agencies, therefore, are usually associated with an excessive amount of rules or red tape that may impede its performance. A third difference between the public and private sectors is that public agencies have more formalized personnel procedures, purchases processes, and other administrative tasks that are regulated by central administrative agencies. There is typically more external oversight of public agencies for personnel and purchasing decisions. Fourth, most studies of work-related satisfaction indicate a lower rating in the public sector than in the private sector, especially at the management levels. This poses a challenge for recruiting and retaining of top workers for the public sector agencies.

Financially, public organizations are funded by government, and private organizations are those owned and funded through sales or private donations (Perry and Rainey, 1988). Organizations that overlap represent mixed types of government corporations such as public utilities and government contractors. The degree of external control by major institutions, such as political authorities and economic markets, is a significant distinction between the two sectors. Ownership of sources of funding reflects a degree of control, and public agencies have a greater degree of institutional control than their private sector counterparts. Privately owned and funded organizations are more likely to be influenced by economic markets.

In addition to these general differences, there are four important distinctions in which public organizations are different from the private sector in regards to public management (Boyne, 2002). These distinctions that public managers face provide challenges for adopting and promoting IT projects in their agencies.

Public Agency and Organizational Environments

As discussed, there is greater complexity in public agencies because of the many stakeholders with which they must contend. Public agencies are also more permeable, meaning they are open systems that can be easily influenced by external events; this poses unique challenges for public managers. Public agencies also are instable, meaning they have political constraints and there is consistent pressure to achieve quick results because of election cycles. Finally, public agencies also face the absence of competitive pressures. Public agencies normally have few rivals, and when there is competition, government frequently enjoys a dominant position. As a result, public managers face a unique and constrained operating environment that they must contend with.

Public Agency and Organizational Goals

Public managers face multiple goals imposed upon them with numerous stakeholders to satisfy. Private organizations pursue a single goal of generating a greater profit, whereas public agencies get pushed and pulled in many directions. In addition, the presence of multiple and sometimes vague goals is a challenge for public sector managers. As a result of this goal ambiguity, it is difficult to know if results are being achieved over the short and long run.

Public Agency and Organizational Structures

The internal characteristics of public agencies, such as more bureaucracy, more red tape, and low managerial autonomy, provide unique challenges for public managers. Public organizations normally have more formal procedures for decision making and less flexibility and are more risk averse than their private sector counterparts. As discussed, public agencies typically have more red tape, which can provide an unnecessary and counterproductive obsession with rules rather than achieving results. Finally, public agencies have lower managerial autonomy, which means public managers have less freedom to react and see fit the circumstances they face.

Public and Managerial Values

Staff attitudes toward work have an influence on public managers' ability to lead and manage. Public managers are believed to be less materialistic than their private sector counterparts and less likely to be motivated by financial rewards. Second, public managers have a greater desire to serve the public and promote the public interest. Finally, there is a lower organizational commitment in the public sector largely because of the inflexible personnel rules and weak link to performance and pay.

Of all the distinctions between the public and private sectors, one that has very serious implications for management is the differences in views of risk between the sectors. There is a familiar view that public sector managers are risk averse, in that they are unwilling to take a chance on something new and different for their organization, compared with their private sector counterparts. According to research, several factors lead to taking more risk in public sector organizations (Bozeman and Kingsley, 1998). First, public managers who trust their employees are likely to have employees who will take calculated risks. Second, if the goals of the public organization are known and stable, people will take risks. Third, red tape undercuts risk because this detracts from managers being entrepreneurial and endorses change. All these differences in the public and private sectors overall translate into important issues for public managers to understand.

Framework for Understanding IT and Public Administration

This book covers three dimensions of IT and public administration examining the external environment, the internal environment, and the major issues that public organizations face (**Figure 1-1**). As discussed, the overriding theory we use to explain public administration and IT is the sociotechnical perspective. Each theme is briefly introduced. All three areas are interrelated; what happens to one area has an impact on another area. These areas are one way of thinking about IT and public administration; they are examined in turn and are the focused discussion of this book.

External Environment

As mentioned, public sector organizations have many diverse interests with which to contend. The external environment can be divided into three factors that influence IT and public administration. The literature on IT and public administration has long argued for the importance of examining the external environment; because change does not merely happen internally within government, many external influences drive IT adoption (Bretschneider, 1990).

First, there is democracy and its influence on IT and public administration. The Internet and other information and communication technologies (ICTs) have influenced the way democracies function. For instance, the Internet can be used as a medium for political candidates running for office to reach a broad audience. They can also target specific individuals they might want to get donations or support from for their election campaign. In addition, the general election in the United States in 2008 was heavily influenced by ICT as seen through a record number of donations to the then presidential candidate Barack Obama. It was also used as a source for

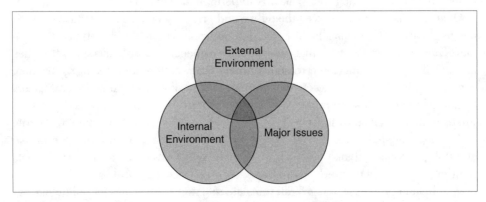

Figure 1-1 *Public Administration and IT Through the Sociotechnical Perspective*

online information on candidates through new social media such as Facebook and Twitter. Indeed, the ways elections are conducted today have been greatly influenced by ICT even in the way citizens vote in the United States at polling places. Some of the most important issues and challenges of e-democracy are discussed in this book.

Another external environmental influence is the participation of citizens in the political and policymaking process. ICT has enabled citizens to participate in their government much more easily as a result of advances in this technology. For instance, before the Internet, proposed policies would be distributed in paper form, which of course is expensive and time consuming to deliver. With ICT, governments can display and customize information for citizens, creating a more transparent government. The policymaking cycle has changed as a result of ICT, where citizens can mobilize support for or against a new government policy because of new social media such as blogs.

The final area of the external environment is e-governance. E-governance is the impact of ICTs on the delivery of services to citizens by their government. E-governance focuses more on how IT impacts change, not just within the organization but externally both politically and institutionally. With advances in ICT, public service delivery has fundamentally changed. It is possible for a government to provide information or a service to its residents through the Internet. This can range from simple things such as looking up a city council's agenda online, to more advanced functions such as renewing a vehicle registration online. E-governance is supposed to create more transparent government and is said, by some researchers, to increase trust and confidence in their governing institutions. E-governance can be driven externally by the interests of citizens and their needs. The second part of this book examines the internal environment of IT and public administration with a focus on leadership and management, e-government, and enterprise architecture.

Internal Environment

Unlike the external environment where change is driven by external stimuli, the internal environment examines change from within public sector organizations. The first area covered is leadership and management and its impact on IT and public administration. We often hear there is a lack of leaders in public sector organizations. Leaders are critical for these organizations because they can move and change them in a defined direction. This book argues that successful IT adoption in public organizations occurs when leaders support the importance of IT to organizational success. Leaders need to provide the vision of where IT fits into the mission of their organization. Management also plays a critical role, because management is responsible for making sure IT projects are properly implemented and produce results. Effective management, according to the literature, is a critical catalyst for the development of IT in public administration.

A second internal environment stimulus is that of e-government and organizational change. Unlike e-governance, e-government deals specifically with the application of IT to public sector organizations. The focus on e-government is more on change within the organization. The e-government literature examines best practices and how this technology transforms organizations. E-government through ICT is said to change the internal structures of government by creating more efficient and effective organizations. Compared to e-governance, e-government deals more with the "nuts and bolts" of ICT application in the public sector. Examples of e-government are the implementation of an information system within a department that can communicate across different departments and share information. The literature on e-government has some scholars arguing it will transform the organization, and it has others arguing it will produce more incremental change.

The third internal environmental influence is enterprise architecture, or the use of IT to map the business processes of the organization. For IT to be integrated holistically with the organization, there needs to be a blueprint mapping out all its functions and how technology fits into these functional arrangements. The U.S. federal government, one of the largest purchasers of IT in the world, is a strong advocate for enterprise architecture because they want new information systems to work in conjunction with the mission of the department or agency. Enterprise architecture is a way to integrate information systems into the mission of the organization, and it is discussed in this book.

Major Issues

Any introductory book on IT and public administration cannot cover all the major issues public organizations face. This book has a selection of what I believe are some of the most important present and future issues to consider for this important topic. First, there is a discussion of e-procurement, e-commerce, and online financial reporting. All three areas involve the use of public resources to provide information or purchase goods to fulfill a service request. E-procurement is the use of ICTs to impact the purchasing function in public organizations. This can range from online ordering systems to the removal of paper-based procurement with electronic processing and digital signatures. E-commerce is using ICT for citizens to complete a transaction online. Unlike e-government, e-commerce involves a transaction or payment of money for a public service. An example of e-commerce is paying for a public utility bill online or registering a car over the Internet. Finally, online financial reporting is the use of the Internet to post information about the financial status of government online. This can take the form of a city's audited financial statements or annual budget being posted on the Web.

The second major issue covered in this book is human resource information systems in public sector organizations. As the result of ICT, the human resources function has been greatly influenced. Some common examples are through the recruitment process, where job advertisement can now be immediately posted online. Employees can look up their benefit plans online or change their plans during the annual enrollment period. Human resource information systems can be used to create databases on employees or to look at trends in employment that might be of value to the government. Essentially, IT in the human resources department has created a virtual department that is explored in this book.

The third and final major issue covered is perhaps the most important for public sector organizations, that of privacy and security of IT. Because we are in a networked and interconnected world, there is great value of knowing the personal information of individuals. For example, if politicians know the profile of a likely voter they can more effectively target that voter in campaign advertisements. Or if a government knows what information and services citizens want, they can better provide these services if they can collect personally identifiable information online. The issue becomes what is being done with personal information, because at the time of collecting the information the individual may not know exactly what it is being used for. Information security is another important issue related to privacy, examining what protections are in place to secure information systems of public organizations. Both privacy and information security are critical issues as governments move forward adopting IT in their public agencies.

Summary

This introductory chapter for *Public Administration and Information Technology* sets the context of the book and provides a framework for thinking about IT and public administration. This book uses the sociotechnical perspective because of its heavy influence on the field, in which readers need to understand both the social and technological aspects of IT to understand its influence on organizational change. There are three parts to the book examining the external environment, internal environment, and major issues in the field. Each part is important to know because of the unique way public organizations are influenced by environmental pressures. One needs to appreciate the unique context of IT in public sector organizations and how it is different from the private sector, and this book addresses this important issue. The purpose of the book is to provide a broad overview of the theories and major issues in this important and growing area of public administration.

Discussion Questions

1. What are the three main theories of public administration and IT? What theory is the most useful?
2. Why study public administration and IT?
3. What are the most important differences between the public and private sectors and how do they frame the study of public administration and information technology?

Closing Case Study

SSA and New Baby Boomer Claims

The Social Security Administration (SSA) has increased its use of electronic transactions, expanding by 50% from fiscal year 2008 to 2009 (Jackson, 2010). The SSA is struggling to keep up with demand, despite a record number of staff increases, and so is increasingly relying on automated services to meet this demand. Three important factors have influenced increased demand for SSA services: a retiring baby boomer population, an aging workforce, and the worst economic crisis in the late 2000s since the Great Depression. This problem is especially acute as baby boomers reach their retirement and disability-prone years in tough economic times.

For fiscal year 2010, the SSA estimated it would receive over 375,000 more retirement, auxiliary, and survivors' claims and over 730,000 more disability claims than were estimated only 2 years before. SSA estimates that over the next 10 years it will see a 14% increase in claims for Old Age and Survivors Insurance, Disability Insurance, and Supplemental Security Income, rising from a combined total of 9.4 million claims in fiscal year 2008 to 10.7 million in 2017.

Budgets and staffing have not kept pace with these increases. SSA has responded to these pressures with a number of strategies, including increased use of online, telephone, and video services; load balancing by shifting work between offices; and deferring less essential jobs. However, key among these strategies are online services. Online services make sense because the public is increasingly demanding them when they conduct business, without having to wait on the phone on hold or take leave from work to travel to an office and wait to meet in person with an agency representative. In addition to being convenient for the public, this approach also reduces the average time spent by employees processing claims. The SSA reported that in fiscal years 2008 and 2009 the total number of electronic transactions jumped from 4 million to 6.1 million. Electronic filings for retirement benefits went from about 400,000 to 833,000 during that period and now account for nearly one-third of total retirement applications being filed. Online filings now account for 83% of total retirement claims growth.

Even though the SSA did not market the option to file for disability benefits online when it launched iClaim, online disability applications have also increased from less than 10% just a few years ago to nearly 25%. SSA launched an improved version of iClaim in December 2008 and saw an immediate increase in the number of retirement applications filed online. In fiscal year 2009, more than 30% of retirement applications were filed online, nearly twice as many as in the prior year.

Part I

The External Environment

Chapter 2

E-Democracy

Opening Case Study

Maryland's New Social Media Campaign Rule

A new law enacted in 2010 in Maryland shows the influence new social media technologies have on political campaigns (Wilkinson, 2010). Maryland now requires political candidates to identify their online campaign material. This legislation passed by a 11-1 vote by the state General Assembly's Joint Committee on Administrative, Executive and Legislative Review after a hearing last month. Proponents argued that by passing this law early it allows candidates for the fall 2010 election to know the rules up front. The law expands the current campaign material law to include electronic media such as social media sites, microblogs, and online ads created by a political committee, making them subject to "authority line" requirements. This authority line is a declaration of approval listing the committee that paid for the space and the campaign treasurer's name. This has been previously placed on broadcast in print, television, and radio advertisements. These ads typically read "I'm Candidate Joe Smith, and I approve this message" or "paid by the Committee to Elect Joe Smith."

With this new law, Maryland is the first state to extend the rule to cover the online realm. Facebook applauded the new law, viewing it as providing clarity on the legal use of social media in campaigns. Other states such as Wisconsin, California, and Texas are expected to follow and produce similar legislation.

Most states have ignored social media such as Facebook and Twitter when it comes to political communication.

Social media is just appearing on radar screens in state campaign finance and has been only minimally addressed. The penalties for not posting the tag lines on social media or other electronic communication depend on the depth of the violation but can include a $1,000 fine or the inability to hold public office for 4 years. In addition, the federal government is also constrained by the Hatch Act of 1939, which generally forbids federal workers from participating in political activity while in the workplace on government time, but social media adds a new dimension to this law (Lipowicz, 2010). Federal agencies posting on Facebook or Twitter may not post web links to political candidates' websites or to online newspaper articles on the political activities of any federal executive, according to a new guidance issued by the Office of Special Counsel.

Chapter Objectives

There are six primary objectives of this chapter on e-democracy:

1. To understand the most important theories of e-democracy in public administration
2. To discuss declining trust in government and how information and communication technology is expected to influence trust
3. To discuss the role that information and communication technology plays on politics and political campaigns
4. To discuss electronic voting or e-voting, examining support for and opposition against this technology
5. To discuss the role of social media technologies on e-democracy
6. To discuss the role of the Internet in the 2008 general election in the United States

Introduction

In this chapter we discuss the role electronic democracy, or e-democracy, has on governments. The first part of this chapter presents some of the most important theories of e-democracy. This is followed by a discussion of trust in government, something that has declined precipitously in the United States since the mid-1960s. The role of information and communication technology (ICT) in politics is also examined. Political campaigns have been influenced by ICT by, for example, the use of websites as a tool politicians can use to provide information to the public. Another important issue of e-democracy is that of electronic voting. We discuss some of the pros and cons of this method of getting citizens more engaged in elections. Social media technologies can be used in e-democracy; their role is discussed as well as some common technologies currently used. Finally, this chapter illustrates the use of ICT in the 2008 campaign for president of the United States.

Framework for Conceptualizing E-Democracy

One framework used to examine e-democracy has four main components, namely stakeholders and policy, methodology, ICT, and environment (**Figure 2-1**). All these components have an impact on creating a more sustainable e-democracy system (Funilkul and Chutimaskul, 2009). This chapter uses this framework to understand the scope of e-democracy in contemporary governments.

Stakeholder and Policy

Stakeholders are citizens, the government, the private sector, and political parties. These stakeholders can be both participants in the system and supporters. Policy for e-democracy involves the regulations written by government to achieve the intended objectives of e-democracy development. To achieve in the development of e-democracy there must be a clear aim to increase transparency and openness in policy development.

Methodology

This provides the right direction of e-democracy development and the guidelines for controlling and monitoring its progress. There are five stages of e-democracy development. The *initiation stage* determines the feasibility, emphasizing the design and implementation of an e-democracy system in accordance with citizens' needs. The *defined stage* is concerned

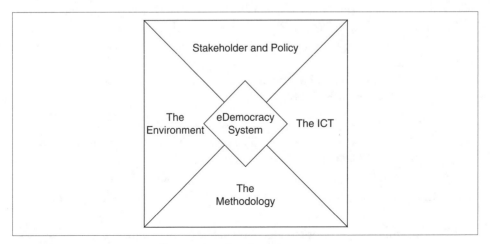

Figure 2-1 *E-Democracy Framework* (From Funilkul and Chutimaskul, 2009)

with clearly defining the personnel involved in its development and understanding the objectives of the e-democracy system. The *repeatable stage* involves the development of e-democracy that has a systematic plan that can be examined. The *management stage* involves the collection of related documents and analysis of strengths and weaknesses of the e-democracy system. The *optimizing stage* is the correcting of the development in a continuous process of the e-democracy system.

Information and Communication Technology

ICT gives citizens the ability to communicate with each other to access and participate in the political process. Internet technology, mobile and wireless technology, collaboration technology, and enterprise applications are examples of common technologies used to facilitate e-democracy. To facilitate e-democracy, the benefits and costs of each of these technologies must be understood to promote its further development.

Environment

The environment in e-democracy development consists of such issues as security and privacy, collaboration, quality, and ethics. These issues all have an impact on the outcome of e-democracy development. Consistent with the sociotechnical perspective, the environment has a tremendous influence on the outcomes of e-democracy. This chapter uses this framework to understand the scope of e-democracy and the issues associated with its development.

E-Democracy Theories

E-democracy is the use of communications devices to enhance the degree and quality of public participation in government (Kakabadse et al., 2003). The Internet can enable citizens to vote electronically in elections and referendums, and it can be used to facilitate opinion polling. Several different perspectives on e-democracy are presented in this chapter.

There are four primary objectives to applying ICT to the democratic decision-making process (Macintosh, 2008, p. 91):

1. Reaching a wider audience to enable broader participation
2. Supporting participation through a range of technologies to cater to the diverse technical and communicative skills of citizens
3. Providing relevant information in a format that is both more accessible and more understandable to the target audience to enable more informed contributions
4. Engaging with a wider audience to enable deeper contributions and support deliberation

E-democracy is a way of broadening political participation by enabling citizens to connect with one another and their elected public officials through ICT (Chadwick, 2006). Information technologies can be used instead of, or in conjunction with, traditional practices of democracy. ICT can have a role in enhancing community cohesion, deliberation, and participation in the democratic process.

One way of assessing the relevance of ICT for democracy is to ask the following four important questions (Anttiroiko, 2003, pp. 125–126):

1. *Institutions:* To what extent are the ICT-based citizen-centered solutions and applications integrated in the practices of existing political institutions and how do they affect actual decision-making processes?

2. *Influence:* Are the e-democracy experiments or practices such that people involved truly influence the issues of interest?

3. *Integration:* Is the potential of technology used optimally in integrating the basic elements of the entire e-democracy process, including agenda setting, planning, preparation, decision making, implementation, evaluation, and control?

4. *Interaction:* Is the potential of technology in disseminating information, facilitating interaction, and conducting political transactions used so as to increase the transparency, efficiency, flexibility, cost-effectiveness, and inclusiveness of a democratic system?

The role of ICT in public sector organizations in relation to e-democracy can be examined in four stages: electronic bureaucracy, information management, direct democracy, and civil society (Kakabadse et al., 2003). Each of these stages of e-democracy can proceed in a linear step-wise fashion, where it is possible for a government to progress from one stage to the next. However, it is possible for governments to combine stages or skip stages to reach higher development.

First, the *electronic bureaucracy* model is the electronic delivery of government services. The focus on this model is to improve efficiency in the operation of delivering government services. Through electronic bureaucracy there is outreach to citizens through simple service delivery improvements, which helps to provide more trust and confidence in government and its institutions. The focus on electronic bureaucracy is outreach to citizens through public service delivery.

The second model is *information management,* which provides electronic information to citizens. For example, presidential speeches, as well as bills introduced by Congress, can be posted online. This involves creating more transparency in government by placing information online. The focus on information management is to improve transparency to citizens, which enables more trust and confidence in government and enhances democracy.

The third model is *direct democracy*, the populist one that enables citizens to register their views on current issues. This model is most often equated with direct democracy of citizens in their government. For example, Web 2.0 technology enables citizens to have a greater influence on government decisions. The focus on direct democracy is that citizens are able to influence policy decisions through the use of ICT.

The final model is the *civil society*, where there is a transformation of the political culture brought about by ICT. There is a strengthening of the connections between citizens and their government (Milward and Snyder, 1996). This is the most difficult stage to achieve because of the dramatic change that needs to take place.

Another perspective by Jaeger (2005) is that e-government and democracy have three main approaches: individualist, communitarian, and deliberative. The *individualist* perspective is that e-government will promote individual empowerment and direct participation in the political process. The individual will be able to make informed decisions because of enhanced access to information. The *communitarian* approach is that e-government will create a community virtually through networks and online town halls. Social network technologies have the potential to drive this approach. The third approach is the *deliberative* approach of e-government by creating a form for democratic interaction through open dialogue and creating a consensus through debate and discussion. E-government in the deliberative view can move citizens toward understanding the issue and coming to some sort of conclusion.

There is a downside of e-democracy, according to Kakabadse and colleagues (2003). E-democracy is mainly an expression of the individual providing input into the government system by digital means. The difficulty lies in aggregating the preferences of these individuals in a meaningful way. Excessive participation can lead to government paralysis. E-democracy can extend the influence of democratic decision making into government responsibility, which is especially problematic in times of crisis in which not being able to reach a decision can have very adverse consequences. Another issue with e-democracy is that ICT is not equitably distributed; therefore, a minority of individuals generally have access. Therefore, information-poor individuals will not be able to influence the political agendas of politicians. ICT can provide better access to individuals who are well equipped, well educated, and well organized, bringing large-scale lobbying to a whole new dimension. The most serious problem of e-democracy is that of the separation of responsibility from accountability. Citizens will be responsible for influencing political decisions but will not be held accountable for the results of these decisions. Therefore, they are free to pursue their own self-interests without thinking about the interests of the collective. As a result, elected representatives would be held accountable for policies over which they had little influence. Essentially, these elected officials would not have any bargaining power, and agreements may be undermined (Kakabadse et al., 2003).

Through focus groups of chief information officers in 37 large local governments, Norris (2007) found that e-government efforts operated principally to deliver government information and services and provide greater access for citizens to government officials. Essentially, Norris found evidence for stages one and two of the Kakabadse et al. (2003) e-democracy model. However, e-government does not operate to enable more citizen participation in government programs, decision making, e-voting, or e-democracy. E-government at the local government level is largely informational and is consistent with Kakabadse et al.'s (2003) model. In the focus group discussions of e-government, Norris (2007) found that none of the participants gave e-democracy as a reason for adopting e-government. Essentially, Norris argued that e-democracy is not on the radar screens of most American local governments as a priority for future implementation.

As an overview, most of the e-democracy models argue for the stages of its development, where governments start initially with providing information for citizens online. They then move to more advanced stages of development, more directly involving citizens in policy development, until they finally reach direct democracy through the use of ICT. Most of these models take a sociotechnical perspective, arguing for the importance of the environment influencing technology adoption.

Trust in Government

One of the often-studied areas of information technology and politics is that of the ability of technology to increase the trust citizens have in their government. Trust in government in the United States has taken a steep decline, especially since the mid-1960s. Trust in government is a measure of whether institutions perform according to expectations. With a decline in political trust there is also declining political participation and turnout at elections. When citizens are more trusting of their government they are more likely to obey laws and regulations. An increase in political trust enhances a democracy. Reversing the decline in public trust of American government is one of the major issues in modern governance, which has been a focus of much research in political science (Tolbert and Mossberger, 2006).

Research shows that e-government may have an impact on citizens and their trust of government. For instance, users of local government websites are more likely to trust local governments, controlling for other demographic factors, and use of these websites was associated with more positive feelings. Research shows that e-government is worth pursuing as a means of enhancing a trusting relationship between citizen and government (Tolbert and Mossberger, 2006). Research shows that e-government satisfaction is positively associated with trust in government (Welch et al., 2004). In the offline world, an individual who is frustrated and disappointed with government services is likely to report lower levels of confidence in government services and less trust; research indicates the same finding for the online world (Welch et al., 2004; Tolbert and Mossberger, 2006).

The primary reasons for citizens distrusting government are government inefficiency or misallocated tax dollars. Some view e-government as a tool for improving efficiency of the government and quality of service delivery as well as enhancing public participation. Research shows that those citizens most likely to gain trust in the government as a result of conducting online transactions are those with existing high levels of trust, not those who just received a positive service experience. There-fore, governments should engage individuals with a high level of trust if their online efforts are to succeed. The overall message is that governments that want to increase trust should devote more resources to non-web-based courses of action (Parent et al., 2005). As a result, the message is clear that e-government does not represent a pana-cea of increasing trust and confidence in government. E-government may enhance the trust of individuals who are already trusting, but it will not bring trust to those who do not trust government in the first place.

ICT and Politics

ICT and its impact on politics and public administration can be divided into two camps, optimists and pessimists (Bimber, 2003; Pole, 2005). The *optimists* believe ICT has the ability to improve democracy. The idea is that the United States is becoming an "electronic republic" where citizens become directly involved in the decision-making process of government. This view was especially enhanced because of the Internet, which could increase citizen participation in the decision-making process. This view shows the potential of the ICT for issues such as voting, campaigns, and advocating issues. The *pessimists* argue that technology will not necessarily im-prove political participation and democracy because the Internet provides another mechanism that can be used by the media and interest groups to dominate discus-sion. This view holds that technology might be undemocratic because it can poten-tially restrict conversation depending on those who have access to the technology compared with those who do not have access.

Bimber (2003) examined four different phases in information revolution and the political system in the United States. The first phase, between the 1820s and 1830s, was when national political information was available for the first time to the public. This phase had a centralized, hierarchical distribution of political information. The second phase, between the 1880s and 1910s, was when more decentralized, special-ized bureaucratic organizations distributed political information. The third phase, from the 1950s until the 1970s, led to the ability of campaigns to influence a mass audience. The fourth and final phase was from the 1990s to the present, with the Internet providing another means of reaching a large audience. Bimber showed that information dissemination has moved from being centralized and controlled to being decentralized as a result of ICT such as the Internet. This decentralization of infor-mation is especially seen with the use of social media technology such as Facebook and Twitter, discussed more thoroughly later in this chapter.

According to Bimber (2001), the rational approach is the most common method that political actors use to acquire information. In this approach, (1) political actors seek information to reduce uncertainty, (2) the cost of information is an indicator of how much new information is acquired, (3) if information is costly there is political activity to arrive at a solution, and (4) there is a point where diminishing returns set in and more information has less of a return. The idea behind the rational approach and information is that the Internet and other ICTs make it much easier for citizens to participate and be engaged in the political process. However, existing research does not support this correlation between political participation and Internet use (Bimber, 2001).

Research by Musso and coworkers (2000) showed that ICT applications government provides tend to focus heavily on information and service provision functions rather than on facilitating communication between residents, policymakers, and democratic discourse. Municipal governments in particular tend to focus on service provisions rather than enhancing the democratic process for their residents. Municipal websites in California demonstrated they tended to improve management through entrepreneurial and managerial reforms rather than improve democracy by enhancing participatory reform (Musso et al., 2000).

Two political factors noted in the literature, which were shown to predict innovation in e-government, were legislative professionalism of a state government and political party affiliation (McNeal et al., 2003). State government leaders involved in professional associations such as the National Governor's Association and the National Conference of State Legislatures were more innovative in e-government. This empirical research also showed that republican-controlled legislatures were more likely to embrace e-government compared with democratic-controlled legislatures. The presumption from this finding was that republicans were more predisposed to small government, and they viewed e-government as providing cost savings. This research essentially shows differences in political parties and the use of ICT, but there is little research on this area and therefore no definitive conclusions can be drawn at this point.

Political Campaigns

The Internet has become an important tool for political campaigns. For instance, the 2004 presidential campaign demonstrated that the Internet could have an important impact on a candidate's ability to raise resources and organize activists. The campaigns of Howard Dean and John Kerry raised tens of millions of dollars from small online donations. They used websites such as Meetup.com to help candidates recruit campaign volunteers. Therefore, the Internet has become crucial to campaign politics. It has the advantage of being a very cost-effective method of communication for candidates with limited resources. However, as with most technology, there is a digital divide, as discussed in Chapter 3, between those with access to the Internet and those without access; this will impact political engagement (Herrnson et al., 2007).

There are four important functions of political campaign websites (Davis et al., 2009). First, the Internet allows the campaign to gather useful information such as background material on an opponent, polling information, and so forth. Second, campaign websites can be used for communication purposes, such as informing voters on the policy positions and biographies of the candidates. Third, campaign websites can be used to mobilize supporters. For instance, blogs can connect supporters with the candidate, providing them with an arena to voice their opinions. Finally, campaign websites can be used for fundraising, with online donations becoming increasingly important because campaign finance laws encourage small donations.

The evolution of the Internet and political candidates indicates that in the mid-1990s, presidential candidates constructed websites and used them to promote their agendas (Greengard, 2009). However, in this Web 1.0 world these websites were merely brochures, allowing candidates to post campaign news and positions on issues. There was no targeting of groups of voters in the Web 1.0 environment. However, in 2004 Howard Dean solicited donations through the Web for his run for the Democratic nomination. In 2008 there was the emergence of Web 2.0 technologies, which are changing how candidates communicate with the public through blogs, wikis, social networking sites, and more sophisticated analytical tools, which has made it easier to target individuals and generate vast amounts of money. The Obama presidential campaign knew well the value of this outreach through Web 2.0 technologies and was able to use the Internet in ways that were not used before, targeting specific audiences for donations.

Online forms such as YouTube, Flickr, MySpace, and Facebook have centralized self-publishing and brought large audiences into campaigns (Davis et al., 2009). A major problem with social networking sites, however, is that the demographic audience may not have a large impact on election outcomes. Typically, these sites attract the least participatory group in an election, with an age range of 18 to 24 years. However, these social networking sites can be used for recruiting volunteers for campaigns. These individuals often become the foot soldiers for the campaign. Overall, the Internet has not changed political campaigns as television has, because the reach is not nearly as great. Websites generally attract a relatively small audience compared with television. However, campaign websites and social media have become just another means to reach voters. Bimber and Davis (2003) wrote that use of the Internet for political campaigns may be capable of performing some functions well, such as reinforcing political attachments and mobilizing supporters to donate and volunteer, but will not revolutionize campaigns and politics as some have predicted. This remains to be seen, and current evidence is very substantial. It is difficult for political candidates to ignore these new social media platforms.

Websites have allowed voters and the media to obtain a more comprehensive picture about the candidate. But with more sophisticated websites, there are increased costs. For example, Howard Dean's presidential campaign made use of a campaign blog, an online updated journal; blogging has been used by other campaigns. Research shows that online campaigns merely reinforce the existing messages found in traditional media and they preach to the converted; therefore, campaigns may not be getting additional voters as a result. Online campaigns did allow for small donations, which substantially impacted fundraising abilities for Barack Obama. Essentially, there has been little research that examines the role of the Internet in campaigns, and much more can be done (Herrnson et al., 2007).

One study of online campaigning found this has less to do with the digital divide than with strategic and structural factors. The incumbency of the candidate, campaign spending, electoral competitiveness, the number of people who live in the district, and the professionalism of the legislature for which the candidate is campaigning for provided the best explanations of why candidates invest in online campaigning. These findings reinforce the existing political science literature, which argues that campaigning is related to strategic factors on which candidates compete (Herrnson et al., 2007).

Digital political information, a relatively new information product, makes it possible for political campaigns to use this information to create strong political messages (Howard, 2005). The market for digital political information is more open in that people can buy and sell this information very readily. A market has opened up for political information about the personal identity and opinions of individuals to allow researchers to draw inferences. Information from individuals can be collected from credit card purchases, Internet activities, surveys, and government information that are readily available. From this, political campaigns can infer political preferences of individuals based on gender, race, and consumer activity.

E-Voting

Electronic voting, or e-voting, is the use of ICT that tries to minimize the human element in the vote collection and tabulation process (Smith and Clark, 2005). The closing case study at the end of this chapter provides an example of how the Internet has changed voting in the county of Honolulu. E-voting can use online information gathering and retrieval technologies to expand the reach of voting. There are two models of e-voting: voting at an official polling place, with votes transmitted through the Internet to election officers, and voting at a remote location with any Internet connection and sending the vote into election officials. With the latter method there is some sort of digital signature to verify the identity of the voter. E-voting has the potential to reduce the cost of staffing polling places and reduce the errors of voters and election officials and allow for more uniform standards of ballot format. There are potential risks of security and privacy, especially as it relates to securing the identity of the voter.

There are both proponents and opponents of Internet voting (Alvarez and Hall, 2004). Proponents of Internet voting offer several arguments. First, Internet voting is thought by proponents to make it easier for voters to participate in elections because every computer that has an Internet connection becomes a potential polling site. Internet voting lowers the cost of participation because voters can do this from the comfort of their own home or at work. Voters who do not have an Internet connection can vote in public places such as libraries or Internet cafes. Second, voters who are disabled and not able to get to a polling place can vote remotely with Internet voting. For example, a study found that more than 80% of polling places had some sort of barrier that prevented disabled voters from getting access. Third, individuals with work schedules or family commitments that prevent them from getting access to the polling place would benefit from Internet voting. A single parent or someone who travels frequently may not have access to a polling place on Election Day. The final reason for Internet voting is that this might attract the hardest to reach voters, between the ages of 18 and 25, to participate in the political process. Internet voting for this group might increase voter turnout because this group has historically low rates of participation. For example, younger voters may be attending college, which means they would not be in their district to vote at election time. In addition, younger voters are much more likely to be online, which should increase participation.

Opponents to Internet voting have their views as well (Alvarez and Hall, 2004). The most commonly cited opposition to Internet voting is the issue of online security. The Internet is vulnerable to viruses and attacks from hackers (discussed in Chapter 10). These attacks can be staged from anywhere in the world. The second major criticism of Internet voting is that the system may favor some voters over others. There essentially is a digital divide in Internet access, where some groups, especially those with greater income, have more access. A third criticism of Internet voting is that this technology could further disintegrate civic life. One of the major issues that the United States faces is decreased civic involvement, with fewer people engaging in political or civic activities. Some argue that if there were no polls on Election Day this would not enable people to participate together in one of the most important functions of citizen engagement.

Using Rogers' (2003) diffusion of innovations theory, Liptrott (2007) examined e-voting issues and its adoption in local governments in the United Kingdom. When comparing local governments that did trial adoption of e-voting to nonadopters, Liptrott found the factors of continuity, security, time, resources, and kudos influenced their decision to adopt e-voting. As far as continuity is concerned, local government may be more willing to adopt e-voting if they do not feel overwhelmed by the central government denying them the opportunity to continue with their e-voting system. Essentially, governments that believe they can continue using the technology after the trial may be more willing to invest time and resources in its successful implementation. Second, local governments were concerned about security of e-voting systems of the vote and voter. Security as previously mentioned is a common issue that impedes the adoption of e-voting systems. Third, many local governments were concerned about the lack of time they faced in establishing a fully functional e-voting system. Fourth, many local governments were concerned about resource issues in the adoption of this new technology, such as who would essentially pay for new systems and updates. Finally, kudos had an impact on adoption; local governments could demonstrate to the public and other stakeholders that they were being innovative by adopting e-voting systems; this would have an impact on some governments adopting this technology.

Results in a field study of e-voting systems indicated that major voting systems used by U.S. governments were viewed favorably by voters (Herrnson et al., 2008). Voters were able to negotiate their way through the systems. However, voters found some of the design features to be annoying, perplexing, and disconcerting. Voters expressed varying levels of confidence that their votes would be accurately recorded. Voters often found the need to ask for help when completing the voting process. This was particularly the case for voters with little computer experience, senior citizens, and individuals whose predominate language was not English. This suggests that voting machine design should take into account usability when testing their machines. Another solution would be to use more poll workers where there is a concentration of those groups that need assistance.

Moynihan (2004) argued that the failure of e-voting technology has profound consequences for the confidence of citizens in the electoral process. This author argued that there is no more central public administration task than administering elections that accurately reflect voters' intentions. The administration of the Florida 2000 presidential election recount had a number of serious implications for public administration and ICT. First, it showed the influence of election board officials and their role in the process of administering elections. Second, the Florida recount showed the importance of voting technology in determining the number of votes counted, with problems most acutely associated with punch-card machines. Third, this recount spurred the development of the Help America Vote Act (HAVA) of 2002, which provided federal funding to replace the antiquated punch-card system and created the Election Assistance Commission to help with information on the running of federal elections (Moynihan, 2004).

How Managers Deal with E-Voting

Public managers have to deal with the operational aspects of e-voting. To provide voting equipment at polling places for elections involves two major tasks (Montjoy, 2008). First, the equipment used at the polling place must be purchased from a vendor according to the standards set by the officials, technology department, and attorneys. The second task is to prepare and deploy the equipment at each election, and this requires vendor support. HAVA 2002 provides incentives for jurisdictions using lever machines and punch cards to replace these systems. This Act also requires that each polling place have at least one device that allows disabled voters, including the visually impaired, to cast their votes without assistance.

HAVA affects nearly every aspect of the voting process, from voting technology to provisional ballots and from voter registration to poll worker training (U.S. Government Accountability Office [GAO], 2007). In particular, the Act authorized $3.86 billion in funding over several fiscal years for programs to replace punch-card and mechanical lever voting equipment, improve election administration and accessibility, train poll workers, and perform research and pilot studies. HAVA also established the Election Assistance Commission to assist in the administration of federal elections and provide assistance with the administration of certain federal election laws and programs. HAVA also established minimum election administration standards for the states and units of local government responsible for the administration of federal elections. The Act specifically tasked the Election Assistance Commission to serve as a national clearinghouse and resource for compiling election information and reviewing election procedures. For example, it is to conduct periodic studies of election administration issues, including electronic voting system performance, and to promote methods of voting and administration that are most convenient, accessible, and easy to use for all voters. Other examples of Election Assistance Commission responsibilities include the following:

- Developing and adopting voluntary voting system guidelines and maintaining information on the experiences of states in implementing the guidelines and operating voting systems
- Testing, certifying, decertifying, and recertifying voting system hardware and software through accredited laboratories
- Making payments to states to help them improve elections in the areas of voting systems standards, provisional voting and voting information requirements, and computerized statewide voter registration lists
- Making grants for research on voting technology improvements

Technical Aspects of E-Voting

In the United States most votes are cast and counted by one of two types of e-voting systems: optical scan and direct-recording electronic (DRE) (GAO, 2007). For the November 2004 general election, optical scan was the predominant voting method for more than half of local jurisdictions nationwide. In contrast, DREs were used as the predominant voting method by an estimated 7% of jurisdictions, although they were the predominant voting method for large jurisdictions. **Figure 2-2** shows the estimated use of predominant voting methods for small, medium, and large jurisdictions in the 2004 general election.

Optical scan voting systems use electronic technology to tabulate paper ballots (GAO, 2007). For the 2004 general election, 51% of all local jurisdictions predominantly used optical scan voting equipment. An optical scan voting system is made up of computer-readable ballots, appropriate marking devices, privacy booths, and a computerized tabulation device. The ballot, which can be of various sizes, lists the names of the candidates and the issues. Voters record their choices using an appropriate writing instrument to fill in boxes or ovals or to complete an arrow next to the candidate's name or the issue. The ballot includes a space for write-ins to be placed directly on the ballot.

Optical scan ballots are tabulated by optical-mark-recognition equipment, which counts the ballots by sensing or reading the marks on the ballot. Ballots can be counted at the polling place. If ballots are counted at the polling place, voters or election officials put the ballots into the tabulation equipment, which tallies the votes. These tallies can be captured in removable storage media that are transported

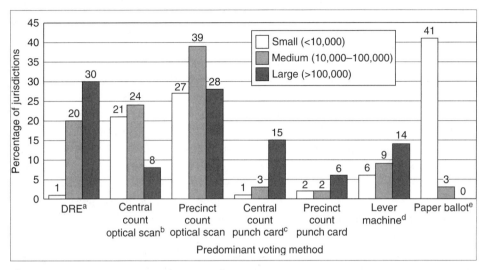

Figure 2-2 *Estimated percentage of jurisdictions using predominant voting methods in 2004 by jurisdiction size* (From GAO, 2006)

to a central tally location, or they can be electronically transmitted from the polling place to the central tally location. If ballots are centrally counted, voters drop ballots into sealed boxes and election officials transfer the sealed boxes to the central location after the polls close, where election officials run the ballots through the tabulation equipment.

DREs capture votes electronically without the use of paper ballots (GAO, 2007). For the 2004 general election, an estimated 7% of all local jurisdictions used DREs predominantly, although 30% of all large jurisdictions used them as the predominant voting method.

DREs come in two basic types: push button (the older technology) or touch screen (GAO, 2007). Push-button and touch-screen units differ significantly in the way they present ballots to the voter. With the push-button type all ballot information is presented on a single "full-face" ballot. For example, a ballot may have 50 buttons on a 3 × 3 foot ballot, with a candidate or issue listed next to each button. In contrast, touch-screen DREs display ballot information on an electronic display screen. For both push-button and touch-screen types, the ballot information is programmed onto an electronic storage medium, which is then uploaded to the machine. For touch screens, ballot information can be displayed in color and can incorporate pictures of the candidates. Because the ballot space on a touch screen is much smaller than on a push-button machine, voters who use touch screens must page through the ballot information. Both touch-screen and push-button DREs can accommodate multilingual ballots.

Social Media Technologies Used for E-Democracy

Social media technologies such as blogs and wikis have the potential to promote openness and transparency in government (Bertot et al., 2010). The opening case study provides an example of how social media technologies have changed political campaign rules. Some essential tools for promoting e-democracy should be outlined. First, blogs represent the Internet's democratization of the publishing industry. Second, wikis are collaborative drafting systems that allow many people to work together on a shared document. Wikis is a website that uses collaborative web-based software that allows users with access to add new edited content to existing content. With Wikis users can collaboratively work together to accomplish this goal of creating a document. Wikis are different from websites because users can add or edit content. Third, collaborative filtering and data mining tools allow for the filtering of news and information into categories that can be pushed out to users. Finally, open government initiatives provide both transparency and accountability of government to citizens. All four of these tools have the potential to allow the inclusion of citizens and to promote e-democracy.

Data mining is a set of automated techniques used to extract buried or previously unknown pieces of information from large databases (Tavani, 1999). Data mining is a technique for the efficient discovery of valuable, nonobvious information. The use of data mining can provide important patterns and relationships that were previously unknown. These data can then be used to make better and more informed decisions. A data warehouse is a highly integrated database, which is typically used to process information. The issue with data mining and data warehouses becomes the invasion of private information of individuals.

Two of the most important technologies for e-democracy that should be discussed further are blogs and political data mining. A blog, particularly important for e-democracy, is essentially a website that has content formatted through a series of postings, often displayed in chronological order. Blogs are often used to share personal information, opinions, and news about a particular subject with others. Blogs are often textual in nature, but they may also have multimedia content such as video and audio embedded in the text. Readers of blogs are often allowed to provide feedback and comments; therefore, content is very open and interconnected. Governments that want to promote transparency and openness of information can use blogs to accomplish this task (Coleman and Wright, 2008).

Political blogs can be individualized, such as a blog of a politician and his or her accomplishments and views on issues. Blogs can also have multiple authors and can represent the views of groups. According to Coleman and Wright (2008), blogs enhance political communication in four key ways:

1. They reduce the distance in communication between messenger and receiver.
2. They can enhance interactive dialogue because the receiver can respond directly to the blog.

3. They present an appearance of being responsive to listeners because their content can be changed in response to comments and criticisms.
4. They can give rise to more grassroots movements, enabling anyone with access to the Internet the ability to comment on news.

Blogs can increase overall accountability of elected officials. Blogs can also reverse political communication by challenging the traditional ways citizens receive information. Blogs can increase public debate and may even reach a consensus from the opinions of citizens and groups on the blogosphere.

Political data mining firms have become commonplace and are used by U.S. legislators and presidential candidates to look for information on electoral behavior (Howard, 2005). Lobbyists, for example, also can use political data mining to target supporters, generate awareness, and solicit contributions. These data mining techniques allow them to reach audiences based on demographic, geographical, and political criteria. Some of the political databases are derived from companies that provide free e-mail service and require subscribers to fill out questionnaires. The initial information collected is basic, containing demographics such as age, gender, income, and education. This information is supplemented using spyware and tracking members' patterns of Internet use. Howard showed that the largest political databases have information from 150 million registered voters in the United States, and this information is taken from state and local boards of elections, departments of motor vehicles, municipal licensing agencies, and social science survey data. Most of these firms compile the digital information without the explicit or informed consent of the individuals in the database. In addition, most of the data is readily available or available by request to the appropriate agency.

Survey Evidence for Social Media Technology Use

During July and August 2010, the National Association of State Chief Information Officers conducted a survey of social media use of all 50 state governments, of which 43 states responded to the survey (NASCIO, 2010). According to state government chief information officers, the primary drivers for social media use are citizen engagement, public information and awareness, and open government (**Table 2-1**). Only one state responded to the survey that did not use any social media technologies.

The five most frequently used social media technologies for state governments were Facebook, Twitter, YouTube, Flickr, and blogs (**Table 2-2**) (NASCIO, 2010). From the survey data it appears states are using very similar social media technologies to engage their citizens.

The greatest concerns for the potential risks associated with social media technology are security, terms of service (legal) issues, records retention issues, and privacy (**Table 2-3**) (NASCIO, 2010). There were not a high number of states that believed lack of management support and resources were an impediment to social media adoption.

Table 2-1 *What Are the Primary Reasons for State Government Adoption of Social Media Technologies?*

Reasons	Response (N = 43)
Citizen engagement	42
Public information, outreach, and awareness	40
Open government	29
Business engagement	23
Government engagement	19
Reduced need for agency resources (e.g., less e-mail, phone calls, open records/freedom of information [FOI] requests)	15
Process improvement	12
State government employee engagement	11
Not using social media technology	1

As one can see from the survey evidence, states do use social media technology to engage citizens in government. But they used a limited number of technologies such as Facebook and Twitter, and security is a major concern for them when they adopt social media technologies.

Open Government

President Obama on his first full day of office issued a memorandum on Transparency and Open Government (Office of Management and Budget, 2009). In this memorandum the Obama Administration called for a system of transparency, participation, and collaboration (McDermott, 2010). According to the Obama Administration, government should be *transparent* and provide information for its citizens on what it is doing. The administration called for executive departments and agencies to use new information technology to put information about their operations and decisions online and make it readily available to the public. Federal agencies should also seek feedback from the public on important issues. The second pillar of open government is *participation*. The idea here is that public engagement in government enhances the quality of decisions. Executive departments and agencies should provide, to the public, knowledge developed by their agencies. This enables citizens to participate in the policymaking process. The third pillar is that government should be *collaborative*. Executive departments and agencies should use innovative tools, methods,

Table 2-2 *What Social Media Tools Are State Governments Using?*

Technology	Response Count (N = 43)
Facebook	37
Twitter	36
YouTube	33
Flickr	20
Blogs	19
LinkedIn	9
Vimeo	5
Ning	4
MySpace	3
Digg	3
Delicious	3
Foursquare	3
Second Life	1
GovLoop	1

and systems to enhance collaboration with all levels of government, nonprofits, and individuals.

Some examples of open government are said to increase transparency, collaboration, and participation (Jaeger and Bertot, 2010). The federal government has developed a website as a way to provide direct access to a substantial amount of government data online (see www.data.gov). This site, it is hoped, will allow users to find new uses for the data and be able to provide unavailable insights into government activities by mining the data. Also, the Obama Administration uses social media such as blogs, wikis, social networking sites, really simple syndication (RSS) feeds, cloud applications, and virtual worlds to make government information available for citizens to have direct contact with their government. The U.S. Department of Health and Human Services contest for the best H_1N_1 flu prevention YouTube video is an example. The federal government created a website (see www.recovery.gov) intended to promote public monitoring of federal spending for the stimulus program. Holding online meetings and soliciting comments to get public feedback on proposed policies and regulations is another example. Mandating that agencies

Table 2-3 *What Are High Concerns Constraining Broader Use of Social Media Representing Potential Risks?*

High Concern	Response Count (N = 43)
Security	25
Terms of services (legal) issues	21
Records retention issues	18
Privacy	18
Employee use/misuse	16
Lack of resources to monitor/control	14
Lack of control over providers	13
Work culture and perceptions	13
Lack of quantifiable business benefit	11
Lack of resources to support	9
Lack of governance framework	9
Lack of executive/management support	6
Accessibility	4

create their own open government plans and web pages has been implemented at the federal level as well.

Dawes (2010) discussed two important principles of information transparency, namely stewardship and usefulness. *Stewardship* is the conservative principle acknowledging that government information has some of the same qualities as clean air and safe streets. Stewardship focuses on ensuring the accuracy, validity, security, management, and preservation of information holding by government. All public officials are responsible for handling information with both care and integrity. There are two important components of being good stewards of information: protecting government information from damage, loss, or misuse and making information fit for use. The principle of information *usefulness* recognizes that government information is valuable and can generate social and economic benefits through its use and innovation. Policies that promote usefulness of information provide agencies with guidelines and incentives to share information to benefit a wide variety of public and private users. They encourage investment in information management to support information sharing. Both principles can check each other: being good stewards of information prevents misuse, and providing useful information enables its use for the betterment of society by providing for greater transparency in government (Piotrowski and Van Ryzin, 2007).

ICT enables countries to promote transparency and reduce corruption in public agencies (Bertot et al., 2010). Many nations have implemented transparency laws that have been tied directly to ways of using ICT to promote transparency. ICT can reduce corruption by promoting good governance, strengthening reform initiatives, reducing potential corrupt behaviors, enhancing relationships with citizens and employees, allowing citizen tracking of activities, and monitoring and controlling behavior of employees and contractors. India provides some examples of ICT used to promote transparency; India put rural property records online, greatly increasing the speed at which records are accessed and updated while removing the opportunities for local officials to accept bribes. In the United States the federal government has created websites that allow access to data of government expenditures (see www.usaspending. gov) and information technology funds (see www.IT.usaspending.gov), thereby promoting more transparency. These websites are intended to promote public monitoring of government spending for elimination of government waste and inefficiencies.

The Internet and the 2008 Presidential Campaign

As an example of ICT in democracy, a case study is provided on the impact of the Internet on the 2008 U.S. presidential campaign. Many believe this election was a turning point in the use of the Internet in electoral politics in America. The 2008 race for president was inspired by factors such as a lengthy contested race in the Democratic primary of Barack Obama and Hillary Clinton and a general election featuring the first African-American Democratic Party candidate and a well-known Republican senator. This general election was especially interesting because it coincided with the collapse of the housing market, banking sectors, and widespread disappointment with the former President George W. Bush. The culmination of these factors makes it an interesting case study of the impact of the Internet on political campaigns.

According to a Pew Internet and American Life 2009 survey, for the 2008 election season more than half (74%) of the entire adult U.S. population went online to learn about the campaigns or the political process (Smith, 2009) (**Table 2-4**). Nearly three-fourths of Internet users can be labeled online political users. Of this percentage, 60% went to get news online about campaigns and politics, 38% communicated with others about politics using the Internet, and 59% shared and received campaign information using specific tools such e-mail, instant messaging, text messages, and Twitter (not shown).

Table 2-5 shows the differences in online political users by demographic characteristics. Online political users are similar in their demographic characteristics

Table 2-4 *Online Participation by Demographic Groups*

	Percent of Internet Users in Each Group Who Are Online Political Users	Percent of All Adults in Each Group Who Are Online Political Users
Total	74	55
Gender		
Male	75	58
Female	73	53
Age		
18–29	77	72
30–49	77	65
50–64	71	51
65+	60	22
Race/ethnicity		
White, non-Hispanic	76	58
Black, non-Hispanic	66	40
Hispanic	64	52
Education		
Less than high school	—	18
High school grad	62	42
Some college	78	67
College grad	87	81
Annual household income		
Less than $30,000	56	31
$30,000–$49,999	70	57
$50,000–$74,999	79	73
$75,000 or more	87	84

Source: Smith (2009).

Table 2-5 *Demographic Profile of the Online Political User Population*

	All Adults (%)	Internet Users (%)	Online Political Users (%)
Male	49	50	51
Female	51	50	49
Age			
18–29	19	24	25
30–49	37	42	43
50–64	26	25	24
65+	17	8	7
Race/ethnicity			
White, non-Hispanic	70	71	73
Black, non-Hispanic	11	9	8
Hispanic (English-speaking)	11	12	11
Education			
Less than high school	13	6	4
High school grad	36	32	27
Some college	23	27	28
College grad	27	34	40
Annual household income			
Less than $30,000	26	19	15
$30,000–$49,999	17	19	17
$50,000–$74,999	14	17	18
$75,000 or more	24	32	37
Geography			
Urban	30	29	29
Suburban	53	55	58
Rural	18	15	13

Source: Smith (2009).

Table 2-6 *How Voters Communicated About Campaign 2008*

	Ever (%)	Daily (%)
Mail	69	17
E-mail	40	12
Text messaging	15	3
Instant messaging	10	2
Twitter	1	
Margin of error is ±2% based on all adults (n = 2,254).		

Source: Smith (2009).

to other groups with respect to gender, race, and geography. Online political users tended to be younger and had a greater level of income and education than the population as a whole. **Table 2-6** shows that e-mail was the dominant form of online political communication, followed by text messaging and instant messaging. Twenty-four percent of online political users contributed to an online political debate by posting questions, comments, or commentary where others read them; this is called the online political participatory class (**Table 2-7** and **Figure 2-3**). The Pew survey also showed that young adults were more likely to use social networking sites in general and were also more likely to use these sites for political purposes.

Table 2-7 *Online Political Participatory Class*

	Among Online Political Users (%)	Among Internet Users (%)
On a social networking site	14	10
On a website of any kind, such as a political, campaign, or news site that allows comments and discussion	12	9
On a blog (your own or someone else's)	11	8
In an online discussion, listserv, or other group forum	10	8
Have done any of these	24	18

The percent within each group who have posted comments, queries, or information about the campaign or election online.

Source: Smith (2009).

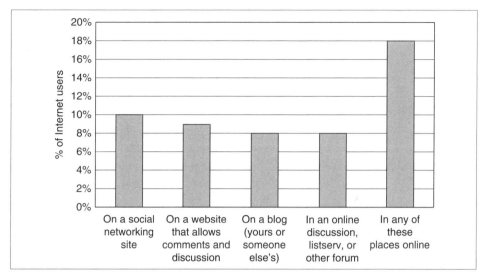

Figure 2-3 *The online participatory class: 1 in 5 users posted political commentary online* (From Smith, 2009)

Summary

In this chapter we discussed e-democracy. ICTs such as the Internet are seen as one way to reach a wider audience and to engage citizens more in the political process (Shane, 2004). Trust in government has declined since the mid-1960s in the United States, and ICT is a way to increase trust and confidence in government. Empirical evidence does not indicate that ICT will enhance trust of individuals who already distrust government. ICT and politics indicate that there are two views on its impact. One view holds that it will enhance citizen participation in a democracy, and the second view holds that it will reinforce existing power structures and just become another mechanism used to not include individuals in the political process. Websites have allowed greater visibility of political campaigns by the public and the media. E-voting is one area that ICT could potentially influence, but the issue of privacy and security of the individual's vote must be addressed before wider acceptance of this technology occurs. Blogs and political data mining are two important social media technologies that can be used in e-democracy. Both of these technologies allow for greater reach to get citizens involved in the political process. Nearly three-fourths of Internet users went online to get information about the 2008 presidential campaign. Therefore, the Internet has provided a valuable source of information for citizens during elections.

Discussion Questions

1. How do you think ICT has changed e-democracy? Has it changed it for the better?
2. Discuss what role ICT will have in enhancing trust and confidence in government?
3. What are some of the pros and cons argued for e-voting?
4. How has ICT changed political campaigns in the United States?
5. What role do social media technologies have on politics and political campaigns?
6. Examining the campaign for President of the United States, has the Internet changed the way a presidential candidate runs for office?

Closing Case Study

First All-Digital Election in the United States

In May 2009 the city and county of Honolulu used an all-digital election to elect members of its Neighborhood Boards (Vander Veen, 2009). Instead of e-voting machines, residents were allowed to vote either online or by phone. In this election no paper ballots were available. This first all-digital election came about not because of the desire to use this new technology but was driven by the need to cut the budget. The elimination of paper ballots reduced the election costs by half. The Neighborhood Commission Office worked with a San Diego–based company, Everyone Counts, which has been conducting digital elections for the last decade in the United Kingdom for military personnel and expatriates.

Security is an issue that has held back e-voting. E-voting, because of the lack of paper trail as well as proprietary code, has been seen as an easy target for hackers. Everyone Counts says its security protocol has a two-key system requirement that is very difficult to hack. When the election begins, voters vote and each ballot is encrypted and stored securely. At the end of the election the encrypted ballots are removed from the Internet and onto a clean personal computer. They are not accessible until election officials come together and provide the unique password to the system, which decrypts the votes. In addition, voters can verify their vote was received and counted by going to a special website and using the unique nine-digit password they received combined with the last four digits of their Social Security number.

The issue with the election was that voter turnout was down 83% from 2007 and the voter participation rate was only 10%. However, the all-digital election costs half of the a paper-based election at $90,000.

Secure web-based voting is not expected to occur for at least a decade, because perfecting the cybersecurity for such a system is a decade away as much more research and development needs to be done (Williams, 2010a). Furthermore, a test of the vulnerabilities of a Washington, DC, pilot system of online-only voting indicated a vulnerability: researchers could log on remotely and change the results.

This disclosure of new vulnerabilities for e-voting coincides with the new Military and Overseas Voter Empowerment Act passed by Congress in 2009. This law mandates that state and local governments put measures in place no later than November 2010 elections to make voting more accessible and reliable for U.S. military and oversees citizens. Under the Act, paper ballots must be mailed to overseas citizens no later than 45 days before an election. Several states, such as Delaware, West Virginia, Tennessee, Arkansas, and Idaho, have begun implementing technology that will digitally deliver the ballot to them and allow them to mail it back through the postal service.

E-Participation

Opening Case Study

Federal Government Contest Website

In September 2010 the federal government launched Challenge.gov, which provides online contests for Americans to vie for cash prizes for solving problems federal agencies cannot deal with by themselves (Sternstein, 2010). The public can also vote on proposed solutions on the website. In early September there were already 35 contests underway. The prize money is awarded through grants. The General Services Administration is in charge of this website. The Challenge.gov website makes it easy for federal agencies to post challenges on the website in minutes without any technical skills by simply filling out an online form. Visitors to the website can search for competitions by subject matter, agency, award amount, time remaining to enter, and recently posted contests (**Figure 3-1**).

The Consumer Product Safety Commission, for example, started a contest to design nine posters that teach Americans how to prevent carbon monoxide deaths. The competition has $2,750 in prize money. The Energy Department and Progressive Insurance has a competition for $10 million in prizes they are offering for engineering vehicles that can travel more than 100 miles on a gallon of fuel. Agencies are not obligated to award funding if competitions do not yield satisfactory submissions.

The origins for the Challenge.gov website can be traced back to President Barack Obama's Strategy for American Innovation, which called for government agencies to foster innovation, among other things, by offering challenges and prize money. Most of the challenges are sponsored by private sector companies.

Figure 3-1   *A sample page from the website Challenge.gov*

Chapter Objectives

The following are the five primary objectives of this chapter:

1. To examine the e-participation perspectives and their importance to understanding civic engagement of citizens
2. To understand the digital divide and how information and communication technologies (ICTs) influence the digital divide
3. To understand the role of ICT in the policymaking process
4. To examine how ICT influences the rulemaking process
5. To examine the various Web 2.0 technologies that can be used in e-participation

Introduction

This chapter examines the role of ICT on participation of citizens in a democracy, or e-participation. The first part of the chapter examines some of the most common e-participation perspectives as a way of understanding this important area of information technology (IT) and public administration (Macintosh, 2008). In this chapter we also examine civic engagement and the role the Internet plays in creating a more active citizenry. The digital divide is discussed, which is the difference between those with access to the Internet and those without access. We examine the role of ICT in the policymaking process from agenda setting, analysis, creation, implementing, and monitoring policies. There is a discussion of electronic rulemaking, or e-rulemaking, as a way for citizens and interest groups to have an influence on new government policies. Finally, Web 2.0 technologies and their potential impact on the participation of citizens in government are discussed.

Framework for Understanding E-Participation

Table 3-1 illustrates the three models of e-participation and the important characteristics of each (Chadwick and May, 2003; Macintosh, 2003; Kamal, 2009)

Table 3-1 *Three Models of E-Participation*

	Level of E-Participation		
	Managerial →	Consultative →	Participatory
Role of government	Efficiency in the delivery of public services to citizens	Better policy decisions with citizen input	Citizen interaction is critical to the development of the policy
Actors involved	Customers as citizens, business, mass media	Interest groups, citizens as customers, business	Voluntary associations, interest groups, and citizens
Flow of information	Directed from government; one-way interaction	Directed by government, but shaped by citizen input; two-way interaction	Complex with both flow from government and citizens shaping governance and policy; two-way multidirectional interaction
Technologies used	Online tax returns, public information on websites	Social media technologies	E-voting, opinion polling, electronic town hall meetings
Logic	To enhance service delivery	To improve policy success	To enhance democracy
Implementation issues	Lack of cost savings	Apathy of the public	No signs of radical change

Adapted from Chadwick and May (2003), Macintosh (2003), and Kamal (2009).

and also shows the different dimensions of e-participation for each model. The three models can be represented on a continuum, with the managerial model being the lowest form of e-participation and the participatory model being the highest form of participation, with the most citizen interaction with government. The consultative model is somewhere in between the managerial and participatory in its level of active e-participation. Governments can work their way up through the different stages in a linear fashion, or they can skip stages to reach a higher level of e-participation.

Managerial

The managerial model of e-participation is much different from the consultative and participatory model in that it focuses on efficiency in service delivery (Lean et al., 2009). This research shows that improvements in service delivery are one of the most important aspects of e-participation. In this model citizens are viewed as customers, and government provides information and services to satisfy the demand of their customers (Morgeson and Mithas, 2009). Therefore, the private sector term "customer" is used to mean that governments merely respond to their desires when making information or services available.

A primary drive toward the managerial model is the public sector mimics the success of private sector entities, which is consistent with new public management (NPM) reform efforts (Hood and Peters, 2004). In the NPM model, private sector principles of performance are applied through the use of e-government to improve service delivery. The managerial model is a directed model by government; therefore, information flows in one direction to citizens (Chadwick and May, 2003). In this form of participation citizens merely use what is provided online by government. Governments choose what to put online, which directs the level of one-way interaction with citizens (Pina et al., 2010).

Some common technologies used in the managerial form of e-participation include online tax forms, licenses, and filing fees to more basic contact information of officials placed online (Norris and Moon, 2005). Some governments provide basic forms of e-participation, where citizens can do research on an issue online, and other governments provide more interactive e-government, with the ability of citizens to conduct transactions online (Anthopoulos et al., 2007). One of the overriding issues faced in the implementation of the managerial model is the lack of cost savings as a result of online government and the difficulty in justifying investment in new technology (Pirog and Johnson, 2008).

One of the major challenges in this form of e-participation is the limited government interaction with citizens. Citizens are given the opportunity to receive information or services from government but are not able to change the service delivery process. The only feedback government receives is through their use of online services, where services that are used more often indicate greater importance to citizens. A second challenge of the managerial model is that it focuses on being responsive to customers, which may not always be a good approach, because citizens are different from customers in that they interact with a single provider for a service.

Consultative

The consultative model is more directed toward citizens and their interaction with government than the managerial model (Kolsaker and Lee-Kelley, 2008). In this model, instead of being focused on providing more efficient service delivery to customers, as emphasized in the managerial model, the role for government is directed toward creating better policy decisions with citizens' input (Macintosh, 2004; Anttiroiko, 2010).

There is a diverse range of actors involved in the consultative model, where there is less focus on customers and more toward satisfying the interests of different stakeholders (Lim et al., 2007). Similarly to the managerial model, the consultative model of participation is directed by government, but unlike the managerial model, citizen input shapes policy. Therefore, this model moves toward two-way interaction, directed by government. In the consultative model there is a movement from viewing citizens as customers in that citizens have more of a stake in governance, as reflected in the model.

Some of the common technologies used in the consultative model are social media technologies such as the Web, Facebook, and Twitter (Anttiroiko, 2010). These technologies allow for greater citizen interaction and are more active than technologies that just provide a Web presence in the managerial model (Pasek, More, and Romer, 2009). The consultative model, therefore, can provide an improvement in public policy, with this directed toward citizens' input being critically important (Kolsaker and Lee-Kelley, 2008).

A notable challenge of this model is that even though citizens have been elevated from their customer status in the managerial model, information is still directed by government. Therefore, the top-down approach to information dissemination remains in the consultative model. Another challenge is that the public may not want to get involved in policy debate, and a limited number of individuals and groups may ultimately influence policy decisions (Shulman, 2005).

Participatory

The final model, which has the greatest degree of e-participation, is the participatory model. In the participatory model, citizen interaction is critical for the development of public policy (Andersen et al., 2007). There is a diverse range of actors involved in the participatory model, ranging from nonprofit organizations, interest groups, citizens, media, and businesses (Kakabadse et al., 2003).

Unlike the more directed managerial model, in the participatory model there is a complex flow of information between government and citizens designed to enhance and shape policy (Jaeger, 2005). The flow of information is multidirectional, and policy changes are the result of citizens' comments (Chadwick and May, 2003). In this model, change can occur in different directions, with citizens initiating change from the bottom up, which is not seen in the managerial and consultative models. Some common technologies used in the participatory model are e-voting, online opinion polling, and online town hall meetings (Andersen et al., 2007).

The ultimate goal of the participatory model is to enhance democracy and citizen participation in governance (Macintosh and Whyte, 2008). The most problematic issues are that there is very little evidence for this occurring at different levels of government and there is little known about what factors cause e-participation (Norris, 2007).

Additional Perspectives on E-Participation

Other authors have shown various ways of conceptualizing e-participation in government. For example, Macintosh and Whyte (2008) proposed a framework for e-participation that has three overlapping perspectives, which are as follows:

1. The *democratic* perspective considers the overarching democratic criteria the e-participation initiative is addressing. Here, one of the most difficult aspect is to understand to what extent the e-participation affects policy.
2. The *project* perspective looks in detail at the specific aims and objectives of the e-participation initiative as set by the project stakeholders.
3. The *sociotechnical* perspective considers to what extent the design of the ICTs directly affects the outcomes. Established frameworks from the software engineering and information systems fields can be used to assess issues such as usability and accessibility.

These authors essentially take the perspective that e-participation is a hybrid of various technologies, social influences, and political systems that requires much more research to properly understand. Therefore, to understand e-participation one must understand democracy, the project that is being worked, and the socialtechnical environment.

A three-stage model demonstrates the commitment to e-participation between citizens and government through the use of ICT: information provision, consultation, and participation (Medaglia, 2007). *Information provision* is the one-way delivery of information to citizens, and in this stage citizens play a very passive role. Participation involves individuals looking up information. *Consultation* is the two-way interaction in which citizens provide active feedback on government policies. This is a more active form of participation with citizen consultation, but there is no guarantee that citizens' input would be taken into account when shaping policy. Finally, active *participation* is where citizens can initiate ideas on policies and shape policy outcomes. This is the highest form of e-participation where citizens can potentially have a substantial influence on policies. In an analysis of local governments in Italy the provision of ICT was directed more toward information provision, but there was some citizen consultation taking place (Medaglia, 2007). Therefore, research shows that most participation is very passive, merely providing information about policies to citizens.

Survey evidence of citizens indicates that online participation is not simply an extension of offline participation in democratic politics and it can be distinguished in several important respects (Jensen et al., 2007). One difference is that political and community participation is different from private online participation. Because it can be easily accessed, the Internet makes private participation much more possible, where someone can participate alone without having to be in a group. A second difference is that online participation is not characterized by socioeconomic status as much as offline democratic participation. Individuals who participate offline tend to be older and more affluent. Therefore, the young are able to be more active as a result of the Internet and participation. Third, there is a strong link between engagement and political associations for those online. Therefore, the Internet provides an easy vehicle for creating political associations and as a result promotes participation. The following section examines why citizens engage online with their government.

Internet and Civic Engagement

Three objectives of e-engagement can contribute to the policymaking process of government. The first objective of e-engagement is information dissemination. This is the one-way relationship between government producing information and citizens receiving the information. Citizens in this form of engagement are very passive, and government is actively disseminating information to them. The second objective of e-engagement is consultation. This is where there is a two-way relationship between citizens and government. In the consultation phase citizens provide feedback to government on policy changes. The third objective of e-engagement is active participation. This is where there is a partnership between government and citizens to actively engage in the policymaking process. Citizens are partners with government and are actively involved in the development of new policies, and that can impact outcomes (Organization for Economic Co-Operation and Development [OECD], 2003).

There are both positive and negative views of the Internet on civic engagement (Jennings and Zeitner, 2003). A positive view is that it will strengthen civil society and democratic politics and institutions by expanding the opportunities for communication and mobilization of citizens. A more pessimistic view is that the Internet could exacerbate existing inequalities in civic engagement because of the digital divide. Survey research does show that Internet users tend to have higher levels of civic engagement than non-Internet users. But this relationship may also be explained by the socioeconomic status of the Internet user, and the models don't take this into consideration.

The Internet is said to be an important tool for democracy because it engages citizens in challenging dominant discourse, allowing individuals to better engage in a range of political and social issues. The Internet can particularly be useful after political shocks, such as major changes in policies, because segments of the population may disapprove of a policy and may find it difficult to voice their dissent through traditional media. The Internet provides free space for dissent and can provide a foundation for activism (Rohlinger and Brown, 2009).

Research shows three ways the Internet can be used as a tool after political shocks. First, the Internet can provide a free space for challengers to form opposition to dominant groups. The Internet provides an avenue for dissent for citizens to express discontent. Second, the Internet provides citizens with the ability to express their dissent anonymously and without retribution. The Internet enables citizens to oppose a policy without having to be identified, reducing risk toward the individuals. Third, the Internet has the ability to move online activism to the streets because of its mobilizing potential (Rohlinger and Brown, 2009).

MoveOn.org provides an example of online activism in the wake of terrorist attacks on September 11, 2001, on the World Trade Center and the Pentagon. This online website mobilized protests against military engagement in the Middle East. MoveOn.org provided a free space away from the control of dominant groups for which opposition could articulate their point of view. Research shows that online organizations such as MoveOn.org can engage citizens to dissent and participate in government, showing that the Internet can be an important democratic resource (Rohlinger and Brown, 2009).

Pew Internet and American Life survey research shows that offline political participation has been associated with a certain group: those with high levels of income and education (Smith et al., 2009). **Table 3-2** compares both offline and online political activities. Some common online activities for political engagement are sending e-mails to government officials, signing a petition online, e-mailing an editor, or

Table 3-2 *Comparing Both Offline and Online Political Activities*

Offline Activities	Online Activities
Contact a government official in person, by phone or by letter	Send an e-mail to a government official
Sign a petition	Sign a petition online
Send a letter to the editor through the U.S. postal service	E-mail a letter to the editor
Make a contribution in person, by phone, or through the mail	Make a political contribution on the Internet
Communicate with a civic/political group by face-to-face meetings, print letter or newsletter, or telephone	Communicate with a civic/political group by messaging, instant messaging, or using a social networking site

making a political contribution on the Internet. Some newer forms of political engagement online are through social networking sites such as Facebook and Twitter.

Pew Internet and American Life survey evidence shows that online activities are marked by the same high levels of stratification by both income and education as offline civic engagement (**Figure 3-2**). As income and education levels rise, community involvement increases, political activity rises, and other types of civic engagement increase. There is no evidence that web-based political participation has fundamentally changed this long-standing finding. Therefore, the Web is just a tool for e-participation; it does not create more participation.

Table 3-3 shows that almost two-thirds of all Americans have participated in some form of political activity in the past year. To measure the amount of political activity in the United States, in 2008 the Pew Internet and American Life survey asked respondents whether they did a range of 11 activities from working with fellow citizens to solve local problems, to participating actively in organizations that try to influence public policy, to volunteering for a political party candidate. The results show that 63% of American adults have done at least 1 of those 11 activities over

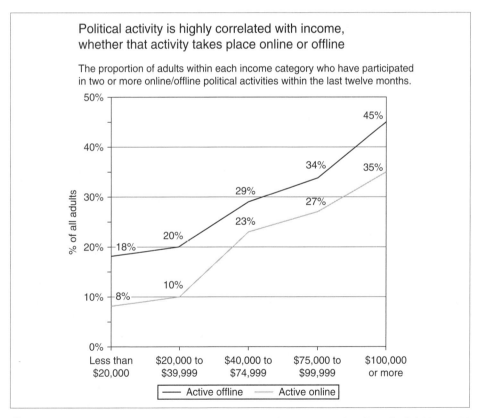

Figure 3-2 *Political activity online and income. Margin of error is ±2% based on all adults (n = 2251)* (From Smith et al., 2009)

Table 3-3 *Civic and Political Involvement in America*

Adults Who Did Each of the Following in the Last 12 Months	Percent
Sign a petition	32
Contact a national, state, or local government official about an issue	30
Work with fellow citizens to solve a problem in your community	28
Attend a political meeting on local, town, or school affairs	24
Contribute money to a political candidate or party or any other political organization or cause	18
Be an active member of a group that tries to influence public policy or government	15
Attend a political rally or speech	12
Send a letter to the editor of a newspaper or magazine	10
Work or volunteer for a political party or candidate	8
Make a speech about a community or local issue	7
Attend an organized protest	4
Any of these	63

Margin of error is ±2% based on all adults ($n = 2,251$).

Source: Smith et al. (2009).

the previous year. The results show that a significant amount of Americans are very civically engaged.

Table 3-4 provides a comparison of income and education and civic engagement. These results show that income and education do have an impact regardless of whether the individual is online for civic engagement. **Table 3-5** also shows that age has an impact on civic engagement. However, there is a small change, by only 2% with younger individuals (18–24 years) going online and being civically engaged.

Table 3-6 shows the new forms of online political engagement such as posting material about political and social issues on the Web and using social networking sites politically. These new forms of civic engagement are dominated by the younger adults. When it comes to online political activities as previously noted, the youngest adults from ages 18 to 24 years were less likely as a whole to take part in online political activities but were more likely to do so than those individuals that are 65

Table 3-4 *Online and Offline Civic Engagement by Different Demographic Groups*

Proportion of Adults Who Have Taken Part in 2 or More Civic/Political Activities in the Past 12 Months	Active Offline (%)	Active Online (Among All Adults) (%)	Active Online (Among Internet Users) (%)
Total	27	18	24
Education			
Less than high school	12	2	n/a
High school grad	18	9	13
Some college	32	23	26
College grad	44	35	37
Annual household income			
Less than $20,000	18	8	15
$20,000–$39,999	20	10	14
$40,000–$74,999	29	23	26
$75,000-$99,999	34	27	30
$100,000 or more	45	35	37
Geography			
Urban	25	17	23
Suburban	29	21	26
Rural	27	13	20

Source: Smith et al. (2009).

and older. But when it comes to new forms of contacting government, such as social networking sites and blogs, this exhibits a different pattern. There is a noticeable decrease in using these new forms of media with age; this is especially the case with the elderly. Survey results show that adults under the age of 35 represent 28% of the respondents of the survey but make up 72% of those who make political use of social networking sites and 55% of those who post comments or visual material about politics on the Web.

Table 3-5 *Online and Offline Civic Engagement by Different Demographic Groups—*

Adults Who Have Taken Part in 2 or More Civic/Political Activities in the Past 12 Months	Active Offline (%)	Active Online (Among All Adults) (%)	Active Online (Among Internet Users) (%)
Total	27	18	24
Gender			
Male	29	18	24
Female	26	18	25
Age			
18–24	18	16	18
25–34	26	20	23
35–44	30	21	24
45–54	28	21	26
55–64	33	22	30
65+	26	10	27
Race/ethnicity			
White, non-Hispanic	28	19	26
Black, non-Hispanic	25	13	18
Hispanic (English-speaking)	23	18	23

Source: Smith et al. (2009).

Digital Divide

Figure 3-3 shows three approaches to understanding the digital divide in regards to e-government: (1) access digital divide, (2) multidimensional digital divide, and (3) multiperspective digital divide (Helbig et al., 2009). The technology deterministic argument contends there is a simple dichotomy between the "haves" and the "have nots" of access to the Internet. This access digital divide is the result of social, environmental, and organizational factors that prevent use of e-government technology. The multidimensional perspective treats not only access to technology as a problem,

Table 3-6 *Young Adults Are More Likely to Engage in "New" Forms of Online Civic Engagement*

Proportion Within Each Age Group Who Take Part in the Following Activities	18–24	25–34	35–44	45–54	55–64	65+	Difference Between 65+ Age Group and 18–24 Age Group
				%			
Two or more offline political activities	18	26	30	28	33	26	+8
Among all adults							
Two or more online political activities	16	20	21	21	22	10	–6
Make political use of social network sites	29	15	5	3	3	1	–28
Post political content online	30	17	11	7	7	3	–27
Among internet users							
Two or more online political activities	18	23	24	26	30	27	+9
Make political use of social network sites	33	17	6	4	4	2	–31
Post political content online	34	19	12	9	10	8	–26
Among home broadband users							
Two or more online political activities	21	25	29	31	35	35	+14
Make political use of social network sites	35	18	7	5	5	4	–31
Post political content online	40	21	14	9	10	9	–31

Source: Smith et al. (2009).

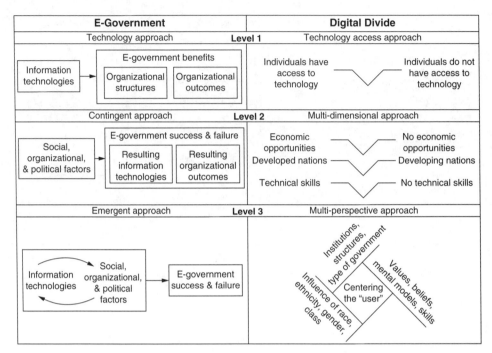

Figure 3-3 *Three approaches to understanding the digital divide* (From Helbig et al., 2009)

but race, ethnicity, income, skills, geography, cultural content, and education as well. Although the multiperspective examines all the above, it also includes the role of institutions of government, values, and beliefs.

In digital divide research there also are different views of the role of e-government in the divide (**Figure 3-3**). The technological approach examines the benefits of e-government on citizens, with a simple focus on technological adoption. In this research the focus is on implementing e-government to change organizational outcomes. The contingency approach to e-government and the digital divide is that social, organizational, and political factors come into play and dictate success or failure of e-government. Finally, the emergent approach is where both the technology and social dimensions collide and dictate e-government success or failure. Essentially, the digital divide and e-government is very complicated and requires multiple social, technological, and organizational perspectives.

Pew Internet and American Life survey data empirically shows a digital divide between individuals who have Internet access and those who do not (**Table 3-7**). As of September 2009, 77% of adults reported going online. There is a digital divide with regards to race, because only 61% of Hispanics and 72% of Blacks reported going online, compared with 80% of Whites. There is also a digital divide with regards to income, with 95% of those earning a household income more than $75,000 per year going online. Education is also a factor; those having less education are much less likely to go online. For instance, 37% of individuals with less than a high

Table 3-7 *Demographics of Internet Users, September 2009*

	Use of the Internet
Total adults (18 and older)	77%
Men	78%
Women	76%
Race/ethnicity	
White	80%
Black	72%
Hispanic	61%
Age	
18–29	93%
30–49	83%
50–64	77%
65+	43%
Household income	
<$30,000/year	62%
$30,000–$49,999	84%
$50,000–$74,999	93%
$75,000 and over	95%
Educational attainment	
Less than high school	37%
High school	72%
Some college	87%
College +	94%
Community type	
Urban	73%
Suburban	75%
Rural	71%

Source: Smith et al. (2009).

school education went online, whereas 94% of those with a college education went online. Age also affects online activity; 93% of young adults (those aged 18–29) are very active online. Therefore, the Internet may not be the ideal medium for providing e-government to all citizens because of this digital divide.

When examining citizen data related to whether they ever contacted government online, recent survey evidence in **Table 3-8** shows the digital divide as well, with only 59% of adults having ever visited a government website. Blacks and Hispanics are less likely than Whites to have visited a government website. Seniors are the least likely to visit a website when compared with 65% of those aged 30 to 49.

One way to understand the diffusion of the Internet and other successful technological innovations is the S (sigmoid)-shaped pattern (Norris, 2001). New technologies under this model experience a slow rate of initial adoption; this is followed by a surge and then by reaching a penetration and then slowing. In this model there are increased returns to scale during the initial innovation followed by diminishing returns as the adoption rate hits most of the population of users. This model argues that a proportion of the population would be left out of Internet access; this is called the digital divide.

Norris (2001) provides two models of technological diffusion that can be applied to Internet diffusion. The more optimistic model shows that Internet diffusion will saturate society much like the telephone did as it becomes easier to use and less

Table 3-8 *Citizens Ever Visiting a State, Local, or Federal Government Website, November 2008*

	Percent
Adults	59
Men	61
Women	56
Whites	63
Blacks	48
Hispanics	44
18–29	52
30–49	65
50–64	61
65+	43

Source: Smith et al. (2009).

expensive. The second more pessimistic view holds that socially disadvantaged groups will not obtain access to the Internet, and this will halt Internet diffusion before it can reach 100%. The more optimistic view is the classic diffusion of innovations pattern where there is slow initial adoption, a surge in the middle, and slowing adoption near the saturation point. The more pessimistic view holds the same pattern, but there will be no saturation point at the top of the curve. Empirical evidence for the digital divide shows that when comparing the United States with European countries, income is important for understanding the digital divide in the United States. In fact, income was the most distinctive source of inequality in the odds of someone using the Internet in America (Martin and Robinson, 2007).

Research shows an urban–rural digital divide in Canada, with the odds of using the Internet almost two times more likely for someone who lives in an urban area than for someone who lives in a rural area (Noce and McKeown, 2008). This finding makes it difficult to separate out other important determinates noted in the literature, such as social economic status of the individual, skills to access the Internet, and infrastructure differences between urban and rural areas that impede access.

Belanger and Carter (2009) identified two major types of digital divides of e-government users, the access divide and the skills divide. Lack of access is the most common one identified in the literature; however, there is a substantial percentage of the population that may not have the skills necessary to interact with government online. The skills digital divide can be further broken down into technical competence and information literacy. Technical competence is the skills needed to do such things as operate hardware, software, typing, and use a mouse. When using e-government, the information literacy is the ability to use information effectively to make decisions. One of the greatest challenges facing individuals when accessing government information is the ability to read and interpret information effectively.

Research on the global digital divide of an analysis of 118 countries and Internet use between 1997 and 2001 found support that it is a result of socioeconomic status and regulatory, political, and sociological variables (Guillen and Suarez, 2005). Therefore, this research essentially shows it is difficult to simplify the digital divide: what happens in one country could be different in another country. The United States, for instance, has a more stable regulatory system that promotes Internet use; other countries may not have these policies, which would have an impact on the digital divide. The digital divide is essential to know in order to understand political participation, because certain groups will not have access to participate online.

Policymaking Process and ICT

Five stages of the policymaking life cycle can be related to e-participation (**Figure 3-4**). There is a direct link in each of these stages between information, consultation, and participation and how ICT can be used in the development of these stages

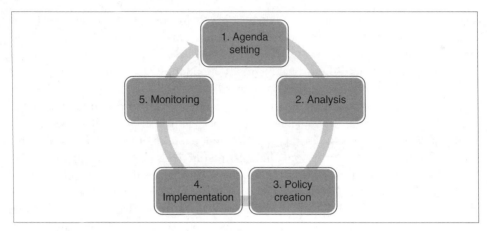

Figure 3-4 *The policymaking life cycle*

(OECD, 2003, p. 35). Each of these stages shows the relationship between e-participation and the policymaking process.

1. *Agenda setting:* Establishing the need for a policy or a change in policy and defining what the problem to be addressed is. This may arise as the result of a change of government, a sudden change in the environment, a growing development, a new problem, or a continuing problem. Information, consultation, and participation are all important for this stage. In particular, active participation allows citizens the opportunity to determine possible agenda items.

2. *Analysis:* Defining the challenges and opportunities associated with an agenda item more clearly in order to produce a draft policy document. This can include gathering evidence and knowledge from a range of sources, including citizens and civil society organizations; understanding the context, including the political context for the agenda item; developing a range of options (including doing nothing) and conducting a cost–benefit analysis for each one; and providing advice to agencies who make a decision on which option to pursue. Again, information, consultation, and participation are all important for this stage. Active participation allows citizens to determine the range of options under review.

3. *Creating the policy:* Ensuring a good workable policy document. This involves a variety of mechanisms, which can include formal consultation, risk analysis, undertaking pilot studies, and designing the implementation plan. At this stage information and consultation are important, but there is possibly limited scope for active participation.

4. *Implementing the policy:* Involving the development of legislation, regulations, guidance, and a delivery plan. At this stage information and consultation are

important, but there is also scope for active participation (e.g., in the delivery of public goods and services by civil society organizations).

5. *Monitoring the policy:* Involving evaluation and review of the policy in action, research evidence, views of users, and horizon scanning. Information, consultation, and participation are all important for this stage. Active participation allows citizens the opportunity to give their views on the policy in action and to suggest changes.

Table 3-9 shows the policymaking life cycle and e-participation as well as the three objectives of e-engagement in the policymaking life cycle. For example, in the agenda-setting stage increasingly more complicated technologies are used moving from information, consultation, and participation. In the agenda-setting phase at the information stage search engines and websites are commonly used. At the consultation stage online surveys, e-mail, and chat rooms can be used as tools in the agenda-setting stage. At the e-participation stage e-referenda and e-petitions can be used as tools for e-enhancing participation.

Three levels of participation should be commented on in relation to the policymaking process (Macintosh, 2004). E-enabling is about supporting who would have Internet access to take advantage of the large amount of data they could access. This has to do with how technology can be used to reach a larger audience.

Table 3-9 *Tools for Online Engagement in the Policymaking Process*

Stage of the Policymaking Process	Information	Consultation	Participation
Agenda setting	Search engines, website, other online information	Online surveys, e-mail, chat rooms	E-referenda, e-petitions
Analysis	Advanced software, data mining	Virtual communities	Virtual town hall meeting
Formulation	Enterprise architecture	Citizen consultation online	Online referenda
Implementation	E-newsletters, websites	Online discussion forms	Online elections, e-mail distribution lists
Evaluation	Online feedback, auditor reports online	Online citizen satisfaction surveys	Elections online

Adapted from Anderson et al. (2007), Kamal (2009), and OECD (2003).

The technology can be used to make sure the information is easily available and easy to read and interpret. The second level of participation used to engage citizens is e-engaging. This is concerned with consulting a wide audience in a top-down citizen consultation model. The third level is e-empowering, in which citizens support active participation and there is bottom-up idea generation. In the bottom-up perspective, citizens act as producers of information rather than merely consumers of information.

According to Phang and Kankanhalli (2008), e-participation initiatives can be deployed to achieve four general objectives for citizen participation: information exchange, education and support building, decision-making supplement, and input probing. E-participation efforts used for information exchange are where planners and citizens are brought together to openly share ideas and concerns. These efforts seek to achieve an open dialogue between planners and citizens. Examples of technology used in this objective are citizen participation with web portals and online chat and online discussion forums that can be used to achieve this objective. The second objective of citizen participation is education and support building. E-participation efforts with education and support-building objectives aim to inform citizens about the why and how of government's policy plans and creating a favorable climate for enabling these plans. ICT tools that can be used here are a selection panel of committee members based on electronic profile of their demographic information. Online chat, teleconferencing, and video conferencing tools can be used to hold meeting sessions among members. Push technology can be used such as e-mail blasts that broadcast items such as newsletters. The third e-participation effort with the decision-making objective aims to extract specific information from citizens, such as preferences. Example of technologies used here are group support systems that aid in the participation process. The final objective of e-participation efforts is input probing. This is where you obtain citizens' views on relatively underexplored political issues. One common technique in this objective is citizen surveys. ICT tools used here are online survey questionnaires, web comment forms, and data analysis tools. Another area of e-participation is citizen involvement in the rulemaking process.

E-Rulemaking

IT-based solutions to rulemaking hold the promise to increase the volume and lower the cost of citizen participation in government (Shulman, 2005). The movement to e-rulemaking is partly attributed to the Government Paperwork Elimination Act of 1998 and other directives to open up the regulatory process to make it more open, transparent, deliberative, efficient, and effective. In addition, in 2002 Congress passed the E-Government Act, which directs agencies to enhance public participation through electronic means. The portal www.Regulations.gov is part of the solution for federal e-rulemaking.

Citizens and their access to rulemaking information, as noted by Schlosberg and colleagues (2009), are much different from what was envisioned in the Administrative Procedures Act. This has all changed with a new era of digital technologies such as blogs, podcasts, mass e-mail, and web services. There are numerous avenues for public comments rather than simply filling out an offline form and submitting the information through the mail. These authors first found that public comments on proposed rules is very high with agency websites as an important source for information for comments. Second, commenters also view the comments of others in the rulemaking process. Third, commenters say they gained an understanding of other positions by reading their comments online, and some even found them persuasive. The elements necessary for online deliberation such as openness to information, willingness to understand others, and the possibility of preferences being changed was present with e-rulemaking (Schlosberg et al., 2009).

Scholars have proclaimed that ICT will "revolutionize" rulemaking from relative obscurity to opening up government to ordinary citizens to participate in regulations (Coglianese, 2007). A more pessimistic view holds that the federal government's current e-rulemaking process is likely to deliver only marginal changes in which citizens participate in rulemaking. As a result of the Internet, regulatory agencies post key studies and other rulemaking documents on their websites. Some agencies allow public comments to be submitted via e-mail. In 2003 there was the creation of www.regulations.gov, which relies on the Office of Federal Register's listing of notices of proposed rules and enables users to search all proposed rules that are open for public comment. For example, the U.S. Department of Agriculture's rulemaking of organic foods garnered more than a quarter of a million comments. However, research shows the more controversial or high profile rules get the most comments, but the more common changes in rules get very few comments. ICT may reduce the costs associated with accessing information on agencies for public comment, but most of the rule changes get little attention. Coglianese (2007) argued that most citizens are already disengaged with politics and policy, and ICT in the rulemaking process is unlikely to change participation.

Web 2.0 Technologies and E-Participation

Web 2.0 technologies are the collection of social media through which individuals are active participants in creating, organizing, editing, combining, sharing, commenting, and rating web content as well as forming a social network through interacting with each other (Chun et al., 2010). The Web 2.0 technologies include blogs, wikis, social networking sites (e.g., Facebook and MySpace), web-based communication (e.g., chatting, photo-sharing using Flickr), video casting and sharing (e.g., YouTube), audio sharing (e.g., podcasts), mashups, widgets, virtual words, and microblogs (e.g., Twitter). **Table 3-10** provides definitions of social media technologies and examples of government applications of social media technologies.

Table 3-10 *Social Media Types and Government Examples*

	Definition	Goals	Government Examples
Blog	A web log (blog) is a web-based interactive application that allows one to log journal entries on events or to express opinions and make commentaries on specific topics. It is a popular content generation tool. Blogs typically consist of text, images, videos, music, and/or audios.	Attract new audience for government information; puts human face on government; opens up a conversation	Federal agency public-facing blogs, elected official blogs, interesting topics blogs, pandemic leadership blogs
Microblogging	The process of creating a short blog that is primarily achieved through mobile devices to share information about current events or personal opinions. A well-known example is Twitter.		
Wiki	A web-based collaborative editing tool that allows different people to contribute their knowledge to the content. One author's content can be modified and enhanced with another author's contribution. A well-known example of this application tool is Wikipedia.	Collaboration (e.g., project management, knowledge management); create a better work product; use mostly enterprise wikis, restricted to community of practice; enhance community participation in decision making	Community support (e.g., GSA collaborative work environment), Intellpedia (wiki for intelligence agencies), diplopedia (State Department wiki), peer-to-patent wiki, NASA wiki for object-oriented data terminology
Social networking	A web-based tool or model that allows individuals to meet and form a virtual community through socializing via different relationships, such as friendships and professional relationships, sharing and propagating multimedia information, exchanging interests and communicating.	Reach people where they are	CIA recruit Facebook

Table 3-10 *Social Media Types and Government Examples* (Continued)

	Definition	Goals	Government Examples
Multimedia sharing	The rich multimedia contents such as photos, videos, and audios are shared through multimedia sharing tools. Typical examples include YouTube, Flickr, Picasa, Vimeo, etc.	Share rich set of governments' multimedia data with people in coordinated manner	Library of Congress Flickr stream, federal photo sharing site (http://www.usa.gov/Topics/Graphics.shtml) (e.g., Air Force photo gallery, federal agency YouTube), state photo sites, White House podcasts, NASA audio/video casts, government services podcasts (us.gov), DOD's TroopTube for troops to connect to their families and supporters
Mashup	An application that uses contents from two or more external data sources, combines and integrates them, and thus creates new value-added information. This is a reuse and repurposing of the source data by retrieving source contents with open APIs (application programming interfaces) and integrating them according to the information needs, instead of navigating them sequentially.	Provide combined content from different government data sources; share contents and expertise from different sources; create more rich contents for decision making	USA search mashup combines search engine results, forms database, FAQ database, images, and categorization related to keyword search; NASA's Atrolicio.us, Google map with government data
RSS	A web application that can pull the content from sources that are structured in standard metadata format called RSS (really simple syndication) feeds such that it is easy to syndicate the contents from RSS-	Get regularly updated content out; link back to authoritative source; ties feeds to e-mail alerts	Usa.gov library of federal RSS feeds, EPA RSS feeds, disaster news feeds, NOAA watch feeds

(Continues)

Table 3-10 *Social Media Types and Government Examples* (Continued)

	Definition	Goals	Government Examples
	formatted documents. The RSS feeds or web feeds can be published and updated by the authors such that the updates can be easily inserted and quickly updated in content aggregation sites. The RSS feeds (also called atoms) are annotated with metadata such as the author and date information. The RSS-based content aggregators include news headlines, weather warnings, blogs, etc. Once the source content is updated, the content aggregator sites will be updated, thus always sharing the updated content.		
Widgets	Small applications either on the desktop, a mobile device, or the Web. The widgets bring personalized dedicated content to the user from predefined data sources.	Prebuilt applications to add more interactivity and functional capabilities on a web page will allow users to develop widgets using government data to expand the reach and functionality and share these widgets	FBI most wanted widget, DHS hurricane info widget
Virtual world	A virtual world is an interactive 3-D computer-simulated world where avatars, controlled and played by the users, interact with each other as inhabitants.	Train and educate with simulations	Departments of Defense and Homeland Security emergency management planning preparation

Table 3-10 *Social Media Types and Government Examples* (Continued)

	Definition	Goals	Government Examples
Social bookmarking and tagging	A tagging system that allows the users to describe the content of the web sources with metadata such as free text, comments, evaluative ratings, and votes. This human-generated collective and collaborative set of tags forms a folksonomy and helps cluster web resources.		

Adapted from Chun et al. (2010).

There are many challenges associated with Government 2.0 technologies (Chun et al., 2010):

- How to analyze the immense amount of data collected, through a vast amount of participation to develop appropriate policies that can be proposed in the data analysis
- How to effectively search and share all these data
- How can governments integrate data from different sources without endangering the privacy of individuals
- What are the interoperability issues of designing Government 2.0 technologies
- How to extract high-quality data from the mass participation through social media
- How to get certain underrepresented groups to participate in the political process through social media technologies.

Web 2.0 is the new generation of Internet applications (Meijer and Thaens, 2010). The basic idea of Web 2.0 is that the old generation of unidirectional technologies has been replaced by multidirectional applications that make users both senders and receivers of information. The Web 2.0 is the new Internet in that it is participatory or social in nature, with communication in many-to-many networks common. These applications are based on the idea that users generate the content. Therefore, user-generated content is one of the second key characteristics of Web 2.0 technologies. Finally, personalization is the third key characteristic of Web 2.0 technologies in that users are enabled to indicate their personal preferences as seen through RSS feeds. Even knowing that Web 2.0 technologies have many-to-many networks, user-generated content, and personalization, their usefulness has not been fully realized in the public sector. These new technologies enable governments to realize the benefits of becoming more efficient, more transparent, and more effective and responsive to citizens. Some argue by using this technology it may be possible to transform government by reducing red tape and gridlock and to enhance democracy (Meijer and Thaens, 2010).

Web 1.0 was the introduction of the World Wide Web (Singh et al., 2010). Web 2.0 technologies focus more on the user. Some may refer to Web 2.0 technologies as a fad, but it is becoming clear that it has growth and will be here to stay. Some of the characteristics of Web 2.0 is its increasing focus on looking at the collective intelligence of users, new ways of presenting data (mashup), reliance on user-generated content, ease of programming, elimination of software upgrade cycles, digital democracy, social networks, collaboration, and rapid development of business models.

Social networking sites model real-world networks in a virtual community. They are web-based services that allow users to (Schellong, 2008a, p. 229)

- Construct a public or semipublic profile within a bounded system
- Articulate a list of other users with whom they share a connection
- View and traverse their list of connections and those made by others within the system

Social networking sites assist each user in creating or seeking a network of friends, acquaintances, and generally people who share similar interests. The members on these sites are encouraged to expand their network by inviting others to join the network (Schellong, 2008a). Empirical studies show that new technologies have not lived up to the revolutionary hype. Most ICT is designed to reinforce existing democratic practices (Wright, 2008). Website use has changed with a movement toward Web 2.0, where there is an emphasis on user-generated content, social networking, interactivity, openness, integration, and adaptability of service channels. Examples of Web 2.0 technologies are blogs, discussion groups, wikis, music streams with rating features, and social networking platforms. These sites are normally self-organized by users bringing together their thoughts and opinions (Schellong, 2008a).

In an analysis of survey research, young people using the Internet for information are more likely to participate in offline clubs and groups and demonstrate more political knowledge (Pasek et al., 2009). Essentially, social networking site users of Facebook and MySpace are more civically engaged. Therefore, social networking sites may provide some explanation to encourage civic engagement, but there is not overwhelming evidence that this will have any long-lasting impacts on public administration and IT.

Summary

This chapter examined e-participation and some of the issues associated with this important area of IT and public administration. There was a discussion of e-participation theories and civic engagement, and one theory advocates that e-participation occurs in different stages ranging from providing information, to consultation, to active participation. Overall, survey evidence indicates that information, the most passive form of e-participation, is most common among governments. Survey research also shows that civic engagement increases with greater income and education, but there are no differences in engagement for those online versus offline.

What is noticeably different in civic engagement is that the new social networking sites dominated by the young, between 18 and 24 years, are a new form of civic engagement. The digital divide is the result of a certain segment of the population not having access to a new technology such as the Internet. There are many theories of the digital divide, but one theory argues that the diffusion of innovations will eventually reach 100%, with the entire population having access to a new technology. The other view is that the digital divide will never be eliminated because the technology may never reach the entire population.

The five stages of the policymaking process where ICT can have an influence are agenda setting, analysis, creating the policy, implementing the policy, and monitoring the policy. Citizen participation can be incorporated into each of these stages through such technologies as virtual town hall meetings, online feedback, discussion boards, and blogs.

The rulemaking process has changed in the United States as a result of ICT. New technologies have enabled the rulemaking process to be more transparent and have provided another avenue for increased citizen participation. There is a new generation of user-generated content online, such as Web 2.0 technologies, providing the next platform for citizen participation in government.

Discussion Questions

1. How has the Internet changed civic engagement, and how does online engagement differ from offline engagement?
2. What is the digital divide and how does it impact e-participation?
3. How has ICT impacted the policymaking process in government? Describe some of the technologies that can be used in policy development.
4. Has the Internet revolutionized the rulemaking process in government? Explain.

Closing Case Study

Social Media Sites and the Visually or Hearing Impaired

Governments have embraced social media sites such as Facebook, Twitter, and YouTube as a new way of reaching the public (Perlman, 2009). The issue is that some would-be followers, especially the visually and hearing impaired, may be cut off from these sites. In fact, Section 508 of the Federal Rehabilitation Act requires that persons with disabilities are able to access information and data on U.S. government websites. Although they do not fall under the federal requirements, many state and local governments have their own laws addressing accessibility based on the federal regulations. For example, the Missouri Department of Conversation uses Facebook and Twitter and does not focus on accessibility. The argument is made that they don't put any original content on either site, and Twitter posts links to the departmental main site, which is accessible. And with Facebook, this is a collection of newsfeeds. Department officials claim that these sites just repackage information that is already available.

The technology to help the visually impaired read the social media sites is very limited and of poor quality. A legal case could be made that Section 508 accessibility rules don't apply to the social media sites, such as YouTube and Facebook, because these are privately owned and operated. But some would argue that this evades the spirit of the law. The issue then becomes as social media sites become more commonly used by the public to get information from their government in such forms as a virtual town hall meeting, those with disabilities will not be able to fully participate. In addition, the www.Recovery.gov website of the Obama Administration, unveiled in 2009, was designed to show where the stimulus dollars were going to create greater transparency (Lipowicz, 2009). The issue with this technology is that it left out one segment of the population. Advocates for people with disabilities found a number of accessibility flaws on the site that jumbled the spending data or otherwise put it beyond reach for individuals using screen readers and other assistive devices.

Advocates for disabilities believe that having more open and transparent government under the Obama Administration should improve access to those with disabilities. Section 508 of the Rehabilitation Act of 1973 governs the accessibility of federal websites, and amendments were added in 1998 that greatly strengthened it. Under the rules, sites must be compatible with assistive technologies for people with disabilities, including screen readers. However, unlike the federal government, state and local agencies have no uniform approach for ensuring that websites are accessible.

Chapter 4

E-Governance

Opening Case Study

New York City Integrates Social Services

New York City is faced with the challenge of integrating data to help those in need of social services (Newcombe, 2009a). Health and Human Service (HHS) Connect was created to address this problem. The hope with this system is that caseworkers, whether they work for the city or a nonprofit agency, are able to see the client's history, family composition, and immediate future needs through HHS Connect. With this system caseworkers can give families the resources to get back on their feet rather than just solve a crisis. But the problem is getting the organizations to share information to make this happen.

Linda Gibbs, deputy mayor for New York City, put faith in the HSS Connect technology to be able to change this situation. Gibbs realized with reform-minded Mayor Michael Bloomberg that the way to reform was through increased collaboration. Gibbs wanted to use HHS Connect to get the resources necessary to treat the family's situation holistically. She believes it is not just the current situation that was important to address but future issues as well that impact homelessness such as unemployment, illness, and incarceration. Gibbs worked with agency commissioners to develop a vision for collaboration and created a strategic roadmap for how the problem could be solved with the help of consulting firm Deloitte. She also brought in chief information officer

Kamal Bherwani to oversee the strategy and architecture across the nine organizations that compose HHS.

Bherwani's strategy was to leverage the information technology assets of the city to reshape how services were delivered. His strategy was to involve input from 13 agencies. He required that all agencies share their data unless it was against the law, and all stakeholders were required to attend all meetings. Bherwani used a model that took the project's various risk factors and placed them in a risk register, which is a dashboard that tracks the probability of a potential problem. This worked well because agencies tended to be risk averse, and they could see potential risks ahead of time.

Other technology in New York City is seen through the City's Department of Homeless Services (DHS), which has deployed mobile handheld devices to field workers enabling inspectors to input and share data, such as condition of the dwelling, documenting housing compliance standards, and completing checklists in real time (Anonymous, 2009). The DHS needed apartments to be approved more efficiently, and mobile technology enables more efficiency. Since deploying mobile devices in the field, this has increased DHS inspections by 57%, and the number of leases signed through its rental assistance program, Advantage New York, has increased by 25%.

Chapter Objectives

The six primary objectives of this chapter are as follows:

1. To understand e-governance and the various models used to describe this theory
2. To describe the importance of e-governance for citizens
3. To understand e-governance and organization change by creating a more transparent government
4. To describe the influence of new public management on e-governance
5. To understand e-governance and its impact on service delivery as seen through street-level bureaucrats
6. To understand citizen relationship management technology and its application to public administration

Introduction

This chapter examines the role of e-governance in understanding information technology (IT) and public administration. E-governance models are described in the literature and are presented in this chapter (Garson, 2007). E-governance is especially important for citizens and their interaction with government, and this chapter covers that important relationship. E-governance is said to influence organizational change and transformation, and here we discuss its impact on public administration, especially in regards to making a more transparent government. New public management (NPM) is one theory of reform in public administration, and some of its principles can be found in e-governance, as discussed in this chapter. One area that e-governance has impacted is the delivery of public services. Most notable is the change in the relationship of the traditional street-level bureaucrat as a result of information and communication technologies (ICTs). Finally, we discuss one of the most important technologies used to enhance citizen interaction in e-governance, centralized customer service systems.

E-Governance Defined

E-governance can be defined as the governmental use of ICT to improve the quality and effectiveness of service delivery for citizens (United Nations, 2008; Chen and Hsieh, 2009). E-governance goes beyond merely improving service delivery for government and delves into the area of enhancing democracy and citizen participation in the policymaking process (Kolsaker and Lee-Kelley, 2008). Most e-governance research has focused on the supply-side metrics such as government output, but the more critical question for e-governance is the demand-side perspective, or citizen's interaction with government.

E-commerce can sometimes be confused with e-governance, but there are three major differences related to access, structure, and accountability (Carter and Belanger, 2005). In e-commerce, businesses are allowed to choose their customers; in e-governance, government agencies are required to provide access to an entire eligible population. These individuals may be of lower income levels or have disabilities. The digital divide makes providing e-governance even more of a challenge for governments. Structure is also different for e-governance compared with e-commerce in the private sector. In business the structure is normally more decentralized and entrepreneurial, whereas in government there is much more structure in the form of hierarchy. Accountability is another difference in e-commerce and e-governance, where public sector agencies are required to allocate resources on the basis of public interest, which recognizes the political nature of decisions. In e-commerce the allocation of resources is done on the basis of profits and investments. Research on e-governance services indicates that when there was a perceived ease of use, compatibility, and trustworthiness, these factors significantly explained citizens' use of state e-governance services (Carter and Belanger, 2005).

When reviewing the e-governance literature, there are several important characteristics (Grant and Chau, 2005). First, most e-governance definitions focus on the service delivery component as being critically important to its development. For example, improvements in tax filing through online systems, payments of public service bills online, and renewal of vehicle registration online are common examples used to successfully implement e-governance. The opening case study shows the importance of e-governance in integrating New York City's social services. Second, there is literature that argues for e-governance as a transformative force of change. This view holds that e-governance will reinvent government, increase its efficiency, decentralize structure, and be transparent and accountable to its citizens. Third, e-governance offers a diverse number of solutions to a problem through applications. The focus here is applications that make improvements in government operations in different countries. The Internet with its universal standards makes it easier for developing countries to offer e-governance services. Fourth, the integration of e-governance with existing IT systems is possible because of the Internet. The argument here is that e-governance is one important dimension of the overall IT architecture. Fifth, there is the maturity aspect of e-governance that argues for different stages of adoption in organizations. Common stages of development of e-governance go from the information, transactions, and integration within organizations. Sixth, there is the international dimension of e-governance. Governments around the world in both developed and developing governments are looking at e-governance as a way to change their operations, reach out to citizens, and transform their organizations. From these six components, Grant and Chau (2005, p. 9) come up with a universal definition of e-governance:

> A broad-based transformation initiative, enabled by leveraging the capabilities information and communication technology: (1) to develop and deliver high quality, seamless, and integrated public services; (2) to enable effective constituent relationship management; and (3) to support the economic and social development goals of citizens, businesses, and civil society at local, state, national, and international levels.

Table 4-1 shows the adoption of e-governance and its different phases and implementation (Dawes, 2008). In the first phase, in the early 1990s, the mainframe computer was predominant. These information systems processed large batch transactions and were centralized in the organization. In the mid-1990s, the second phase of e-governance was where the desktop computer became the norm of government, with local area networks connecting up these computers, and Internet access became more common. It was not until the late 1990s with the commercialization of the Internet that the Web proliferated through both business and government. As a result, citizens had more access to government online, and there arose the issue of the digital divide, or those individuals without access to the Internet. Early 2000 was a period of the development of wireless networks, mobile computer, and other advanced applications that built on the early developments of the Web. The third phase brought about the issue of privacy and security, and enterprise architecture was used to connect the government together with IT. The last phase, in late 2000, saw the development of social networking technologies and advanced programming languages such as extensible markup language, or XML. This was a time of increased collaboration and potential for citizen participation in governance.

Table 4-1 *E-Governance Phases and Implementation Issues*

Time Period	Adopted Technologies	Implementation Issues
Until early 1990	Mainframe computers	High-volume transactions, very centralized IT
Mid-1990s	Desktop computing, local area networks, and web browser	Performance management, create internal efficiency, decentralization of IT
Late-1990s	Commercially available Internet, e-mail, networks	Websites, online citizen services, digital divide
Early 2000	Wireless networks, mobile computing, advanced applications such as search tools, data mining, and GIS	Privacy and security, Y2K issue, enterprise architecture
Late 2000	Web 2.0 technologies, and XML	Information sharing and collaboration, online voting and citizen participation

Adapted from Dawes (2008).

Two defining features of e-governance make it different and important for the study of IT and public administration (Chen and Hsieh, 2009). The first is the seamless integration of government. Essentially, the integration of government information and services to promote better governance are important for e-governance. The second defining feature is the online citizen participation in governance, which includes access and use by citizens. How have citizens' lives been changed as a result of e-governance? In a comparative case study of the United States and Taiwan and their e-governance, Chen and Hsieh showed the United States has done better at showing the importance of building democratic institutions and technology infrastructure to foster e-governance. With regards to integrating e-governance, Taiwan showed the importance of having a lead agency to coordinate e-governance projects. Essentially, e-governance is important because it addresses the use of IT to increase citizen participation in government.

Models of E-Governance

Three policy phases of e-governance are important to discuss to understand its influence on policymaking and public administration (Snellen, 2002). The first phase, ICT in the pre-implementation phase, is indicative of the network model of public administration with interactive policymaking taking place. Policymaking is also proactive in that different groups mobilize because of an issue. There is the coproduction of policies in which different groups that are impacted by the policy will try to influence its development. The second phase is ICT in the implementation phase. This is where street-level bureaucrats play an important role in how the policy is implemented. There is a tendency in a networked organization to downgrade the work of street-level bureaucrats, which is in line with the hollowing out of their discretion. There is the creation of expert systems, which translate the policy into actionable behavior. Data mining and databases play a key part in the implementation phase to identify clients and determine their status of their application. The final phase is ICT in the post-implementation phase. In this phase there is the handling of administrative complaints and judicial appeals of citizens, performance indicators and benchmarking, and freedom of access to policy documents.

Chadwick and May (2003) demonstrate three models of e-governance, namely the managerial, consultative, and participatory models, which are shown in **Table 4-2**. The managerial model of e-governance focuses on efficient public service delivery through ICT. In this model change is incremental depending on the challenges and opportunities available. This is a push model in which e-governance is provided to the public without any input. The consultative model is more of a pull model. In this model the public is consulted on various e-governance projects, but the parameters of input from citizens are set in advance in the system. The final model is participative, in which there is more of a complex horizontal and vertical flow of information. The difference between the consultative and participatory models is that the latter participation percolates from the bottom up. The consultative model still has the bureaucracy setting the parameters of participation, whereas the participatory model has citizens driving change. In an examination of the United States, Great Britain, and the European Union, Chadwick and May (2003) found these governments were relying more on the managerial model of using e-governance to promote efficient government rather than the consultative and participatory models. Individuals might get better services from their government, but there is little interactivity with them on the types and effectiveness of the services that they received.

There are six important dimensions of e-governance, which Dawes (2009) identified as essential for any future research agenda. With these factors it is hoped that e-governance research will move beyond its main focus on services to citizens, some believe the true potential of e-governance. The first is the purpose of e-governance. What is the role for government in society? Issues such as accountability, transparency, and stewardship are important for this dimension. Second, societal trends impact e-governance such as demographic trends, digital divide, and political participation is important in this dimension. Third, the changing technologies of e-governance are another dimension. Here there are issues of security and privacy, wireless technologies, social networks, and sensory technology that need to be further studied. The fourth dimension is information management through digital archives and libraries, databases, and retrieval systems. Information management is extremely important because

Table 4-2 *Managerial, Consultative, and Participatory Models of E-Governance*

	Managerial	Consultative	Participatory
Role for government	Regulatory; responding to the needs of the "new economy"; efficient and faster delivery of government information to citizens and "users."	Regulatory; responding to needs of societal interests as expressed electronically; *better* policy provision to citizens and "users."	Protector of free speech and rights of expression, regulator of infrastructure, but little beyond that; civil society exists away from the state and (will be) mediated electronically.
Principal actors and interests	Government and its "customers"; business; the mass media.	Government; "customers"; businesses; interest groups.	Voluntary associations and interest groups spontaneously interacting within "cyberspace"; groups use information gleaned through deliberation to influence government.
Flow of information	Unilinear from government to "customers," customers to government, but main emphasis on improving flow of information within government.	Unilinear from government to citizens or citizens to government.	Discursive and complex—citizens to citizens, citizens to government, government to citizens.
Principal mechanisms for interaction	Online tax returns; benefit claims; "one-stop shops"; updating of personal information held by public bureaucracies; government gathering and aggregation of "market research" data; government provisioning of information about its activities to media and public.	"E-voting" at elections; instant opinion polling; electronic input from voters and interest groups to government; "advisory" referendums; "electronic town meetings," and so on.	Autonomous pluralist mechanisms, such as discussion lists, Usenet, peer-to-peer technologies; time and distance become compressed, facilitating increased political participation and a "cyber civil society."

(Continues)

Table 4-2 *Managerial, Consultative, and Participatory Models of E-Governance* (Continued)

	Managerial	Consultative	Participatory
Usage issues	Market-based access and usage patterns; minimal state regulation and public education programs to equip consumers.	Market-base access and usage patterns; minimal state regulation and public education programs to equip citizens.	Universal access and widespread usage are prerequisites.
Defining logic	"Service delivery" and policy presentation.	"Technical accuracy" and improved policy success rate.	"Deliberation," participation, and enhanced democracy.

From Chadwick and May (2003).

these new technologies make it much easier to store and manipulate information. The fifth element is the human element, which deals with trust, user friendliness, and e-learning. The final dimension of e-governance is interaction and complexity in which there is collaboration, multichannel service delivery, and system interoperability. With this knowledge of the various models of e-governance, the following section further elaborates on citizens and their impact on e-governance.

E-Governance and Citizens

E-governance has provided the potential of tapping new ways of relating to citizens (Welch et al., 2004; King, 2007). In the first phase, information/transaction, e-governance is more directed toward the needs of government through an information/transactions relationship with its citizens (King, 2007). The aim of such a system is to provide an efficient response to citizens' inquiries and complete their necessary transactions. This citizen relationship is driven more by the needs of the government in regards to service delivery. The second phase is the insightful citizen relationship, which is still government driven. ICT systems can be used here to segment citizens depending on their needs, providing operational analytics to improve performance of the organization. There also is a wall between the second and third phases, citizen-centric government. The wall represents a significant barrier for citizen-centric government, created by bureaucratic, political, and the general government resistance to change. If governments are able to get past this wall, they can achieve citizen-centric government through ICT. In this phase there is extensive citizen access to data and coproduction of data and decisions made with citizens. Therefore, to understand e-governance there needs to be more research on the demand by citizens for online information and services.

One such study was a survey of residents in the state of Georgia. Thomas and Streib (2005) examined the demand for e-governance; most of the existing research has examined what government offers online. Their research focused more on citizens and their experiences with e-governance. These authors examined e-commerce, which can be defined as online transactions with governments that involve an exchange of money. This could be either citizens paying government for income taxes owned or governments paying citizens for a tax refund. E-democracy, as discussed in Chapter 2, deals with citizens who engage in online activities in the political process. Finally, e-research refers to the use of a government website to look up information when citizens need help with a problem. The results of their survey of citizens revealed, not surprisingly, that e-democracy was the least used online service, whereas e-research and e-commerce were used more often. Essentially, their survey showed the importance of citizens and their role in governance.

Accountability refers to the answerability of government to the public on its performance. E-governance is said to promote accountability because more information is delivered in a timely fashion to citizens, there is an increased transparency of government to citizens, and citizens are empowered to monitor the government's performance (Wong and Welch, 2004). Research shows that the relationship between e-governance and public accountability is conditional, depending on the characteristics of the organization and its environment. ICT is said to reinforce existing systems and processes in organizations rather than change them (Kraemer and Dedrick, 1997). The following section examines further the impact of e-governance on organizational change, an important area in public administration.

E-Governance and Organizational Change

There are two schools of thought on organizational change as a result of ICT (West, 2004). The transformationalists believe ICT will have widespread consequences for society and government at large. The incremental perspective, by contrast, argues that there will be more of a constraining influence because of economic and institutional constraints that prevent wholesale change. Examples of technological changes that can be viewed as transformational are the printing press in the 15th century, the telegraph is the 1840s, the telephone in the 1870s, the rise of the radio in the 1920s, and coast-to-coast television broadcasting in the 1940s; these technologies all had dramatic and enduring consequences for business, government, and society. However, e-governance's potential to transform service delivery and democratic outreach has followed more of an incremental path and has not created a wholesale transformation as many of the earlier scholars predicted (West, 2004).

With this incremental pace of change as the result of e-governance, governments have not made much progress in enhancing the power of the Internet to increase accountability and representation (West, 2005). West's (2005) extensive analysis of federal and state government websites found very few interactive features. This limits the ability of governments to use e-governance to transform the public sector as much.

There are two important developments in modern public organizations according to Snellen (2002). First, the traditional vertical command and control relationship between governments and societies is being replaced by a horizontal network relationship that is much more complicated and has many interests involved. The horizontal network relationship is much more fluid and influenced by public, private, and nonprofit agencies. The second development is the introduction of ICT, which will change the control, surveillance, communication, and knowledge of this horizontal network relationship. ICT has the potential to make the horizontal organization a reality. Therefore, decentralization of the organization is a common change as a result of e-governance.

Allen and colleagues (2001) challenged the transformational shift to the administrative culture as a result of e-governance. In a case study of the implementation of e-governance in Canada, these authors noted that e-governance requires horizontal governance, but the Canadian government has relied on a vertical architecture of power and decision making. E-governance refers to the new patterns of decision making, power sharing, and coordination made possible with the advent of IT. However, the Canadian federal government has taken on a more incremental approach to adopting e-governance but has the potential to embrace full-scale change if it accepts a more transformational aspect of this technology. Essentially, the research shows that e-governance and organizational change has been more incremental than transformation. Another dimension of e-governance is its impact on transparency of government.

Transparency

Government transparency can be defined as the ability to find out what is going on inside government (Piotrowski and Van Ryzin, 2007). Transparency is fundamentally important to democratic governance. Some avenues of government transparency are open meetings, access to records, proactive posting of information on websites, whistle-blower protection, and illegally leaked information. There are some common reasons for not releasing information to the public such as national security, homeland security, law enforcement, propriety information, and personal privacy. E-governance will be able to increase the transparency of government to its citizens. This is especially the case with the Internet and Web being able to display government information online. The closing case study shows the impact on transparency on the federal government.

Countries are more likely to exhibit government transparency if they have the following four key components (Relly and Sabharwal, 2009). First, there is more government transparency in countries where citizens have access to information through laws. Freedom of information laws are written to increase government transparency and advance accountability, and many countries use these for that purpose. Second, high-income countries should exhibit more transparency with government information than poorer nations. These countries have more resources and can support requests for government information. Third, telecommunication infrastructure, if this is well developed, should increase government transparency. For instance, disseminating of information on the Web is likely to increase government transparency. Countries that provide greater access to e-government websites to its citizens should be more likely to promote government transparency. Fourth, political institutions and government transparency are said to be important for government transparency. Having a democratic system should also increase transparency. Democratic government promotes openness and accountability to citizens and is likely to increase government transparency. In a study of 122 countries and these four factors, the most important were telecommunications infrastructure and free press, as both influenced the perceptions of government transparency in a positive way (Relly and Sabharwal, 2009).

As an example of transparency, the City of Portland has launched an open source design contest where innovators use data sets to create applications that address civic issues and benefits in the greater Portland community (Nichols, 2010a). Developers that have the most innovative applications can win prizes totaling more than $10,000. CivicApps for greater Portland is similar to Washington, DC's Apps for Democracy and New York City's BigApps. However, Portland's version is different because it offers interjurisdictional agencies' information such as city, county, regional, and transit. As part of Portland's Open Data Initiative there are 100 data sets released that include information regarding crime, building permits, parks, transportation, liquor license applications, and so forth. Some of the top ideas for applications include a mobile construction app that would allow citizens with smartphone's to pull up geographical information systems (GIS) data-based maps and data about public works and transportation projects. Portland's CivicApps shows the extent to which governments can use social media technology to change their organization.

New Public Management

One common theory of organizational change and reform in the public sector is new public management (NPM). This theory is important because reform can be accomplished through the use of ICT. NPM has been defined as tactics and strategies to seek the improvement in the ability of government agencies and nonprofits to produce results (Homburg, 2004). NPM focused more on outcomes rather than processes and inputs. NPM was part of the greater movement to reinvent government and was a rejection of the traditional Weberian classic public management paradigm, which remained embedded in public bureaucracy until about the mid-1980s. E-governance has been said to be consistent with the movement of NPM, introducing ICT as a way of modernizing government to focus more on its effectiveness of serving citizens. Research shows that NPM and e-governance are two types of reforms that are consistent with one another (Homburg, 2004). Concepts found in both of these reforms in their technological and organizational impacts suggest similarities with one another.

Some of the most important characteristics of NPM that can be related to e-governance are (Homburg, 2004)

- Customer orientation
- Performance orientation and systems
- Continuous quality improvements
- Lean and decentralized structures
- Empowered employees

- Tight cost control
- Emphasis on accountability
- Breaking down of larger bureaucracy into smaller division structures that focus on results
- More proactive management that focuses on results

With NPM there is a movement to bypass the traditional hierarchical system, which is viewed as cumbersome, slow, inefficient, and unproductive. NPM is a reform that focuses on customers and is accountable to their needs.

Peters (1996) came up with four basic principles of NPM: (1) market government with an emphasis of pay for performance, (2) participatory government with an emphasis on empowerment that enables citizens to have a say in decisions, (3) flexible government with more fluid organizations that change with projects and over time depending on the task at hand, and (4) deregulated government offering managers more freedom to make decisions while being accountable for results. Under NPM, good governance in public administration requires having more transparent and accountable institutions (Perez et al., 2008). ICT is becoming an important means of improving access to government services and information, which improves accountability and good governance.

Dunleavy and colleagues (2005) believed NPM had been a predominant set of management principles for several decades. But there is not much evidence of its impact on changing the overall effectiveness of government. These authors believed e-governance offers the potential to change NPM. There are three themes of NPM as outlined by these authors: disaggregation, competition, and incentivization. Disaggregation is the splitting up of large public sector hierarchies into smaller more flexible organizations. Competition allows for the separation of public structures to create multiple forms of the provision of a service. Finally, incentivization is rewarding managers and staff for performance. The three themes of e-governance are reintegration, needs-based holism, and digitalized changes. With reintegration there is the ability of ICT to put back together many of the elements NPM separated. Needs-based holism is the ability of ICT to create a larger and more encompassing organization and to strip down the unnecessary steps. Finally, digitalized changes create productivity changes with fully digital operations. E-governance, according to these authors, offers an opportunity to create real change in public management, rather than NPM.

New Public Service

Starting in early 2000 the concept of public service became increasingly more important for governments. The new public service (NPS) is a movement built on the importance of democratic citizenship, community and civic society, and organizational humanism (Denhardt and Denhardt, 2000). Democratic citizenship stresses the importance of citizens in a democracy and their impact on public service. NPM does not place citizens at front and center for the development of public management. Civic society stresses the importance of community in the development of public service. Organizational humanism stresses the importance of the bureaucracy being permeable and fluid. **Table 4-3** provides a comparison of old public administration, NPM, and NPS (Denhardt and Denhardt, 2000).

After reviewing Table 4-3, one can see that many of the features of e-governance can be found in the NPS framework. For example, the role of citizens is stressed in e-governance, as well as in the NPS model. There also is the importance of civic participation in NPS, and this can be seen through the various social media technologies used to promote e-participation. In addition, discretion is constrained in the NPS model, with use of ICT minimizing administrative discretion. Collaboration is emphasized in NPS, and ICT can be used effectively to promote collaboration in organizations with citizens (e.g., wikis).

E-Governance and Service Delivery

Survey research shows that e-governance initiatives are still predominately noninteractive and nondeliberative (Torres et al., 2005). They tend to reflect the present service delivery model rather than transformational aspects of e-governance. The focus is on efficiency in service delivery rather than more interaction and participation of citizens in governance. These authors argue that because e-democracy initiatives are not at the forefront of e-governance, there will not be transformational change in the near future.

Grant and Chau (2005) provided a very comprehensive explanation of what e-governance is and its most important components as discussed earlier in this chapter. Early efforts to define e-governance have largely focused on ICT as a way of improving service delivery in public sector organizations. Grant and Chau believed that e-governance is much more than a technological phenomenon because of its transformative nature of this ICT. Defining e-governance means different things to different stakeholders. These authors proposed a more generic framework of e-governance to bring the most important definitions of e-governance together in a comprehensive way, not to just focus on service delivery. One aspect of service delivery that has changed as a result of e-governance is the traditional role of the street-level bureaucrat.

Street-Level Bureaucrats

In many public sector agencies, ICT has been adopted in organizations more reactively to cope with a loss in workers and other resources because of budget cutbacks. Because of the high cost of service delivery for many public sector agencies, they are

Table 4-3 *Comparing Old Public Administration, NPM, and NPS*

	Old Public Administration	New Public Management	New Public Service
Primary theoretical and epistemological foundations	Political theory, social and political commentary augmented by naive social science	Economic theory, more sophisticated dialogue based on positivist social science	Democratic theory, varied approaches to knowledge including positive, interpretive, critical, and postmodern
Prevailing rationality and associated models of human behavior	Synoptic rationality, "administrative man"	Technical and economic rationality, "economic man," or the self-interested decision maker	Strategic rationality, multiple tests of rationality (political, economic, organizational)
Conception of the public interest	Politically defined and expressed in law	Represents the aggregation of individual interests	Result of a dialogue about shared values
To whom are public servants responsive?	Clients and constituents	Customers	Citizens
Role of government	Rowing (designing and implementing policies focusing on a single, politically defined objective)	Steering (acting as a catalyst to unleash market forces)	Serving (negotiating and brokering interests among citizens and community groups, creating shared values)
Mechanisms for achieving policy objectives	Administering programs through existing government agencies	Creating mechanisms and incentive structures to achieve policy objectives through private and nonprofit agencies	Building coalitions of public, nonprofit, and private agencies to meet mutually agreed upon needs
Approach to accountability	Hierarchical—administrators are responsible to democratically elected political leaders	Market-driven—the accumulation of self-interests will result in outcomes desired by broad groups of citizens (or customers)	Multifaceted—public servants must attend to law, community values, political norms, professional standards, and citizen interest

(Continues)

Table 4-3 *Comparing Old Public Administration, NPM, and NPS* (Continued)

	Old Public Administration	New Public Management	New Public Service
Administrative discretion	Limited discretion allowed administrative officials	Wide latitude to meet entrepreneurial goals	Discretion needed but constrained and accountable
Assumed organizational structure	Bureaucratic organizations marked by top-down authority within agencies and control or regulation of clients	Decentralized public organizations with primary control remaining within the agency	Collaborative structures with leadership shared internally and externally
Assumed motivational basis of public servants and administrators	Pay and benefits, civil-service protections	Entrepreneurial spirit, ideological desire to reduce size of government	Public service, desire to contribute to society

From Denhardt and Denhardt (2000).

turning to automating services through ICT. For citizens, rather than speaking with a street-level bureaucrat, they are communicating with a system-level bureaucrat through the Internet. In essence, ICT is a way of exacting control and accountability over the bureaucracy (Milward and Snyder, 1996).

Bovens and Zouridis (2002) believe the traditional street-level bureaucracy has been replaced by a system-level bureaucracy, stating as follows (p. 175):

> Meanwhile, the large-scale executive public agencies of the welfare state appear to be quietly undergoing a fundamental change of character internally. Information and communication technology (ICT) is one of the driving forces behind this transformation. Window clerks are being replaced by Web sites, and advanced information and expert systems are taking over the role of case managers and adjudicating officers.... Today, a more true-to-life vision of the term "bureaucracy" would be a room filled with softly humming servers, dotted here and there with a system manager behind a screen.

Essentially, Bovens and Zouridis provided a sobering account of the change in the organization because of ICT.

Table 4-4 compares the characteristics of street-level bureaucracy and system-level bureaucracy. The role of ICT for street-level bureaucracy is support for the organization, whereas the role of system-level bureaucracy is decisive, preprogrammed by the system designer. In addition, with the system-level bureaucracy there is limited human interface because ICT works behind the scenes to complete the service request. The system-level bureaucracy, most importantly, removes administrative discretion.

Table 4-4 *Characteristics of Street-Level and System-Level Bureaucracies*

Factors	Street-Level Bureaucracy	System-Level Bureaucracy
Role of ICT	Supportive	Decisive
Functions of ICT	Data entry	Execution, control, and external communication
Human interface with individual cases	Full contact	No contact
Organizational structure	Case managers	System designers
Organizational boundaries	Strict boundaries and separation to other agencies	Fluid boundaries within and between organizations
Legal	Ample discretion	No discretion

Adapted from Bovens and Zouridis (2002).

The street-level bureaucrat has discretion in their interpretation of laws, but system-level bureaucracy removes this discretion because it is preprogrammed by the system designer.

Geographic Information Systems

GISs are analytical tools used for decision making that organize, compare, and analyze data (Haque, 2001). GIS is as a method of map overlays using IT (Haque, 2003). GIS is especially powerful because it can display information on a map and can compare data to examine changes in social, economic, and political circumstances. GIS has a significant impact on public administration and public policy because it can be used for planning and community development, environmental protection, integrated public safety response, infrastructure management, transportation planning and modeling, election management, and economic development. One of the top issues with GIS is that it is no better than the data entered into the system. Therefore, the reliability and accuracy of data collection is extremely important for a well-functioning GIS (Haque, 2003).

The Virginia Department of Emergency Management implemented a GIS-based system that impacted how it handles emergencies (Hughes, 2010). Virginia Interoperability-Picture for Emergency Response (VIPER) displays real-time geospatial information to monitor the day-to-day picture during a disaster as it unfolds. VIPER enables Virginia's Department of Emergency Management to assess the wider situation and scale the response to the disaster accordingly. VIPER is a web-based GIS enterprise platform that uses existing information such as live feeds from many sources such as traffic cameras, social networking sites, photographs, and the National Weather Service to show dynamic relationships. VIPER brings the same information to first responders as well as different levels of government. VIPER has been used to track the spin of tornados, the spread of the N_1H_1 virus, the sprawl of traffic accidents, the aftermath of earthquakes and floods, a plan to respond to terrorist attacks, and chemical and nuclear disasters plans.

Citizen Relationship Management

A technology used to enhance citizen interaction with government is customer service systems. Schellong and Goethe (2005) and Schellong (2008b) provide a definition of customer relationship management (CRM) as a holistic management approach that uses ICT to enable broad customer focus that optimizes the firm's relationship with its customers to create more profitable and loyal relationships. Citizen relationship management (CiRM) in the public sector is a strategy enabled as well with ICT to optimize relationships and encourage citizen participation. In the e-governance literature, CiRM is part of the broader NPM approach.

Some of the major differences between CRM used in private sector organizations and CiRM used in public sector organizations are seen through the differences in these sectors. For instance, in the private sector CRM can be justified through increased profitability and customer loyalty, whereas in the public sector CiRM can be justified through enhancing democratic accountability to the public. Although CRM originated in the private sector there needs to be more research that concentrates specifically on its public sector application (Fjermestad and Romano, 2003).

An increasing number of cities in the United States use a nonemergency hotline number, normally 311, to provide customer service support to their citizens (Schwester et al., 2009). These hotline numbers tend to use technology such as CiRM to integrate customer service in the city. Baltimore was the first city to implement a 311 system, and its purpose was to reduce the number of nonemergency calls to 911. The Department of Justice predicted between 50% and 90% of 911 calls being deemed nonemergency. This slowed down the response time of first responders in true emergencies because the 911 system was being clogged up by nonemergency calls. President Clinton requested the Federal Communications Commission to set aside 311 for the use as a number for help in nonemergencies. Potentially, 311 systems could improve the relationship between governments and its citizens because these systems would enable citizens to make service requests and provide feedback.

An effective CiRM system enables citizens to rise above traditional departments and bureaucratic lines when they need information or services from government. These systems simplify the government bureaucracy for citizens when they want information or a service. CiRM systems have the potential to manipulate data to get a better picture of citizen behavior. Therefore, CiRM has the potential to work across departments and break down the functional silos of traditional public sector service delivery (Kannabiran et al., 2004). CiRM does provide the potential to change government by breaking down the traditional way citizens receive information and services. CiRM is a way to integrate multiple channels of contact with government either over the counter or through the phone, the Web, or the mail into one central system. This system potentially could connect up these different channel choices into one system to make service delivery for citizens a seamless experience. Case studies of CiRM adoption show the benefits and challenges of this technology for the public sector.

Case Studies of CRM Adoption

In case studies of five cities and their adoption of 311/CRM done by the International City/County Management Association, some interesting results surfaced (Fleming, 2008). These case studies looked at local governments that had successfully adopted 311/CRM systems and the key elements that supported their implementation. San Antonio, Texas, was the largest city, having a population of almost 1.3 million. Their 311 system was built in-house and was designed by the city's information technology department in 2000; the 311 department reports to the assistant city manager. Los Alamos County, New Mexico, was the smallest local government studied and has a public information officer reporting to the county administrator for their 311 system. Lynwood, California, did not have a 311 system but rather a seven-digit hotline number. Minneapolis, Minnesota, has one of the youngest systems of the group of cities with an integrated 911/311 department reporting to the city coordinator. Finally, Hampton, Virginia, has the oldest and most established 311 system of the group.

A common feature among the systems for the five cities studied was that a centralized customer service system was part of an effort among elected officials and other community leaders to make customer service a priority. The idea that 311 was a front door to local government was mentioned in interviews of these officials. No longer was it necessary for citizens to guess which department they needed to call for information or services; with 311 this made it happen with one phone call. Essentially, the challenge that citizens face is that they do not always understand what department to call, and through one phone call the customer service agent can connect them with the right information. This can be a challenge because departments in the past have controlled information; 311/CRM systems essentially break down these silos of information dissemination. Citizens viewed it as favorable because of the easy access to their government; it essentially made it easier for citizens to get involved. Providing excellent customer service makes for happier citizens and enhances the community's overall reputation.

In these interviews, International City/County Management Association found that all five cities used data collected from 311/CRM systems to measure the performance of the call center but also the effectiveness and efficiency of local government programs. But all of the local governments struggled with how best to use the data they collected, and the degree that these governments used the performance data varied. Most local governments had service-level agreements that focus on the completion of meeting customer needs, which is a cultural shift. These service-level agreements can inform citizens when they can expect to get the work completed and their service request fulfilled. This essentially holds departments accountable for results in their performance.

311/CRM systems offered an opportunity to promote change within a local government. Many of the officials interviewed believed it could lead to a major cultural change in the way the local government does business. These systems reengineered government processes because cities have to spend time working on mapping business processes and procedures to complete their work orders. This allows local governments to determine where the bottlenecks occur and put resources into these areas to remedy the problems. 311/CRM can streamline processes in city government to create more efficiency for their operations. There are some challenges with the implementation of 311 for city governments, most notably the difficulty of departments giving up control of their customer service, lack of use by citizens, and lack of resources to properly fund these systems.

Summary

E-governance can be defined as the use of ICT to improve the quality of public service delivery. Most models of e-governance emphasize the importance of citizens in enhancing service delivery. There are three models of e-governance, managerial, consultative, and participatory. The managerial model, which involves the least level of citizen participation, is most often used in governments. The managerial model primarily focuses on efficiency in service delivery. E-governance is thought by many scholars to be able to transform government, but the evidence shows only incremental change to public service delivery. As a result of ICT, the traditional street-level bureaucrat is being replaced by a system-level bureaucrat. Essentially, e-governance is said to hollow out the administrative state.

CiRM technology is being used to integrate the operations of government, where citizens can call a single number and get access to the information and services of government. Therefore, citizens no longer need to know which department they need a service from, and the customer service representative can help direct them and answer their inquiry. CiRM systems are a new area of research in e-governance on channel choice in public service delivery, where citizens use different channels depending on what they need from government.

Discussion Questions

1. What is e-governance? Explain some of the models associated with this theory.
2. How has e-governance impacted citizens and organizations?
3. How is NPM different from the Weberian bureaucratic model? Explain this with regards to e-governance.
4. E-governance has created a system-level bureaucracy. How has this changed public service delivery?
5. What is CiRM? How will this technology impact public service delivery in government?

Closing Case Study

Data.gov

In March 2009 federal chief information officer Vivek Kundra launched Data.gov, which offers an index of data generated by government agencies rendered to be in open, machine-readable formats such as extensible markup language

(Williams, 2009; Jackson, 2009a). When Kundra was chief technology officer for Washington, DC, his prior appointment, the city set up a website that would offer raw feeds to the data the city routinely collected, such as crime reports and permit applications. The idea behind this system was that outside developers would create public-oriented applications that would reuse the data feeds. With a city-sponsored contest called Apps for Democracy, this resulted in many applications being created that used crime reports to show late night tavern patrons the safest neighborhood.

Data.gov was part of the Obama Administration's push to provide more transparency and open government. Data.gov was using the same premise as what Kundra did in Washington, DC, of providing raw data feeds that can be picked up and reused by outsiders. Data.gov was set up and managed by the Federal Chief Information Officers Council. The debut of Data.gov featured 76 data sets, and within the month there were more than 100,000 additional data sets added. Some data placed on this site were the Bureau of Labor Statistics' Consumer Expenditure Survey and the Justice Department's Uniform Crime Reporting Program.

In addition to providing raw feeds, there is the ability of users to rate the data sets and tools to view the data sets. Data.gov can improve government transparency by releasing these data sets so that citizens are able to analyze them and build mash-up applications.

Not all data can be released on Data.gov, and all information posted on the website must abide by privacy regulations. On Data.gov, national security information will not be released. The problem with the Data.gov website is that if the average person cannot consume the data, it would not contribute to open government.

The barriers to getting the data are high because developers would have to convert the data into usable formats. Right now Data.gov forces people to download the whole data set when they only want a certain part of the data set, which gives users information overload. But others argue that despite these problems, at least providing the data online is a step toward more open government. Other criticisms leveled at Data.gov are omission, formatting, accuracy, and labeling errors of the data (Daconta, 2010). There were also quality issues with poorly structured data and incomplete data in the website.

Part II

The Internal Environment

Chapter 5

Leadership and Management

Opening Case Study

Leadership and the Public Sector CIO

Teri Takai, California's chief information officer (CIO) in 2009, was one of the country's leading information technology (IT) executives in the public sector (Newcombe, 2009b). Takai advanced the role of CIO to a leadership one in the public sector. However, when she began her career, leadership was not her strong suit. She became an IT manager at the age of 28, and she had no background in managing people. Takai began as a manager in a foreign country, as a Japanese-American working for Ford Motor Company, which taught her the valuable lessons of communications, perceptions, and leadership. "Being exposed to different cultures makes you appreciate all three factors," says Takai.

The public sector CIO was not traditionally viewed as a positive career move in the IT community. The CIO was viewed as a good IT engineer and was expected to manage people competently. This changed with the ability of IT, and in particular the Internet, to exchange information, integrate disjointed work processes, and digitalize services. As a result, the role of the CIO was elevated in most public sector organizations as a leader rather than a manager and technology person.

One of the reasons is the growing dependence of organizations on technology, which has changed the role from relative obscurity to one of strategic importance for the organizations. Increasingly the CIO reports to the chief executive officer or other top executive in the organization, such as the mayor, county executives, governors, and, at the very top, the president and the Cabinet. These CIOs are increasingly being called upon to get government to reinvent itself. This task of reinventing government can be seen through the severe economic recession faced in the United States in late 2000.

One of the most important qualities of a CIO is collaboration. Takai learned she needed to be much more collaborative when she worked for government. In government, CIOs tend to have many bosses, as Takai noticed. These bosses are the governor, state legislature, other cabinet members, a peer group of CIOs, and the media. Working across a very diverse group of stakeholders requires a great deal of collaboration in state government.

One of the most important lessons to learn as a public sector CIO is that of politics. Takai learned that you have to understand how the legislature works. Many issues CIOs need to address, such as being politically astute, a great communicator, and a relationship builder, do not come from textbooks; they come from on-the-job training and being sensitive and responsive to the operating environment.

Chapter Objectives

This chapter examines leadership and management in information technology (IT) and public administration, exploring five main objectives:

1. To describe the differences between public and private sector information systems
2. To discuss the role of leadership and management in the public sector
3. To discuss the role and characteristics of chief information officers in the development of IT and public administration
4. To examine the most common IT support systems public managers use
5. To explore the most important pieces of federal legislation that examine IT and public administration

Introduction

Leadership and management are two critical components for the advancement of IT in public administration. This chapter explores these issues through an examination of differences in public and private sector environments. This is important to know, because management and leadership are different in both sectors. The role of leadership and management in the public sector are discussed, and how this role influences IT and public administration is explored. The importance of the CIO is discussed in this chapter, and the unique characteristics of these leaders are presented. Finally, there is a discussion of the major federal legislation passed by the U.S. Congress as a way to understand the environment that leaders and managers face in the public sector. The opening case study shows the importance of leadership in public administration and IT as seen through the state government CIO.

Differences Between Public and Private Sector

Leaders in public sector IT normally deal with the strategic direction of IT and its role in the broader organization, whereas public managers deal with operationalizing IT in their agencies. This is not to say leaders and managers do not perform these other tasks; they do, and it is difficult to separate the operation from the strategic direction in public sector organizations.

Leadership in the public sector compared with the private sector requires paying attention to the different environments of each and how this impacts leadership and management, as discussed in Chapter 1. Because the public sector is known to be different from the private sector in regards to having more ambiguous goals, a more complex multi-stakeholder environment, and lack of incentives due to not having competition like the private sector, this translates into a different operating environment and something that impacts leadership of public sector IT.

Bretschneider (1990) examined whether information systems in public sector organizations differ from their private sector counterparts. Through a review of the literature, Bretschneider suggested two key differences in managing information systems in both sectors. First, the organizational environment that public managers must contend with has greater levels of interdependence than private sector organizations. For example, public sector organizations face many institutional checks and balances that are not prevalent in the private sector, most commonly referred to as "red tape." Second, in regards to management activity, public sector organizations are more concerned with controlling costs and private sector entities are concerned with the profitability of information systems. For example, due to lengthier budget cycles in the public sector, it sometimes takes longer to start a new initiative using information systems than in the private sector. Therefore, managers in the public sector have very unique environments and constraints that differ from the private sector, which translates into impacting leadership.

Goal complexity and ambiguity is said to be one of the most important differences between public and private sector organizations (Rainey and Bozeman, 2000). Public agencies generally have greater ambiguity in their goals because of the nature of the work. Public managers face more complexity, difficulty in measuring outcomes, and harder to reach goals than private sector managers. As a result of ambiguous goals, this makes it particularly challenging for public sector entities to invest in IT because it is difficult to measure outcomes from purchases.

Some common differences noted in the literature on public and private sector information systems and challenges that public managers face are as follows (Rocheleau and Wu, 2002):

- Extreme risk aversion that makes public agencies less likely to invest in risky technologies
- Divided authority over IT decisions because of legal, bureaucratic, and political constraints that makes it difficult to manage IT projects
- Multiple stakeholders with competing goals
- Budget cycles that are normally 1 year, making it difficult to do long range planning
- Highly regulated procurement process
- Multiple links of agencies with other programs and organizations, making change difficult

Some of the findings on a more recent survey of the differences in public and private information systems indicate that private sector organizations invest more resources in IT training; however, despite this, both sectors view IT as important for their organizations. The differences in investing in IT may be the result of the different views on risk. Where private sector managers would view risk as a way of increasing profits and spur innovation, without the profit motive public sector managers would not be as willing to take the risk of investing in a new and perhaps untested technology.

One study examines the differences in the strategic orientation of public and private sector senior information resource managers and found, contrary to the literature, no statistically significant differences between these sectors (Ward and Mitchell, 2004). Through a survey of information resource executives, no pronounced differences existed between public and private sector management of information resources through an examination of environmental and organizational factors, internal structures, and processes. Early researchers have commented that as IT diffuses into government institutions, the differences between management practices, priorities, and so on between the two sectors become pronounced. The research results of their survey indicate the opposite has occurred.

There are three reasons Ward and Mitchell (2004) speculate on the lack of differences in IT in the public and private sectors. First, IT software is becoming commoditized. As software in the private sector has matured, it has become more generic and readily usable by public sector entities as well. Another possible reason was that President Bush's 2002 President's Management Agenda was an attempt to make the public sector more efficient and effective. E-government is thought of being a way, according to the Bush Administration, to create a more market-oriented approach to service delivery. This approach to the use of IT is commonly used in the private sector. Finally, the Bush Administration emphasized outsourcing to private contractors, and there may be more of a blurring of the lines between information resource executives' views in the two sectors. Therefore, Ward and Mitchell argued that because of these three factors the difference between the sectors has become blurred.

Despite some studies that do not find many significant differences in leadership and management challenges between the sectors, we should still be aware of the differences as public managers. With these unique differences in the public and private sectors, public managers must be cognizant of them when implementing IT in their organization. The following section examines the role leadership plays in the development of IT and public administration.

Leadership

Fountain (2009) provides an institution perspective on e-government, which focuses on the internal workings of the state. Both Presidents Clinton and G.W. Bush focused on bureaucratic reform initiatives as part of e-government. The Clinton Administration from 1993 to 2001, with the proliferation of the Internet, used this as a platform to allow citizens access to government. The federal government first organized students.gov, seniors.gov, and business.gov portals as a way of providing citizens better access to their government. The National Performance Review was a bureaucratic reform that began during the Clinton Administration; in this report IT was viewed as one of the major elements of a larger bureaucratic reform effort. The G.W. Bush Administration in 2002 used e-government also as a tool for bureaucratic reform, and this was articulated in the President's Management Agenda. Developed in the President's Management Agenda was the notion that IT should be used strategically and that IT systems must be aligned with performance goals.

IT leadership is the support of senior management for the use of information and communication technology to improve organizational performance (Lim and Tang, 2008). These leaders understand the strategic value of information systems for their organizations. Leadership promotes and encourages the vision and values of the organization to its external environment, managing conflicts, and making sure IT is maximized. Leaders are able to align IT to improve organizational goals, which will improve outcomes. Leaders can create a culture that promotes IT literacy among their employees. To promote good leadership, research shows that leadership-training programs are needed to help managers understand the strategic value of technologies for their organizations.

In survey evidence on county government officials and e-government adoption in Iowa, Ho and Ni (2004) found that common factors noted in the literature on adoption of this technology did not come through in their statistical analysis. For example, budget and technical capacity, economic considerations, and constituency pressure did not show a significant relationship with e-government adoption. These results suggested that e-government was not merely driven by rational economic and political factors, and technical or fiscal factors did not seem to constrain its development. However, political leadership does make a difference in adoption showing that elected officials can bring about innovation and change as a result of e-government. As a result, leadership is important for implementation of IT and public administration.

Management Support Systems

There are several information systems that public sector agencies can use to support decision making at different levels of their organization (Laudon and Laudon, 2009). Each of these uses a different type of system to deliver the information that is required by the agency. These systems are transaction processing systems, management information systems, decision-support systems, and executive support systems.

Transaction Processing Systems

Operational level managers need to have information systems that keep track of basic transactions that frequently occur in their organizations. Transaction processing systems (TPS) are computerized systems that perform and record daily routine transactions necessary to keep the organization going, such as budgeting, account reconciliation, payroll, purchasing, and employee record keeping. The purpose of these systems is to answer routine questions and to track the flow of transactions within the organization. Because they work at the operational level, TPS have goals that are predefined and highly structured. For example, a payroll system keeps track of money paid to employees through an employee time sheet with information on the employee such as their Social Security number, employee number, and number of hours worked per week. These data can be combined with other data to create routine reports for those in management. TPS are essential to public sector organizations and downtime, for even a few hours can be detrimental for the organization.

Management Information Systems

Middle management will use management information systems (MIS) to help monitor and control decision making and administrative activities in the organization. MIS serves middle management with reports on the organization's current performance. This information can be used to monitor the performance of the organization for middle managers to make adjustments. MIS uses data provided by the TPS reports and have reports for middle management produced on a regular basis. MIS serves middle managers primarily interested in weekly, monthly, and yearly results. This enables public managers to drill down from the information on the reports. Most MIS reports provide answers to routine questions that have been specified in advance. These systems are not flexible and have little analytical capability. These reports can be used, for instance, to see what trends are taking place in overtime expenses for police officers in order for middle management to determine how much additional money needs to be requested.

Decision Support Systems

Decision support systems (DSS) support nonroutine decision making for middle management. They focus on problems that are unique and change very quickly. TPS have predefined information, MIS problems are not predefined and are ambiguous, but DSS answers more "what if" type of questions. These systems use a large amount of data, both internal and external to the organization, that is analyzed to help make better decisions. For example, Canadian National Railway uses DSS to detect worn-out or defective rails to prevent derailments.

Executive Support Systems

Executive support systems (ESS) are used by senior managers to address strategic-level issues and long-term trends. These systems answer bigger picture questions such as what will happen to the organization in 5 years. These systems help senior management make nonroutine decisions requiring judgment and insight from the data. ESS uses graphics and data from management sources to provide a user friendly view for other managers to see. An example is a digital dashboard that combines data from different sources to see what the impact would be of a policy change on the public sector agency.

Public Managers' Perspectives

Public managers have different perspectives when it comes to IT and their organization. Each of these is assessed in regards to the stakeholders they deal with on a daily basis when performing their jobs.

IT End Users

The IT end users are the individuals in the departments or agencies that work with the systems provided to them from the IT department. The end users are the ultimate testers of the IT systems that are in place in public sector organizations. It is imperative that IT managers get them involved in the early stages of development of new IT systems. Without "buy in" from the end users, it is very difficult to have successful implementation of information systems in public sector organizations.

IT Personnel

The IT personnel are the individuals who work on making the systems purchased by IT managers functional for the end users. This can involve IT personnel working behind the scenes or working directly with the end users. Behind the scenes, IT personnel could make sure that servers are functional, so e-mail and the Internet work for the government agency. They also could work around the organization helping end users with problems or issues they have with existing IT systems.

Public sector information systems managers place more importance on managerial issues than on technical ones (Swain et al., 1995; Moon and Norris, 2005; Norris, 2008). Essentially, most public sector information systems managers deal with management issues and have their staff specialize in technical issues. Important management issues identified in a survey of information systems managers were strategic planning, organizational structure, and organizational learning. By contrast, the lower ranked technical issues were in the areas of work support, internal management, and software and were more effectively dealt with by operational staff.

The success in implementing information systems is very much dependent on top management support of the project, according to much of the public information systems literature (Biehl, 2007). If top management does not perceive the project as useful for the mission of the organization, this could severely jeopardize the success of the project. In fact, when difficulties arise in the implementation of an IT project, top management support is critical for getting the project completed on time and on budget.

Public administration programs play a critical role in promoting the benefits of IT for public managers (Brown and Brudney, 1998). Effective and efficient technology depends on the training of public managers. The National Association of Schools of Public Affairs and Administration has called upon the importance of computers and information systems for public affairs education. Brown and Brudney argued that information systems failures are not merely the result of technical problems but have more to do with management issues. Schools of public administration should offer a broad array of courses that deal with the importance of management of information systems; this would ensure greater success in the implementation of these systems in government. Therefore, higher education has an important role to play in training leaders and managers for the public sector and should be recognized. The following section discusses the most important leader for IT in public administration, the CIO.

Chief Information Officers

A TechAmerica (2009) survey of 53 federal CIOs showed the challenges they faced in 2008 as they looked forward to the future. These are in order of priority for CIOs:

- IT security (focusing on compliance and operational security)
- IT infrastructure (consolidating, standardizing, and modernizing)

- IT management (coordination with other agencies regarding IT investment and issues)
- Resources (doing more with less resources)
- IT workforce (shortage of skilled workers)
- Application systems (development and implementation of new applications)

The closing case study at the end of this chapter provides a profile of the new federal government CIO. The U.S. Government Accountability Office (2004) identified the following 13 major areas of CIO responsibilities as either statutory requirements or critical to effective information and technology management:

- *IT/IRM strategic planning.* CIOs are responsible for strategic planning for all information and IT management functions—thus the term IRM strategic planning [44 U.S.C. 3506(b)(2)].
- *IT capital planning and investment management.* CIOs are responsible for IT capital planning and investment management [44 U.S.C. 3506(h) and 40 U.S.C. 11312 & 11313].
- *Information security.* CIOs are responsible for ensuring compliance with the requirement to protect information and systems [44 U.S.C. 3506(g) and 3544(a)(3)].
- *IT/IRM workforce planning.* CIOs have responsibilities for helping the agency meet its IT/IRM workforce or human capital needs [44 U.S.C. 3506(b) and 40 U.S.C. 11315(c)].
- *Information collection/paperwork reduction.* CIOs are responsible for the review of agency information collection proposals to maximize the utility and minimize public "paperwork" burdens [44 U.S.C. 3506(c)].
- *Information dissemination.* CIOs are responsible for ensuring that the agency's information dissemination activities meet policy goals such as timely and equitable public access to information [44 U.S.C. 3506(d)].
- *Records management.* CIOs are responsible for ensuring that the agency implements and enforces records management policies and procedures under the Federal Records Act [44 U.S.C. 3506(f)].
- *Privacy.* CIOs are responsible for compliance with the Privacy Act and related laws [44 U.S.C. 3506(g)].
- *Statistical policy and coordination.* CIOs are responsible for the agency's statistical policy and coordination functions, including ensuring the relevance, accuracy, and timeliness of information collected or created for statistical purposes [44 U.S.C. 3506(e)].
- *Information disclosure.* CIOs are responsible for information access under the Freedom of Information Act [44 U.S.C. 3506(g)].
- *Enterprise architecture.* Federal laws and guidance direct agencies to develop and maintain enterprise architectures as blueprints to define the agency mission and the information and IT needed to perform that mission.

- *Systems acquisition, development, and integration.* Successful IT management is effective control of systems acquisition, development, and integration [44 U.S.C. 3506(h)(5) and 40 U.S.C. 11312].
- *E-government initiatives.* Various laws and guidance direct agencies to undertake initiatives to use IT to improve government services to the public and internal operations [44 U.S.C. 3506(h)(3) and the E-Government Act of 2002].

Figure 5-1 provides a comparison of the extent to which public and private sector CIOs view their responsibilities as being influenced by the management areas of federal government CIOs. Figure 5-1 shows that many of the management responsibilities are the same across both sectors. However, some areas viewed as being more important by federal CIOs are enterprise architecture, strategic planning, information collection, and information dissemination and disclosure. These four areas comprise a greater percentage of time of CIOs and their responsibility in the public sector. On the surface, it appears, regarding responsibilities, that CIOs in the public and private sectors have fairly similar roles.

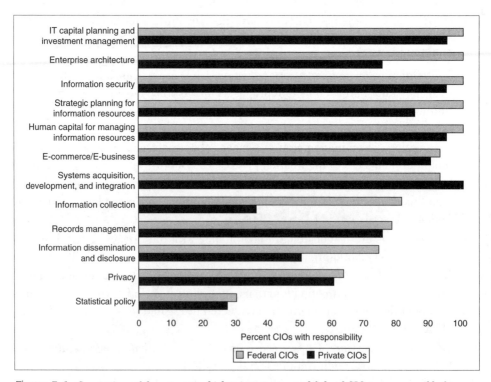

Figure 5-1 *Comparison of the extent to which private sector and federal CIOs are responsible for management areas* (From U.S. Government Accountability Office, 2005a)

Characteristics of CIOs

In a survey of federal government CIOs administered in the summer of 2005, there were 115 federal departments and agencies that had a designated CIO official. The author of this book sent them a short survey that examined their views on the effectiveness of IT to their role as CIO. In total, 38 CIOs responded to the survey, which is a response rate of 33%. **Table 5-1** shows the characteristics of CIOs that responded

Table 5-1 *Characteristics of Federal Government CIOs*

Characteristic	Percent
FTE employment in department/agency	
499 or less	22.2
500 to 4,999	22.3
5,000 or more	55.6
Age	
35–44	16.7
45–54	50.0
55–64	33.3
Gender	
Female	25
Male	75
Years employment federal government	
≤10	25
11–20	16.7
>20s	58.3
Years worked as a CIO	
≤10	75
11–20	9.4
>21	5.6
Advanced degree (i.e., master's, law, doctoral)	
Yes	63.9
No	36.2

to the survey. Most CIOs that responded to this survey were from large departments or agencies that employed 5,000 or more full-time equivalent employees. Large-size departments represented 56% of CIOs surveyed. Smaller agency CIOs employing 499 or less employees represented 22.2% of CIOs. The typical age range of CIOs was between 45 and 54 years, representing half of those surveyed. A third of federal CIOs were between the age of 55 and 64 years. The smallest number of CIOs surveyed were between the age of 35 and 44 years, representing 17% of the sample. More than half of the CIOs worked for the federal government for over 20 years; therefore, the average tenure in the government is very substantial. However, the tenure as CIO was much shorter, with 75% of them working 10 years or less. Most CIOs had an advanced degree such as a master's, doctorate, or law degree. Having an advanced degree is what one would expect for this executive level position. The characteristics of federal government CIOs show they are generally from large agencies. They tend to be baby boomers, be male, and have many years of experience in the federal government but far fewer years as CIOs. Most CIOs are well educated. These findings provide a view of what characteristics federal CIOs have as a way of understanding their leadership role.

The following section outlines some of the most important federal laws that influence IT and public administration. It is important to understand these laws to realize the context of IT in public administration.

Major Federal IT Laws

Mullen (2005) discusses some of the most important pieces of IT legislation passed by Congress since 1980, as shown in **Table 5-2**. All these Acts relate to the performance enhancement of the federal government and IT.

Paperwork Reduction Acts of 1980 and 1995

The purposes of the Paperwork Reduction Act as reauthorized in 1995 were to (1) minimize the public's paperwork burdens from the collection of information for the federal government, (2) coordinate agencies' information resources management policies, (3) improve the dissemination of public information, and (4) ensure the integrity of the federal statistical system. There is an effectiveness component to this piece of legislation discussing the improvement of operations through the reduction in paperwork.

Government Paperwork Elimination Act

The 1998 Government Paperwork Elimination Act required federal agencies to make electronic versions of their forms available online (Relyea, 2000). This Act would allow individuals and businesses to use electronic signatures to file these

Table 5-2 *IT Performance Based Laws and Their Purpose*

Federal IT Legislation	Purpose of the Law
Paperwork Reduction Act of 1980 and 1995	Minimize paperwork burden for the public, coordinate federal information resource management, improve the dissemination of public information
Computer Security Act of 1987	Improve security and privacy of sensitive information
Clinger-Cohen Act of 1996	Improve acquisition, use, and disposal of IT resources; elevate the importance of IT in strategic management
Government Paperwork Elimination Act of 1988	Require federal agencies to disclose, maintain, and submit information electronically
Government Information Security Reform Act of 2001	Require federal agencies to conduct annual IT security reviews and report to OMB
E-Government Act of 2002	Promote the use of IT to provide government services electronically to citizens

Adapted from Mullen (2005).

forms digitally (Mullen, 2005). This act made it possible to use e-government without having a paper trail.

Computer Security Act of 1987

The purpose of the Computer Security Act was to improve the security and privacy of sensitive information in federal computer systems. Under this law all operators of federal computer systems must establish security plans (Mullen, 2005). This act solidified the importance of information security for federal departments and agencies.

Clinger-Cohen Act of 1996

At the federal level, before the Clinger-Cohen Act of 1996, most agencies and departments had an information resource management (IRM) official as their top information person (Buehler, 2000; Relyea, 2000). IRMs were "techies" who believed implementing IT was the most important job function, not examining the business process and how IT fit into the mission of their organization. IRMs were removed from the agency's strategic decision-making process and program offices. IRMs basically operated on their own with little support when making these very expensive and important IT purchasing decisions. There also was the oversight responsibility of IT handled by the General Services Administration, which created an additional level of bureaucracy.

The Clinger-Cohen Act stated that CIOs would report directly to agency directors, empowering them to take responsibility for IT to be carefully planned, executed, and evaluated. Unlike the IRM, the CIO was raised to the executive level. The CIO was more focused on the strategic nature of information systems and how they fit within the mission of the agency. The Clinger-Cohen Act calls for a higher level of personal communication between the CIO and the agency head, focusing more on best practices. CIOs are expected to manage information systems in more of a business-like fashion.

The purpose of the Clinger-Cohen Act is to improve the productivity, efficiency, and effectiveness of federal programs through improved acquisition, use, and disposal of IT resources. This Act streamlines the IT acquisition process by eliminating the General Services Administration's central acquisition authority and replaces this authority with the federal agencies (Mullen, 2005). Essentially, the purpose of the Clinger-Cohen Act was to elevate the profile of IT in federal departments and agencies.

Government Information Security Reform Act of 2001

The purpose of the Government Information Security Reform Act of 2001 was to establish a comprehensive framework for ensuring effectiveness of controls over information resources, while recognizing the interoperability of federal computer systems in a highly networked world, provide government-wide management and oversight of security risks, and provide oversight of information security programs in federal agencies (Mullen, 2005).

E-Government Act of 2002

The E-Government Act of 2002 was designed to enhance management and promotion of e-government services and processes (Mullen, 2005) and to increase citizen access to government information and services by establishing a federal CIO in the Office of E-Government in the Office of Management and Budget (OMB) that oversees e-government.

These important pieces of federal legislation, mentioned above, have impacted IT and public administration now and for years to come.

Planning for Public Information Systems

Strategic planning in government is the effort to produce decisions and actions that will shape the organization in the future (Ring and Perry, 1985; Andersen et al., 1994; Poister and Streib, 2005; Rocheleau, 2006). There is a systematic process involved with gathering information about the big picture and using this information to establish a long-term direction of the organization. Strategic planning involves translating specific goals, objectives, and actions into outcomes. Strategic planning impacts the culture of the organization, creating a sense of where it is going in the future. Municipal managers from cities that engaged in strategic planning are enthusiastic about it, with a large majority of these managers reporting they are satisfied with the implementation of the strategic planning initiatives and the achievement of strategic goals and objectives (Poister and Streib, 2005). Ninety percent of them believe the benefits outweigh the costs of undertaking these efforts. Some of the positive benefits of strategic planning are performance measures, evaluating the feasibility of public programs, tracking performance over time, targeting new money to achieve strategic goals, and involving stakeholders in the process. Strategic planning incorporates IT systems as part of the mission of the public sector organization to move and shape the organization to reach outcomes (Rocheleau, 2006).

Strategic planning is the central management process that integrates all activities and functions of the organization to advance an agenda (Poister and Streib, 1999). The focus on strategic planning is strengthening the long-term effectiveness of the public sector entity to advance a policy or management agenda. Public sector agencies are increasingly being asked to provide proactive leadership, improved performance, and customer service to manage results in their organization. It is difficult for any agency to focus on the long term without a strategic plan to guide their actions. A strategic plan in the public sector is much more difficult because of the changing environment they face. However, research shows that good leaders produce more effective strategic plans for the government. Good leadership in strategic planning is especially the case with the development of IT in the public sector, where the price tag for many information systems is very high and the outcome not always certain.

There are three issues in strategic planning and information system development in organizations that public managers need to address (Dufner, Holley, and Reed, 2002). First, the loose structure of government impedes consideration of operational issues in the strategic plan. There might be a certain objective of preventing a terrorist attack at a specific point in time, but this objective may change with new priorities of the next administration. In addition, in government the processes are not directly connected in that different agencies within government have different objectives that make integrating systems a challenge. In addition, in government there is the lack of a long-term planning horizon that is needed for IT planning. The focus on many governments is budgetary and operational efficiency, which are not strategic objectives. Finally, there is greater stakeholder involvement in strategic planning of information systems, with a diversity of interests impacting the process. This results in goals that can conflict with the different stakeholders, for example, the differences in views of environmentalists and the petroleum industry. Examining empirical results from state governments indicated that much of the strategic planning for this government was not done by top management, it was done by career managers in the hierarchy, which is different from the private sector. Overall, strategic planning is essential for the management of public sector IT.

Y2K and Planning

Year 2000 (Y2K) is a good example of IT planning working effectively, showing the importance of effective leadership and management. There was a goal to prevent a problem of the switch-over of dates for the new millennium and a solution was to fix the dated information systems that experienced these problems. Given that there were few incidents after the year 2000 began, one can say that this is an example of the success of IT planning in public organizations. The Y2K problem provided a lens to examine how governments plan for IT (Ho and Smith, 2001). The Y2K problem was when computer systems that used two digits to represent the year might interpret 2000 as 1900 and as a result shut down or make errors in their calculations. A survey of local governments in Iowa indicated the importance of senior management attitudes toward IT had a large impact on planning. The more concerned senior management was about Y2K, the more likely they were to participate in planning. Essentially, a positive attitude toward IT planning means it would be viewed as not merely a technical issue, but something critical for organizational success. If leaders embrace the strategic importance of IT in their public organization, this will most likely impact change. The literature argues that leadership is essential for the successful development of IT in public administration, as was evident for Y2K planning.

Summary

This chapter examined the role of leadership and management on IT and public administration. One of the most important differences leaders and managers face in government is the goal ambiguity of their organization. Unlike the private sector, where the goals of the organization are stable and known, the public sector faces ambiguity in their goals. This translates into uncertainty in their mission, which makes it more difficult for managers to effectively incorporate change in IT and public administration. Leadership is critically important for the development and advancement of IT in public sector organizations. It is important for public leaders to incorporate IT into the mission and strategic direction for the organization. The literature on the adoption of IT argues that top management support is critical for its development. Public managers must be trained in the latest technology and the importance of systems to change their organization. Federal government CIOs have to balance many competing issues in their departments or agencies, with information security demonstrated as one of the most important issues. Federal CIOs tend to be baby boomers, be male, to have many years of experience in the federal government, and be well educated. Several important federal laws have impacted IT and public administration; some of the most notable are the Paperwork Reduction Act, the Clinger Cohen Act, and the E-government Act. All three pieces of legislation have influenced performance and management of federal departments and agencies.

Finally, strategic planning is essential for IT and public administration to ensure that the organization is able to move towards its mission.

Discussion Questions

1. What are the major differences in public and private sector organizations and how does this impact leadership and management of IT in public administration?
2. Why are leadership and management so important for the development of IT and public administration?
3. Why are CIOs important for the advancement of IT and public administration?
4. What are the most important laws passed by Congress that impact IT and public administration?
5. What role does strategic planning have in IT and public administration?

Closing Case Study

Vivek Kundra

On March 5, 2009, President Barack Obama named Vivek Kundra, who had been chief technology officer for Washington, DC, to the job as federal CIO (Jackson, 2009b). This new role encompassed the former title of the Office of Management and Budget's Administrator for E-Government and Information Technology, the job that was previously viewed as the federal CIO. Federal agencies can expect to see more calls for change, with greater transparency and more use of Web 2.0 and cloud computing technologies, because these were some of the initiatives Kundra developed in Washington, DC.

Kundra believes one of the biggest issues government faces is that the process has overtaken the outcome that government wants to achieve. Everyone is thinking about compliance, rather than innovation, according to Kundra. Kundra mentioned that his career goal is to "affect change as a public servant." Not surprisingly, he was a supporter of presidential candidate Barack Obama, who also spoke of change.

Similar to Obama, Kundra had an international upbringing. He was born in India and grew up in Tanzania speaking Swahili as his first language. When he was 11 his family moved to Gaithersburg, Maryland. He majored in psychology as an undergraduate and earned a master's in IT from the University of Maryland. He spent time in the private sector and brought about innovation so common in the business world as the chief executive of Crestar, a startup company. A brief profile of this young federal government CIO is provided on the next page (Mosquera, 2009).

Profile: Vivek Kundra

Position: Federal chief information officer and Office of Management and Budget administrator for e-government and information technology

Previous positions:

- District of Columbia chief technology officer
- Commonwealth of Virginia's assistant secretary of commerce and technology
- Arlington County, Virginia, director of infrastructure technology

Sample Projects as Washington, DC, Chief Technology Officer (CTO):

- Contracted Google Apps licenses for 38,000 users to reduce cost of enterprise software and to encourage DC employees to create their own sites and collaborate with co-workers.
- Tested the migration of e-mail to cloud computing.
- Sponsored AppsForDemocracy contest, which led to 47 new applications, to motivate volunteers to build apps for web or mobile phones.
- Office of CTO established Digital Public Square for data feed access.
- Managed IT portfolio management like stock market trading floor.

Chapter 6

E-Government and Organizational Change

Opening Case Study

IRS E-Filing

People used the Internal Revenue Service's (IRS) e-file technology to submit 95 million federal income tax returns in 2009, up almost 6% from the 2009 total of nearly 90 million (Mosquera, 2008; Beizer, 2009). Of the 141 million returns filed, more than 67% were filed electronically, compared with 59% last year (**Figure 6-1**), according to the IRS. Although the total number of tax returns increased 10% in the past decade, the number filed electronically has increased 168% in the same time, according to the IRS (Mosquera, 2008).

Taxpayers who use a home computer to file taxes electronically are an increasingly significant segment of e-filers, IRS officials said. More than a third of electronic returns—more than 32 million—were filed from a home computer, which represents an increase of almost 19% from last year's record of 27 million. Other e-filers use accountants and tax-preparation services. More than 3 million taxpayers filed their tax returns for free through the IRS Free File program, officials said. Congress wanted the IRS to expand the e-file return to 80% as a target for 2012.

The IRS wants to motivate people who have resisted e-filing, primarily those who prepare their returns with commercial tax preparation software, print the returns, and send the paper version into the IRS. Some professional tax preparers do not e-file.

YEAR FILED	TOTAL RETURNS	E-FILED RETURNS	PERCENT E-FILED
2000	128,430,000	35,412,000	27.57%
2001	130,965,000	40,244,000	30.73%
2002	131,728,000	46,892,000	35.60%
2003	131,557,000	52,944,000	40.24%
2004	132,200,000	61,507,000	46.53%
2005	133,933,000	68,476,000	51.13%
2006	136,071,000	73,255,000	53.84%
2007	140,188,000	79,979,000	57.05%
2008	153,650,000	89,853,000	58.48%
2009	141,376,000	94,980,000	67.18%

Figure 6-1 *Electronic tax filing is on the rise* (Source: IRS)

Some argue government should mandate it for taxpayers, which would get it above 80%. According to surveys done by the IRS, 92% of users would use Free File again and 98% would tell a friend. The dilemma the IRS faces is closing the gap between those 5 million who use Free File and the 98 million Americans who are eligible. Boosting adoption is also an issue in the 21 state governments that have income tax. In the future, it is hoped that taxpayers can file their return via their cell phone and there should be enough computational power in a cell phone to file a simple return.

Chapter Objectives

The four primary objectives of this chapter are as follows:

1. To examine the role of information and communication technology on bureaucracy and e-government
2. To discuss e-government and the different stages of its evolution
3. To discuss some of the benefits and challenges to the adoption of e-government
4. To examine the role of e-government in promoting organizational change and effectiveness

Introduction

In this chapter we discuss e-government and its impact on organization change. E-government is the use of information and communication technology (ICT), such as the Internet, to make government accessible to citizens and businesses, 24 hours a day, 7 days a week. We also discuss the impact ICT has had on bureaucracy and the movement from the bureaucratic paradigm to the e-government paradigm. We examine the evolutionary theories of e-government development as well as the benefits and challenges of e-government adoption. Finally, we consider e-government effectiveness, showing how it impacts organization change and development.

Bureaucracy and ICT

Weber (1919) defined bureaucratic structures as being well suited for a highly effective organization, where power was concentrated on the top. However, the bureaucratic structure created an organization that had continuity and stability, which are major inhibitors of change (Bannister, 2001). The culture of the Weber model created an organizational culture that was essentially risk averse. Because of the large, diverse, and unintegrated nature of this structure, a silo or stovetop problem was created in public sector organizations, where one department did not communicate with another. Weber's bureaucratic structure has been challenged by many public administration theorists, and information technology (IT) is seen as one way to create a more dynamic, less rigid, and more effective public sector organization.

Computing and Bureaucratic Power

The introduction of computers and information systems into bureaucracies is an intervention of technology into a complex political environment (Berman and Tettey, 2001). Danziger and coworkers (1982) believed computers directly control and reinforce the existing structures of power and the political and organizational culture of the organization. Computers lead to an introduction of new power groups into the structure of the bureaucracy. Their power is based on their control of expertise in the use of the technology that may threaten the authority and status of higher officials in the organization.

Weber's rational-legal model showed how bureaucracy could enable government to work efficiently in society (Fountain, 2001). However, ICT can be seen as a way of changing the bureaucracy in ways that Weber could not have imagined. Weber's definition of bureaucracy shows how the division of labor can create an efficient organization. Weber strongly believed in hierarchy, which enables the decomposition of complex problems in organizations. In addition, Weber advocated for files being an important component of an organization. Written rules were key to ensure the adherence to rules. Weber also believed that the bureaucracy should be neutral and impersonal, and a key component of this is professionalism. Finally, Weber's bureaucracy was characterized by rules and procedures that must be followed. Essentially, Weber was writing about enhancing efficiency in organizations, and bureaucracy was seen as one way of making this happen.

Bannister (2001) provided examples of issues associated with ICT and bureaucracy. Information systems in the Irish civil service have developed into silos of processing without much integration for the following reasons (Bannister, 2001, p. 71):

- The nature of the bureaucracy itself tends toward specialization. This specialization is reflected in the information systems that serve it.
- Political control of these organizations can lead to systems being developed or prioritized for short-term reasons.
- Internal politics occur where control of information systems is a key form of power and influence within departments.
- Pressure for specific solutions forms lobby groups and systems to meet short-term crises.
- Information systems managers in some departments have relatively uninfluential positions.
- Authority is fragmented, which diffuses systematic decision making.
- There is an interdependence, particularly of larger departments of state, from central control and standards and a lack of lines of authority.
- The size and breadth of the range of services offered have an effect.

According to Bannister, this silo structure is inefficient and leads to frustration, waste of resources, and a poor image of government by citizens.

Red tape is a procedural safeguard that uses excessive paperwork to provide protection against arbitrary use of power (Pandey and Bretschneider, 1997). Red tape can serve a useful purpose because it holds public agencies accountable and at the same time ensures fairness and equity in the treatment of clients. Major drawbacks of red tape are public dissatisfaction with the functioning of organizations regarding delays in processing paperwork, excessive reporting requirements, and excessive rules. Because red tape is part of a problem of information processing and communications in an organization, IT can be part of the solution to relieve the burden of red tape. A negative organizational factor such as red tape is said to spur the development of more innovative responses through the use of IT (Moon and Bretschneider, 2002). As the cost of red tape increases, it is more likely that a public sector organization would enable real change through IT.

Revitalized management practices promote increased openness, mutual support, and risk taking by employees and public managers (West and Berman, 2001a). First, risk taking promotes productivity in employees and managers by encouraging them to seek out new opportunities for change. Essentially, risk taking allows employees and managers to experiment with new ideas and ways of doing things. Second, management efforts to increase openness increase dialogue and consensus in the organization. If there is no openness in the organization, then problems and issues may be ignored. Third, management initiatives to promote mutual support increase the problem-solving abilities of employees and managers. Managerial actions that

Table 6-1 *Changes Seen in a Shift from Bureaucratic to E-Government Paradigm*

	Bureaucratic Paradigm	**E-Government Paradigm**
Service delivery	Standardized and impersonal, face-to-face contact	Non–face-to-face, electronic exchange, customized and personalized
Leadership	Command and control	Entrepreneurial
Internal and external communication	Top down, hierarchical, directed	Decentralized, multidirectional
Management	Departmentalization	Networked
Technologies	Written documentation	Electronic documentation

Adapted from Ho (2002) and Moon (2002).

promote risk taking, openness, and mutual support can be promoted by the use of IT. In a study of American cities, the use of IT strengthens revitalized management practices by increasing new opportunities for risk taking, enhancing open communication, and providing opportunities for mutual support (West and Berman, 2001a).

There has been a movement from a bureaucratic paradigm to an e-government paradigm. As a result, some aspects of public service delivery have changed (**Table 6-1**) (Ho, 2002). One characteristic of this movement can be seen through changes in service delivery. The bureaucratic paradigm emphasizes impersonal contact, whereas the e-government paradigm provides a more customized and non–face-to-face contact. The bureaucratic paradigm has management in departments, whereas the e-government paradigm has a networked model. In regards to leadership, the bureaucratic paradigm emphasizes command and control from the top of the organization, whereas the e-government paradigm leadership is more entrepreneurial.

IT and Organizational Structure

The implementation of IT in an organization can have some distinct impacts (Heintze and Bretschneider, 2000). IT has the potential to reduce the number of organizational members across the organization and to effectively reduce the size of the organization. It may also significantly reduce or expand the structure of the organization. Research on IT and organizational structure indicates a managerial employment impact by removing middle management layers and concentrating power at the top of the organization, essentially increasing the span of control of upper management. Essentially, it will increase the manner in which decisions are made and decrease the number of units involved by centralizing decisions.

IT and Centralization Versus Decentralization

There are three views on the impact of IT and centralizing and decentralizing the organization (Bloomfield and Coombs, 1992; Welch and Pandey, 2006). One view is that IT is able to control more information in the organization and therefore centralizes power. The second view holds that IT will decentralize power and control to individuals. This is especially seen with the Internet, where different levels of the organization can have access to information. The final view holds that there will be a bit of both centralization and decentralization of power in the organization (Currie, 1996).

Centralization is the extent to which decision-making authority is dispersed or concentrated in an organization (Dewett and Jones, 2001). The question is whether IT will lead to centralization or decentralization of decision making. Centralization enables managers to obtain more information more quickly and accurately, and IT reduces the uncertainty for lead managers to make decisions. Decentralization through IT enables lower and middle managers to stay better informed about the organization's overall situation and about the nature of the problems and issues that it faces.

There is continual debate on the merits of a decentralized versus a centralized information systems structure (Kraemer and Dedrick, 1997). Those in support of decentralization believe it brings computing under the direct control of the end user, who is able to use this to control his or her department. For example, client-server computing decentralizes computer systems. Centralization should increase economies of scale and provide less control by the user. The literature does show that information systems can have an impact on organizational structure through both centralization and decentralization. The centralization/decentralization debate continues, but this may depend on the type of organization examined. Smaller governments or nonprofit organization may benefit from decentralization, and larger governments may prefer more centralized information systems. Therefore, the organizational context and environment dictate the use of a centralized system versus decentralized information systems.

IT and Administrative Reform

Kraemer and King (2006) concluded that IT has never been a solution to providing administrative reform; rather, it merely reinforces existing administrative and political arrangements in government. Administrative reform is the ability to transform government dramatically through the use of IT. These authors argue for the potential for administrative reform of government through IT, but there is the lack of evidence for this actually taking place. Kraemer and King (2006) test several propositions of the impact of IT on administrative reform in the public sector. The overall findings for each of these propositions are presented:

- *Proposition 1:* Computers have the potential to reform public administration and their relations with their environments.

- *Finding for Proposition 1:* Experience with IT and administrative reform indicates that technology may be useful for administrative reform in some case, but IT does not cause reform and cannot encourage it where the political will to pursue reform is not there.
- *Proposition 2:* IT can change organization structures and thereby is a powerful tool of reform.
- *Finding for Proposition 2:* IT applications have brought about very little change to organization structures and seem to reinforce existing structures.
- *Proposition 3:* IT will be beneficial to administrators, staff, citizens, and public administration as a whole.
- *Finding for Proposition 3:* The benefits of IT have not been distributed evenly within government; the primary benefits are the dominant political and administrative coalitions, not those in the technical, middle management, and clerical staff within the organization.
- *Proposition 4:* The potential of IT is underused because of the lack of managerial understanding of what the technology can do for the organization and the unwillingness of the manager to pursue the potential of technology.
- *Finding for Proposition 4:* Government managers have a good sense of the potential and uses of IT for their organization, and they push IT heavily when it is in their interest.

Essentially, Kraemer and King (2006) made the argument that IT merely reinforces existing structures and power relationships in public sector organizations. These authors did not find any evidence for radical administrative reform in the public sector.

E-Government as a Management Strategy

According to some, e-government can be seen as the merger of several core values from new public management (NPM) and traditional bureaucracy theory (Persson and Goldkuhl, 2010). E-government is essentially seen as a synthesis of these two core management values (Ingraham et al., 2003). A synthesis takes some of the best properties of NPM and traditional bureaucracy and combines them into a new model. The core elements of e-government as a management strategy are outlined below (Persson and Goldkuhl, 2010, p. 48):

- A means of decreasing the impacts of dysfunctional bureaucracy
  - Less impact of rigidity
  - Less fragmentation
  - Less proceduralism
  - More tailor-made solutions
  - Higher degree of personalization

- Vertical and horizontal integration
- Reducing face-to-face contact to ease the effect of functional borders
- A means of strengthening bureaucratic values
  - Centralization
  - Legality
  - Limited discretion
  - Efficiency
  - Productivity
  - Distinct rule application through automation
  - Predictability
  - Reducing face-to-face contact in order to automate
  - Improving transparency
  - Improving accountability through equal treatment and legality
- A way of building on NPM and taking it a step further
  - Performance orientation
  - Citizen or user focus
  - More responsive to citizen needs
  - Focusing efficiency
  - Focusing effectiveness
  - Improving accountability for results
  - Better service provision
  - More accessible services
- A step back from NPM, replacing it with
  - Focus on bureaucratic values and discovery of e-bureaucracy
  - Refocusing impartiality
  - Refocusing equality
  - Refocusing legality
  - Move from dysfunctions of NPM and the discovery of digital era governance

Several core values are associated with traditional bureaucracy (Persson and Goldkuhl, 2010, p. 51):

- Legitimacy
- Rule of law
- Application of detailed rules
- Efficiency
- Effectiveness
- Equality

- Legality
- Impartiality
- Objectivity
- Transparency
- Accountability
- High specialization
- Citizen as subordinate to the administration

In addition, core values of NPM can be extracted from the literature (Persson and Goldkuhl, 2010, p. 53):

- Customer orientation
- Decentralization
- Mission and goal orientation
- Improved accountability for results
- Improved responsibility to address client needs
- Focus on cost-efficiency
- Focus on productivity
- Shift from idea of spending to earning
- Introducing market mechanisms (competition, incentivization)
- Introducing a higher degree of flexibility and discretion
- Empowering of street-level bureaucrats
- Deregulation as reform strategy
- Pushing control from hierarchy of bureaucracies to community
- Preventative and proactive approach rather than reactive and curing
- Separating policy formulation from implementation

Essentially, e-government combines many of the best practices associated with the NPM model with traditional bureaucratic theory. E-government would provide elements of efficiency in the bureaucratic model and combine it with effectiveness and results as noted in the NPM model. In addition, the NPM model calls for bureaucratic discretion; this would be combined with the bureaucratic theory of providing more control over administrative discretion through IT in e-government.

E-Government Evolution

There are many different models on the development of e-government, but the first and most important model was by Layne and Lee (2001) (**Figure 6-2**). Most of these models advocate for a linear, step-by-step maturity of e-government. In these maturity models governments progress from one stage to the next, more developed,

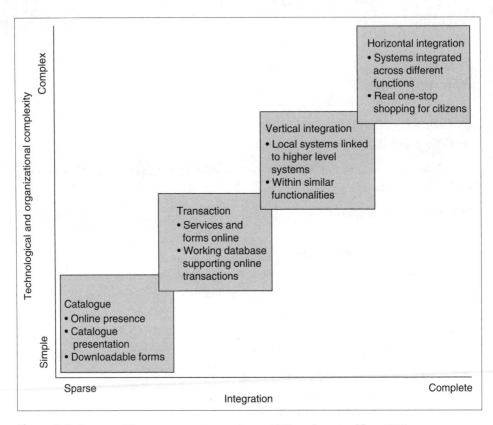

Figure 6-2 *Layne and Lee e-government maturity model* (From Layne and Lee, 2001)

stage of e-government development in which the first stage is usually providing information on a government website, the second stage is transactional, and the latter stages involve a more wholesale change of the organization. Evidence exists for the first two stages to differing degrees, but there is not much conclusive research on latter stages of vertical and horizontal organizational change.

One unique maturity model of e-government compares its evolution in the public sector with e-commerce development in the private sector. Premkumar and colleagues (2006) concluded that e-government development mimics private sector e-commerce in three phases (p. 180):

- *Content phase*, in which a website is used as a one-way communication channel to provide public information to citizens
- *Commerce phase*, in which citizens can make online requests for specific information and conduct e-transactions with government
- *Community phase*, in which a website helps build a virtual community by providing a platform for citizens and community organizations to conduct policy discourses, organize community actions, and make collective decisions

There are several reasons e-government and e-commerce have evolved differently (Premkumar et al., 2006). There are differences in incentive structures between the public and private sectors, as noted in Chapter 1. Because businesses are concerned with profitability and return on investment, websites need to provide greater pressure to get a return on investment. Government websites do not face this pressure because they are financed through tax revenues. In addition, public sector organizations do not face the pressure to keep up with other governments as the private sector does when it develops a website. Budget constraints are another issue for local governments and the development of a website, where it may be difficult to justify given other priorities of the city. The private sector has been able to develop in all three phases, whereas the public sector has only been able to master the content and community phases.

Survey evidence shows that municipal size and type of government are significant institutional factors in the development of e-government (Moon, 2002). Larger local governments are expected to be more proactive and strategic in supporting the development of e-government than smaller governments. In addition, the increased professionalism through a dedicated city manager is said to increase the development of e-government, because they are dedicated to promoting good management practices in the city. However, barriers to the adoption of e-government are technical, personnel, and financial capacities, which may be lacking in many city governments.

The e-government maturity studies as discussed have many of them examining e-government development through the sophistication of a government's website. These studies essentially benchmark the development of e-government. One of the most important criticisms of the benchmarking studies is that they only measure the supply side of e-government (Sharma, 2004). These studies mainly count the number of services offered online by governments to citizens. All these studies do not discuss the actual demand and use of these services by citizens and businesses. Another criticism of the benchmarking studies is that they define it as online service delivery, but the scope of e-government is much broader than that. There is no measure of the quality of services that citizens receive online, or how successful they were at engaging government. Therefore, most of these benchmarking studies are void of any discussion of the impact of e-government on participation of citizens in their government.

E-Government Benefits and Challenges

As noted, Layne and Lee (2001) provided one of the first models of e-government maturity. This model and similar models have been criticized as they reinforce a technical bias when promoting e-government. These models label maturity as the opposite of immaturity (Andersen and Henriksen, 2006). These models assume that a higher stage of development is better than a lower stage. They are normative models explaining what ought to occur. They all predict a state that is progressive and stepwise (Reddick, 2004a). Some scholars have argued that these models are purely speculative, in that they are not even models but guesses about what e-government might be and how it might evolve (Coursey and Norris, 2008).

The two models of e-government and its impact on service delivery are the maturational model and the adaption model (Brown, 2007). The maturational model fits into the notion of incremental change, where innovation of e-government occurs in small incremental steps. In this model productivity gains occur at higher degrees of maturity, which also have greater benefits. The maturational model assumes that change is linear, sequential, and hierarchical. Progress occurs in a stepwise fashion: as the organization master's one stage it can move onto the next stage. Therefore, higher order stages incorporate the learning and initiative of lower order stages. The adaption model shows that change can occur in a nonlinear fashion as a result of environmental shocks that trigger this behavior. Therefore, innovation can occur because of certain circumstances the organization faces. Research shows that technological innovation in local governments occurs incrementally according to the maturational model at the macro level. But this model is less useful at explaining individual organizational-level behavior, which occurs at a more adaptive manner responding to change within and outside of the organization.

There are several important benefits related to the implementation of e-government (Joseph and Kitlan, 2008, p. 4):

- Lower the overall administrative costs to government
- Provide more efficient government operations
- Create a stronger and closer relationship between citizens and government
- Provide easier access to government for all
- Improve the level of service to citizens
- Allow greater access to decision-making
- Empowerment of citizens
- Provide more transparency in government with more responsibility

The main advantages of e-government to public administration are paperwork reduction, greater efficiency, and improved governance (Joseph and Kitlan, 2008). To correct the paperwork problem that governments have faced, the U.S. federal government created the Paperwork Reduction Act of 1998, which required the use of electronic means, when possible, for official business. For greater efficiency the use of electronic systems through e-government saves both time and money. Finally, there is increased accountability because of the rise in transparency from e-government, which provides a platform for citizen participation.

The challenges of e-government for public administration are as follows (Joseph and Kitlan, 2008, p. 5):

- Concerns about inadequate security and privacy of data
- Unequal access to computer technology by citizens
- High initial costs of setting up an e-government solution
- Resistance to change

The issue of security and privacy is evident in the use of personally identifiable information of citizens, where safeguards are needed to protect this information. The digital divide has been well documented and discussed in previous chapters and is a major challenge for e-government advancement. The initial cost of e-government can be a prohibitive factor for smaller and less resource rich governments. There often is resistance to change to do something new and different with e-government.

For e-government to be successful, governments need to market what they offer online to build constituents and interest (Edmiston, 2003). They need to use marketing to educate the public about the benefits of going online to complete a registration form or renew a driver's license online. Governments, unlike the private sector, have not put much time and resources into marketing their services to citizens.

Kraemer and King (2008) argued that IT has never been an instrument of administrative reform. IT has been used to reinforce existing political and administrative arrangements. IT has been touted in many studies as a catalyst for administrative reform. E-government is the latest instrument of administrative reform, but according to Kraemer and King (2008) it is no different from past IT reform efforts where incremental change occurs. The U.S. experience with IT and administrative reform indicates that IT is often used to focus on administrative efficiency and not on reforming administrative organizations. Essentially, e-government can be used to create marginal changes in efficiency and effectiveness but will not transform government as was envisioned by many scholars and practitioners.

In an analysis of government documents and the literature on e-government reform, Bekkers and Homburg (2007) believed that e-government had a mythical quality. An analysis of e-government policy in several countries suggests this technology by itself does not enable or cause public sector agencies to transform them from self-centered organizations to citizen centric. Four myths are associated with the use of e-government to transform government: (1) the myth of new and better government, (2) the myth of technological progress and instrumentality, (3) the myth of e-government as rational information planning, and (4) the myth of citizen as empowered consumer (Bekkers and Homburg, 2007). Bekkers and Homburg believe these four myths indicate that e-government has not transformed government as it has been envisioned. The following section provides an empirical analysis on how effective e-government has been for changing government through a survey of public managers.

E-Government Effectiveness Survey of Public Managers

Rainey and Steinbauer (1999) stated that government effectiveness refers to whether an agency does well at accomplishing its mission. Effectiveness focuses on the organization's administrative and operational tasks and not on the design of the public policy. In a survey of e-government and its effectiveness for American city governments,

Table 6-2 *E-Government and Management*

	Strongly Agree	Agree	Neutral	Disagree	Strongly Disagree
	%				
E-government has made me a more effective manager	14.3	37.5	34.8	7.1	6.3
E-government has been adopted widely and quickly	11.6	38.4	20.5	25.0	4.5
E-government has empowered employees to make more decisions on their own	9.8	30.4	35.7	17.9	6.3
E-government has enabled us to achieve greater performance milestones and results	13.4	53.6	22.3	6.3	4.5

Reddick (2008) found evidence for this occurring. **Table 6-2** shows that in regards to e-government and its impact on management, there seemed to be some evidence that it was able to change this function. The highest level of agreement (summing up "agree" and "strongly agree" responses) showed that e-government enabled city government to achieve greater performance milestones and results (67%). There was agreement that e-government has made the IT director a more effective manager (51.8%). Half of IT directors agreed that e-government has been adopted widely and quickly in their organization. The least level of agreement was for e-government empowering employees to make more decisions on their own (40.2%). Overall, there is evidence that e-government had an impact on management effectiveness in American city governments.

Table 6-3 shows the survey results for the impact of e-government on leadership of American city governments. As discussed in previous chapters, effective leadership is critical for the promotion and support of e-government. For instance, having a champion of e-government is a critical success factor for e-government advancement with 91.1% of IT directors agreeing to this statement. Top management support is also critical for the advancement of e-government, with 46.5% of IT directors agreeing they have a vision and strategic direction for e-government. Over half of American IT directors believed top management dictates what e-government initiatives their governments chose (50.9). Finally, 68.7% of IT directors believed top management was very supportive of their participation in e-government initiatives. The results from the survey of American city government indicate that management had an impact on e-government; therefore, public managers have an important role in the advancement of e-government.

Table 6-4 examines the impact of e-government on project management using survey evidence from American cities. The survey evidence indicates that e-government

Table 6-3 *Leadership and E-Government*

	Strongly Agree	Agree	Neutral	Disagree	Strongly Disagree
	%				
Having a champion of e-government is one of the most important critical success factors for e-government advancement	51.8	39.3	6.3	1.8	0.9
Top management has a vision and strategic direction for e-government	17.9	28.6	30.4	18.8	4.5
Top management dictates what our e-government initiatives will be	9.8	41.1	25.0	19.6	4.5
Top management is very supportive of my department's participation in the decision making process for e-government	35.7	33.0	19.6	8.0	3.6

Table 6-4 *E-Government Projects*

	Strongly Agree	Agree	Neutral	Disagree	Strongly Disagree
	%				
E-government projects have created a more citizen-focused government	12.5	55.4	25.9	5.4	0.9
E-government projects require some input from stakeholders such as city council, citizens, and businesses but ultimate decisions tend to rest with city government	12.5	63.4	16.1	6.3	1.8
E-government projects have increased citizen interaction with city government	17.9	62.5	15.2	3.6	0.9
E-government projects are a top priority of city government	14.3	29.5	30.4	19.6	6.3

Table 6-5 *E-Government and the Workforce*

	Strongly Agree	Agree	Neutral	Disagree	Strongly Disagree
	%				
Recruitment and retention of qualified e-government program management and support staff is one of the most critical issues	12.5	28.6	24.1	27.7	7.1
E-government has allowed a greater degree of information sharing among departments	20.5	40.2	25.0	11.6	2.7
E-government has fostered greater teamwork in employees	7.1	33.0	39.3	16.1	4.5
E-government has developed a new level of collaboration among departments	8.9	29.5	39.3	17.9	4.5

projects have increased the level of citizen interaction with government (80.4%). Furthermore, only 43.8% of IT directors believe e-government projects are a top priority of their city government. The majority of city IT directors believed e-government projects have created a more citizen-focused government (67.9%). Ultimate decisions on e-government projects tend to rest with city government rather than stakeholders such as city council, citizens, and businesses (75.9%). The results of the survey show that citizens have a role in e-government projects and have increased citizen-interaction with government.

Table 6-5 provides survey evidence on the perceived impact of e-government on the city government workforce. The survey evidence indicates that e-government has allowed a greater degree of information sharing among departments (60.7%). E-government has fostered a greater level of teamwork in employees (40.1%). E-government has also developed a new level of collaboration among departments (38.4%). Recruitment and retention of e-government program management support staff was critical, according to 41.1% of IT directors. Essentially, the survey evidence showed that e-government had an impact on collaboration and teamwork in organizations.

Table 6-6 provides information on e-government and resources for American city government. Most IT directors agree their city government has the critical information infrastructure to promote e-government adoption (80.4%) and their city government manual processes have been decreased as a result of e-government (72.4%). City governments take a holistic view of e-government when implementing

Table 6-6 *E-Government and Resources*

	Strongly Agree	Agree	Neutral	Disagree	Strongly Disagree
	%				
Has the critical information technology infrastructure to promote e-government adoption	24.1	56.3	11.6	6.3	1.8
Has adequate budget resources to fund e-government projects	8.9	34.8	17.9	34.8	3.6
Has seen manual processes being reduced as a result of e-government	17.9	54.5	19.6	6.3	1.8
Takes a holistic view of e-government when implementing e-government projects	10.7	32.1	38.4	15.2	3.6

e-government projects, according to 42.8% of IT directors. Not surprisingly, there was not much agreement that cities have adequate budget resources to fund e-government projects (43.7%).

Table 6-7 shows the impact of e-government on administrative discretion in organizations. There is not much agreement that e-government had an impact on discretionary decision making in American cities. For instance, only 33.1% of IT directors agreed that when e-government was used there was greater control over the implementation of policies. Only 22.3% of IT directors believed when e-government was used there was minimal contact by employees with citizens. A small number of IT directors believed decisions were not often questioned when e-government was implemented (16.1%). There was greater accuracy of decisions made by employees when e-government was adopted, according to 26.8% of IT directors. The results showed that when e-government was used it did not have a substantial impact on administrative discretion.

Overall, the survey evidence on e-government and managerial effectiveness shows it has impacted management and leadership the greatest. The least impact was on administrative discretion. The results indicate that the organizational change through administrative discretion was not a great factor in e-government effectiveness.

Summary

This chapter discussed the shift from the bureaucratic paradigm, which stresses that power and authority rest with the top of the organization, to the e-government paradigm.

Table 6-7 *E-Government and Administrative Discretion*

	Strongly Agree	Agree	Neutral	Disagree	Strongly Disagree
	%				
When e-government is used, decisions are not often questioned	2.7	13.4	55.4	25.0	3.6
When e-government is used, there is greater control over the implementation of policies	3.6	29.5	49.1	16.1	1.8
When e-government is used, there is minimal contact by employees with citizens	2.7	19.6	36.6	39.3	1.8
When e-government is used, there is greater accuracy of decisions made by employees	0.9	25.9	59.8	11.6	1.8

The e-government paradigm argues that power is dispersed throughout the organization and decision making is decentralized. Models of e-government articulate that it proceeds in a linear fashion from information, to commerce, to community phases. Research shows that most of the evolution has taken place at the first two phases; not much of a virtual community occurs in government. Much of the e-government research argues that it will transform government and offer a new higher level of public service delivery. However, the results of these studies indicate that change is more incremental than a fundamental transformation. Finally, survey results indicate that e-government has made public managers perform their duties more effectively. E-government has impacted management, projects, and resources, but administrative discretion is an area it has not substantially impacted. Essentially, e-government does have an influence on organizational change and service delivery, but the impact is probably less than what was originally envisioned by earlier scholars.

Discussion Questions

1. How is e-government different from or similar to e-governance, as discussed in Chapter 4?
2. What is the e-government paradigm and how does it differ from the bureaucratic paradigm?

3. What are three phases of e-government development? In what phase of e-government development do governments currently reside?
4. What are the benefits and challenges of e-government adoption?
5. Has e-government had an impact on managerial effectiveness? If so, provide some survey evidence that shows its impact.

Closing Case Study

Charles County, Maryland: Digital Counties Award Winner 8 Years Running

The Center for Digital Government announced the winners for its 2010 Digital Counties Survey. Charles County in Maryland has been the winner of the Digital Counties award for 8 years running in the population category of less than 150,000 (Hanson, 2010). Areas of reported collaborative projects and projects that motivated greater transparency both got high marks by the judges. Another area that got high marks was the deployment of green technologies to reduce energy consumption (Opsahl, 2010).

To learn more about the success of this county in digital government, one needs to talk with the chief information officer (CIO), Richard Aldridge, who became CIO in 2000. Aldridge promised the staff they would never get bored and they would be using state-of-the-art technology. Today, the IT department serves 650 users; however, when Aldridge started, the county went from 7 servers to 79 and 98 physical buildings were being connected through 350 miles of fiber. The IT team in the county site had everything from a green program to an online county checkbook and many interactive applications. The county was the first in the area to allow residents to pay taxes and utilities online.

Their website gets 3 to 4 million hits per month. The IT department has a staff of 16 people who will do what it takes to do it right and keep the website going. Aldridge reads over 30 technical publications per month as well as books, and his staff is deeply immersed in e-government. Most learning is done in-house with books and teaching. Aldridge says the county, a few years back, was the first in the state to put election results online. Aldridge was also selected to represent the counties in a touch screen voting machine deployment. For instance, the night after polls closed the results were posted online. Aldridge says that their county does not buy a lot of software like most counties in the state.

In Charles County their software programmers write nearly 200 Web-enabled applications through Java, JSP, and Java scripting. For example, one of the in-house applications helps senior citizens sign up for activities. When seniors come in they can work with a touch screen computer to see all the events for the day. Another application keeps track of when the Sheriff's Department officers are scheduled to appear in court.

Chapter 7

Enterprise Architecture

Opening Case Study

Ohio Shared Services

Ohio has faced its share of hard economic times since the recession of 2007 (Williams, 2010b). Ohio's tax base has dropped 12% over 2009–2010, causing a $3.1 billion reduction in revenue. There are 4,500 fewer state employees. As a result several Ohio agencies banded together in 2008 to build a state-of-the-art shared services center that would use the new enterprise resource planning (ERP) system for answering invoicing and related questions for government agencies and vendors and provide shared back-end financial services for participating agencies. This resulted in a new division called Ohio Shared Services, designed to maximize the new ERP suite's value. The Center makes a wide use of virtual servers and desktops so that information technology resources can be easily deployed where needed. The Center's employees, who voluntarily came from other state agencies, work under innovative new rules and sophisticated performance measures.

Ohio Shared Services performed a number of back-end tasks such as accounts payable and invoice processing, fielding invoice inquiries, documents imaging, travel expense reimbursement, and vendor maintenance and management that were in the past "siloed" in individual agencies. Participation is voluntary for state agencies with the exception of the Center's travel reimbursement and expense reporting capability. Fifteen state agencies participated in the design and launch of Ohio Shared Services, although they pick and choose which functions they actually use. Only eight agencies were using accounts payable in the summer of 2010.

What was once a tedious workflow handled by finance officers of individual agencies has been transformed into a mostly paperless process in which state employees fax and scan their receipts to the Center, creating a more efficient system that allows the state to cut checks in as few as 2 days. The recession of late 2000, with a very restricted budget climate, has made shared services more popular with state and local governments (Williams, 2010b). The financial motive to adopt shared services is very significant, with a generic shared services system cutting costs by approximately 20%. With the economic downturn in late 2000 in revenue growth for state and local government, which could last 10 years, this creates a new operating environment; governments have no choice but to streamline operations, and shared services is essential for this. Governments may delay implementing shared services in the hope that revenues will improve; however, if this does not materialize, governments will be in a more difficult position in the future.

Chapter Objectives

The four primary objectives of this chapter are as follows:

1. To understand public management information systems (PMIS) and how it is different from private sector management information systems.
2. To understand what enterprise architecture means for information technology (IT) and public administration
3. To understand some of the most pressing issues of IT and public administration, such as enterprise architecture, cloud computing, interoperability of information systems, and enterprise resource planning
4. To understand the strategic factors of PMIS and some frameworks for understanding these information systems in public administration

Introduction

In this chapter we examine the concept of enterprise architecture and its application to public administration. In the first part of this chapter, the concept of PMIS is introduced and the difference in this system compared with private sector management information systems (MIS). In the second part we examine what enterprise architecture is and how it can improve IT in public administration. There also is a discussion of interoperability, which is a major issue in the enterprise architecture model. There is a presentation of strategic factors and frameworks for understanding the impact of IT on public administration.

Public Management Information Systems

PMIS are IT that store, analyze, collect, and display information for public sector organizations. PMIS are information systems in the public sector and are different from MIS in the private sector (Bozeman and Bretschneider, 1986). This is primarily because MIS often ignore environmental variables and focus more on the improvement of performance in the business organization. Therefore, prescriptions for MIS solutions developed for business administration may not altogether be appropriate when applied to public sector organizations.

Table 7-1 shows the differences in MIS and PMIS in structure, motives, and environment and their impact on organizations. For structure, the public sector organization is generally very hierarchical and has a centralized MIS system to control the flow of information throughout the organization. In the private sector structure very much depends on the size of the organization and its mission, although the second difference between PMIS and private sector MIS is the motives of the organization. In the private sector there is primarily a profit motivation, whereas in the public sector the motives often are decentralized and come from the departments, where departments may work on expanding their operations to meet the needs of their clients but not altogether thinking about the organization as a whole. Essentially, for the public sector the motives are much more nuanced and varied than for the private sector. The most important difference between PMIS and private sector MIS is the environment, as noted in previous chapters (Bozeman and Bretschneider, 1986).

Table 7-1 *Differences Between PMIS and Private Sector MIS*

	Private Sector MIS	**PMIS**
Structure	Depends on organizational size and mission of organization, more decentralized information systems	Hierarchical and centralized systems because of strict accountability
Motives	Profit and shareholder wealth, greater integration of information systems across organization	Bureaus shaping through resource maximization, silos of information systems based on departments
Environment	Responsive primarily to clients and customers	Responsive to multitude of stakeholders, i.e., politicians, citizens, business, and interest groups

Adapted from Bozeman and Bretschneider (1986).

In the private sector the organization is responsive to their customers and clients, whereas in the public sector there are multiple stakeholders to take into account, such as politicians, the public, and interest groups. These three differences make PMIS very important to study.

Andersen and Dawes (1991) discussed four phases of PMIS in government. The first phase, between the late 1950s and early 1960s, witnessed the development of new digital computing technology. Large repetitive jobs were processed to support programs such as motor vehicle registration, tax processing, and payrolls. The second phase, in the mid-1960s and much of the 1970s, saw the development of mainframe computer systems. These mainframes were very expensive to purchase and operate and were not accessible for many smaller local governments. The third phase took place in the late 1970s and 1980s with the dramatic growth of microprocessing. The prices of computing power dramatically reduced, and the microcomputer became more popular than the typewriter. IBM-compatible systems with MS-DOS operating systems emerged as the leader. In this phase the workforce became more sophisticated in its knowledge and use of microcomputers. In an examination of personal computing in cities, Norris and Kraemer (1996) argued that mainframes and minicomputers had limited impact on government because they are centralized and mainly used in the financial area and accessed mostly by a MIS department. However, personal computers allowed computing to be decentralized and available to managers and staff outside of IT departments. The fourth and current phase is the networked organization. This is where information systems are integrated into the fabric of the organization through Internet servers. MIS has spilled out into the daily operations of government impacting virtually all employees in the organization. The following section discusses enterprise architecture, one of the most exciting emerging topics in IT and public administration research.

Enterprise Architecture

Enterprise architecture can be defined as the analysis and documentation of an organization and its current and future state of integrating IT into its operations (Hjort-Madsen, 2007). In this system there is an enterprise-wide documentation and analysis that aligns technology with the organization's mission. In the public sector organization, enterprise architecture is part of e-government reform, where IT is a way of providing administrative reforms and transformation. Research shows the neoinstitutional view of organizations can explain the impact of enterprise architecture on an organization. Neoinstitutionalist, unlike the rationalist (the Weberian model of bureaucracy), organizations are dynamic and interlinked systems, which is similar to the enterprise architecture method of analysis. This theory of institutions is used to explain the development of enterprise architecture in public sector organizations, where these organizations can use this framework to map out the dynamic process that is taking place in their organizations. By contrast, a rationalist view would not map the interlinked system of the organization but would focus instead on departments and their structure and functions.

Enterprise architecture was developed with the proposed framework of Zachman (1987) with the purpose of aligning business with information systems. Enterprise architecture aligns strategy, people, technology, and knowledge through the management and governance process (Grego et al., 2007). First, enterprise architecture can enable architecture in that business and information systems come together under a common organizational framework. The architecture is a graphic communication model that allows people to see how the various parts of the organization fit together. Second, in an enterprise architecture framework there is the current and future state of IT defined in detail. Business structures can be built to support outcomes of the organization on the basis of this plan.

Federal Enterprise Architecture

The federal enterprise architecture is an organizing mechanism for managing the development and maintenance of blueprint for IT development in federal agencies (Chief Information Officers Council, 1999). The purpose of Federal Enterprise Architecture, which is led by the Office of Management and Budget's E-Government and Information Technology Office, is designed to help agencies maximize the impact of IT investments on their organization (Office of Management and Budget, 2009). The Federal Enterprise Architecture, in particular, is envisioned to increase the performance of IT to improve the mission of the agency, which is noted to be done in four ways:

- Creating mission performance gaps identified via agency performance improvement and strategic planning activities
- Saving money and avoiding cost through collaboration and reuse, process engineering and productivity enhancements, and elimination of redundancy
- Strengthening the quality of investments within agencies that are related to security, interoperability, reliability, availability, end-user performance, flexibility, serviceability, and reducing costs
- Improving the quality, validity, and timeliness of data and information regarding program performance

Federal government IT projects have been framed using an enterprise architecture model. Peled (2007) made the argument that the enterprise architecture framework used by the federal government encourages bureaucrats and consultants to ignore and even destroy computer achievements of the past. This author believed that federal information systems should use a more incremental approach, rather than the holistic enterprise architecture approach, when modernizing their systems. Peled believed the enterprise architecture system is flawed because it is historical, not considering

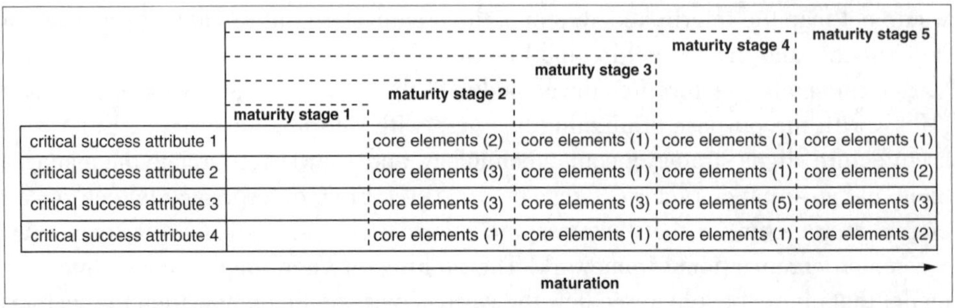

	maturity stage 1	maturity stage 2	maturity stage 3	maturity stage 4	maturity stage 5
critical success attribute 1		core elements (2)	core elements (1)	core elements (1)	core elements (1)
critical success attribute 2		core elements (3)	core elements (1)	core elements (1)	core elements (2)
critical success attribute 3		core elements (3)	core elements (3)	core elements (5)	core elements (3)
critical success attribute 4		core elements (1)	core elements (1)	core elements (1)	core elements (2)

maturation →

Figure 7-1 *U.S. Government Accountability Office (GAO) enterprise architecture framework* (From GAO, 2003)

IT accomplishments of the past. Peled stated since the 1960s new federal computer systems have been layered on top of old systems. Therefore, before enterprise architecture, advocated by the U.S. Government Accountability Office starting in the mid-1990s, a new generation of software and hardware was layered on top of old proven systems. The argument by Peled is that incremental change to systems is preferable rather than the wholesale change from the enterprise architecture model.

The Government Accountability Office (2003) advocates an enterprise architecture framework (EAF), which has five stages of maturity (**Figure 7-1**). Each stage of maturity has core elements, which are essentially what is required at each stage, and critical success attributes or ways to identify if the organization has been successful in implementing its EAF. Stage 1 creates an awareness of enterprise architecture in the organization. At this stage there is no plan for enterprise architecture, just a discussion of the idea, and most efforts are unstructured and a lack of leadership prevents implementing them. Stage 2 builds the enterprise architecture foundation, and the organization recognizes that enterprise architecture is an asset for the organization. There is a management role for enterprise architecture and responsibilities, and plans are developed toward creating the architecture. At this stage, there is an enterprise-wide campaign of awareness of the architecture. There is a framework and methodology that will be used to develop an enterprise-wide architecture plan. In stage 3 architecture products are developed, according to the selected EAF. The scope of the architecture is defined for the organization. The elements of the architecture are used to describe the organization in business, performance, information/data, service application, and technology. At this stage the organization will be tracking progress against the plans and addressing variances from the plan. At stage 4, completing the enterprise architecture, there has been approval of the products that are now being implemented. At stage 5 there is the leveraging of enterprise architecture to manage change in the organization. Management and leadership are required throughout all stages to continually identify ongoing and proposed IT investments so they fit into the EAF. At stage 5 the organization tracks benefits or returns on investment from enterprise architecture. Essentially, the EAF has a progression of development, where the current stage builds on the previous stage. However, the issue with any maturity model of IT development is that change does not always occur in this linear stepwise fashion.

Potentially, there are four layers to enterprise architecture in government: access layer, e-government layer, e-business layer, and infrastructure layer (Ebrahim and Irani, 2005). **Figure 7-2** shows an example of enterprise architecture applied to e-government service. **Tables 7-2** and **7-3** show the applications and technologies, respectively, that can be used to support the e-business and infrastructure layers (Ebrahim and Irani, 2005). These applications range from database management systems that serve the back end of the organization to customer relationship management technologies that serve the needs of citizens. Some of the hardware technologies are Internet and Intranet servers that support IT and public administration.

The access layer is used to access various government services (Figure 7-2). Government users are citizens, businesses, employees, other governments, and community members. Some common channels used are the website, call centers, and information kiosks. The access layer provides a common entry to government information and services. Therefore, the look and feel of each of these contact channels should be similar for consistency. The e-government layer is the integration of digital data of various organizations into a web portal of government services. The e-government layer provides a one-stop shop for government services. A government web portal is essentially a gateway to government information and services, which should reduce processing times, reduce duplication of services, and increase quality. Because governments are complex entities with numerous agencies, a web portal makes sense to sort out this complexity. The third layer is the e-business layer, which uses IT tools through various applications such as customer resource management, enterprise resource planning, document management systems, and so forth. The focus of the e-business layer is on integrating various applications of the organization. Finally, the infrastructure layer is the technologies that need to be in place before e-government services can be offered. Examples of the technologies are hardware, software, servers, Intranet, and extranet. The infrastructure layer provides the foundation for the other layers to function, offering the necessary standards and protocols for effective communication within the organization.

For enterprise architecture to work, major stakeholders and how their demands should be balanced for successful design and implementation of enterprise architecture need to be identified (Veasey, 2001). The five important elements of enterprise architecture are culture, competencies, process, technology, and organization. Culture is the values, management style, and employee attitudes of the organization. Competencies are the skills, aptitudes, knowledge, and experience. Process is the management, support, and operational aspects. Technologies in enterprise architecture are the buildings, workplace, equipment, software, and hardware. Organization is the power relationships, formal communication channels, informal networks, trust, and communication.

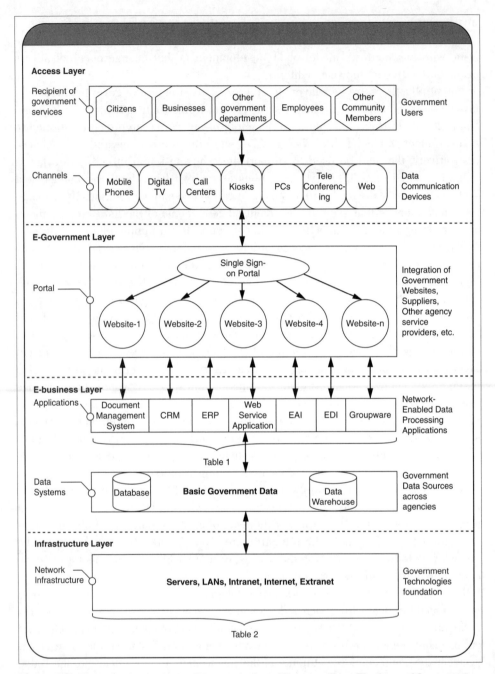

Figure 7-2 *Example of enterprise architecture in the public sector* (From Ebrahim and Irani, 2005)

Table 7-2 *Applications Used in Government Enterprise Architecture*

Application	Description
Database management system (DBMS)	Organization of components that define and regulate the collection, storage, and management of data
Customer relationship management (CRM)	Alignment of business processes through customers in a centralized information system
Enterprise resource planning (ERP)	Business management system that integrates information across functional areas of the organization
Web service application	Governments can host their own website, which will be open to the public and businesses
Data warehouse	Databases that store information from various sources
Electronic data interchange (EDI)	Electronic transfer of data and services using the same standards
Document management system	Stores and manages different formats of documents that are used in the organization
Data and knowledge management	Systematic approach of capturing information and knowledge about an organization
Groupware	Collaborative tools that allow employees to work as a team regardless of physical location

Adapted from Ebrahim and Irani (2005) and Laudon and Laudon (2009).

Some resistance can be expected with the implementation of enterprise architecture. First, management of information systems is an art, not a science. Because there are such complex relationships established with enterprise architecture, it is not just the technical aspects but also the soft management side that makes the difference. Some may fear a loss of power and others may fear change. Therefore, managers will need some convincing that they will not lose power as a result of enterprise architecture. Some believe that natural selection would be a better solution than enterprise architecture because the strongest will survive. This would, however, involve letting strategic change be dictated by survival of the best, which can be very shortsighted.

The main benefit of enterprise architecture is that it is able to define its concepts and instruments to predict and control complex technological systems in organizations

Table 7-3 *Technologies Used in Government Enterprise Architecture*

Technology	Description
Local area network (LAN)	Computer network connecting a geographical area such as a building or campus
Server	A powerful computer that runs applications and connects computer terminals providing service requests
Internet	A collection of global communications that connects users using the same protocols
Intranet	A secure network that connects a specified subpopulation of Internet users
Extranet	A wide area network that links those outside the organization with government inside the organization

Adapted from Ebrahim and Irani (2005) and Laudon and Laudon (2009).

(Weerakkody et al., 2007). Other models are more one-dimensional and therefore are not as holistic. Enterprise architecture emphasizes preplanning and well-defined procedures, which has a good basis for communicating the information systems to others in the organization. Enterprise architecture is also oriented toward efficiency and effectiveness in the management and implementation of information systems. In case studies of enterprise architecture in e-government, some of the most notable challenges were interoperability concerns at different levels of government. A challenge particularly evident in the public sector for enterprise architecture is decentralized information systems.

Interoperability

Interoperability in computing systems can be defined as the ability to exchange information and mutually use this information (Guijarro, 2007). Interoperability between information systems of different agencies is a way of providing services to citizens and businesses in an integrated manner. Public administration has long been concerned with avoiding vendor lock in its IT infrastructure. Standardization has been a response in the 1980s to concerns related to interoperability. Enterprise architecture is a way of aligning information systems to promote interoperability in public organizations.

Interoperability has the goal of getting people and organizations to share information through IT. Landsbergen and Wolken (2001) believed that we are in the fourth generation of computer technology through the networking of information systems. The third generation of computers was the personal computer, which provided the ability of a person to collect, manipulate, and store information on his or her desktop. Interoperability is used to take this information on a personal computer and share it with others in and outside of the organization. The Internet is a prime example of interoperable systems. With the advent of the Internet, the impact of providing interoperability in information systems has become extremely important for public sector organizations.

Some benefits of interoperability are effectiveness, efficiency, and responsiveness (Landsbergen and Wolken, 2001). Effective policies require the sharing of information across agencies and different governments, the private sector, and nonprofit organizations. Interoperable systems provide a greater level of effectiveness of developing policies that take into account the views of multiple stakeholders. Once the information is collected, it is much easier to duplicate and manipulate with interoperable systems. Essentially, interoperable systems promote efficiency by reducing the paperwork burden and facilitate access to information by stakeholders. Finally, interoperable systems are more responsive by providing better access to information, and government can act faster and more effectively to solve problems.

There are also political, organizational, economical, and technical barriers to interoperable systems (Landsbergen and Wolken, 2001). The political barrier encompasses issues of privacy, in which privacy rights are protected while also providing more openness to public scrutiny because of the increased access to information. Organizational barriers comprise issues of trust, developing it with agencies so they share data and educating about the benefits of sharing; agencies may be collecting the same information, of which they might not be aware. There are economic barriers to the adoption of interoperable systems such as the lack of resources. Finally, technical issues with hardware and software for these systems may be incompatible, or there may be different data sharing standards that need to be reconciled for sharing information. Interoperability plays a crucial role in enterprise architecture; there also is the importance of strategic factors in the selection of a system that meets the mission of the public sector organization.

Strategic Factors

Strategic information systems are designed to be positive and proactive and have consequential outcomes for changing the organization (Bajjaly, 1998), whereas operational information systems focus on productivity and controlling costs in performing existing activities. Operational information systems are very important, but focusing on this alone limits the organization's ability to see information as a strategic resource rather than a cost-containment measure. Strategically, information resources provide a way for government to address the demand for more and better services in the face of declining resources. Management plays a critical role in identifying the strategic nature of information systems for the organization as seen through the development of enterprise architecture. This involves creating a supportive IT environment through support from top managers within the agency who understand what benefits can result from the effective deployment of IT.

Much of this book deals with organizations; nonprofit organizations face unique challenges in their adoption of IT. Nonprofit organizations work under greater scrutiny and greater demand with fewer resources and increased competition (Hackler and Saxton, 2007). IT is a way for these organizations to address these challenges. Research examines the impact of IT on the mission of nonprofit organizations. Survey results show that nonprofits need to be more aware of IT's impact to further the mission of their organization. The successful implementation of IT has the potential in nonprofits to transform these organizations. Nonprofits can be assessed in six key strategic areas: (1) IT planning; (2) IT budgeting, staffing, and training; (3) Internet and website capabilities; (4) measurement of IT effectiveness; (5) board support and involvement in IT decisions; and (6) leaders' understanding of the strategic nature of IT. These six components should improve the use of IT to advance the mission of the nonprofit organization. Nonprofits and their use of IT as a strategic resource understand the importance of mission valence for IT development.

Enterprise Resource Planning

Enterprise resource planning (ERP) is an integrated enterprise computing system (Kumar et al., 2002). ERP has an integrated, customized, packaged, software-based system that handles most of an enterprise's system requirements in all functional areas such as finance, human resources, procurement, and customer relations. This software architecture facilitates the flow of information among all functions within an enterprise. It has a common database in which information is stored and retrieved. The most important capability of ERP systems is its ability to integrate enterprise-wide resources. Most ERP systems are generically designed for private sector organizations, which is problematic given the different environment and constraints that public sector organizations face.

ERP software suites are business applications that integrate across the enterprise and link them to a common data repository (Ward, 2006). These business applications are used to manage and integrate financial, administrative, and operational processes across multiple divisions and organizational boundaries. ERP acts as the backbone of the organization and is designed to automate the processes of the public sector agency. Private sector ERP systems implemented in the late 1980s were viewed as a way to increase competitiveness. Some of the benefits noted for the private sector were cost reductions, productivity improvements, and improved business processes. Governments have been late adopters of ERP systems and lag behind industry in implementing these systems. The public sector has different reasons for adopting ERP systems as they are concerned about attaining greater management control, enhance supply chain responsiveness, and lower overall costs.

Empirical research has examined the motivations for adopting ERP systems within e-government (Raymond et al., 2006). The three types of motivations for adopting ERP are *process efficiency*, *technology perspective*, and *strategic perspective*. Efficiency motivation encompasses process modernization and lower maintenance costs. The government administration may be motivated by the technology integration to transform its IT infrastructure into an integrated management system. The strategic perspective views ERP as closely connected with external partners such as other public agencies, citizens, and businesses. Raymond and colleagues (2006) argued that governments should use this framework to understand the motivations of adopting ERP systems. The results of an analysis support this framework in that different public sector organizations' success stores indicate that government organizations adopt ERP systems primarily to integrate their information technology, whereas the private sector seeks greater efficiency or is strategy driven.

Cloud Computing

Cloud computing has the core element of delivering over the Internet, on demand, from a remote location, rather than residing on a desktop, laptop, or mobile device and an organization's server (Wyld, 2009). This means computing will become location and device independent. This enables computing tasks and information to be available anytime as long as the device is connected to the Internet. For cloud computing to exist, users must have (1) universal connectivity to the Internet, (2) open access to the Internet, (3) a reliable system, (4) interoperability to move across cloud platforms, (5) security in that the data must be safe, (6) privacy in that users' rights and their data must be protected, and (7) a tangible economic value.

There are some benefits of cloud computing for government (Wyld, 2009):

- Rapid scalability and deployability
- Decreased maintenance costs
- Improved resource utilization
- Improved economics of scale
- Improved collaboration capabilities
- Ability to engage in usage-based pricing, making computing a variable expense rather than a fixed cost
- Reduced IT infrastructure needs
- Capacity for on-demand and computation power
- Green friendly
- Improved disaster recovery capabilities

As governments become more cash constrained, cloud computing becomes a viable option for them as shown in the closing case study at the end of this chapter.

Project Management IT Projects in Public Sector

The management of IT projects is particularly important in the public sector, especially as budgets get more stringent (Cats-Baril and Thompson, 1995). Four issues account for implementation problems of IT projects. First, there is the issue of not assessing the risks of failure for the individual project at the time a project is funded. Second, there is a general failure to determine whether the level of risk is counterbalanced by the commensurate benefit if implementation was successful. Third, there is a failure to recognize that different projects require different management approaches. Fourth, there is a failure to delegate the implementation of the risk of the project under development to an IT group within the organization.

There are several approaches to manage risks of IT projects in the public sector (Cats-Baril and Thompson, 1995):

1. Evaluate whether the proposed project is aligned with the mission of the organization. The more aligned to the strategic plan, the more likely the project can be easily justified and political support can be garnered.
2. Evaluate the benefits the project will bring to the organization. The benefits can be both tangible, as seen through costs savings, and intangible, such as political good will from greater response time for citizens.
3. Evaluate the risk inherent with the project by examining the project size, experience with the technology, and project structure.
4. Evaluate the expected benefits from the project against its inherent risk. Projects should only be considered that have a proven benefit.

Information Systems Success and Failures

Most information systems projects fail, and the larger the development of the project, the more likely the risk of failure (Goldfinch, 2007). It is difficult to know the exact percentage of failure, but around 20% to 30% are estimated total failures in which the project is abandoned. Around 30% to 60% are partial failures in which there are cost overruns and other problems. In the United States the success rate of government IT projects is only 18%, much lower than private sector rates of success.

The success and failure of information systems can be related to three factors (Heeks, 2002a). First, some systems are total failures. These systems were never implemented or were implemented but abandoned. Some systems, despite years of preparation, never become operational. The second type is partial failure of an information system. This is where the major goals are unattained or there are significant and undesirable outcomes. There could be a situation with an information system working in some areas and not in others, which represents a partial failure. Third, information systems success is where most stakeholders attain the major goals of the system.

Hard and Soft Measures

The two important measures of the success of e-government projects are hard and soft. Hard measures are cost–benefit analysis and benchmarks of e-government

(Gupta and Jana, 2003). Information is being weighed against the cost–benefit analysis. It seeks to answer how much money is being spent to acquire the e-government project and how much benefit is being obtained. The drawback of this approach is that of operationalization. Because e-government service benefits are often intangible, it is sometime impossible to quantify the cost and value associated with obtaining and using it. Benchmarking provides a numeric measure of performance, for example, IT expenses as a percentage of total revenue, percent of downtime, CPU usage, and percent of information systems projects completed on time and within budget as part of e-government projects. Soft measures are benefits such as improved decision making, customer or citizen satisfaction, and employee productivity that can contribute to higher performance. Soft measures use multidimensional attribute measures of information value, which can be more difficult to measure.

External Factors

Political mandates dictate the priority and timeline of IT projects. For example, the Bush Administration's emphasis on homeland security dictated that projects in this area would have a higher priority for funding. Second, the IT marketplace is the availability of vendors that can engage in competitive bidding. The reliability and quality of vendors affect the amount of risks involved in outsourcing of government IT. Third, the characteristics of the technology services are the compatibility and complexity of outsourcing IT services relationships. The more compatible the IT services are with the public agencies, the less difficulty of coordinating them.

Internal Factors

Internal factors are when top management support leads to more successful IT projects that are outsourced. Top management support fosters collaboration between IT personnel and managers that implement the IT outsourcing arrangement. Other factors in this area are the ability to secure partnerships between the public agency and the vendor. A strategic plan is needed to find the appropriate fit with the vendor that can provide the service. A solid commitment of financial and human resources is necessary for the entire duration of the outsourcing project. Performance measures that ensure the quality of IT outsourcing services are important, such as service-level contracts being maintained.

Information Systems Failure

One of the most important reasons for failure of information systems is the overblown expectations of IT projects in their development (Goldfinch, 2007). Three issues are related to this problem of enthusiasm and computer failure. First, there is *idolization* of technology that is believed to transform the organization. A second issue is *technophilia*, which is the belief that there is a technological fix for problems. Third, *lomanism* is significant enthusiasm presented by the vendor for the product that does not deliver after it is implemented. Fourth, managerial *faddism* is the tendency of consultants and managers to eagerly embrace the newest management fad.

There are three types of information systems failures (Goldfinch, 2007):

1. *Project failure:* The project does not meet the agreed-upon standards, including the functions provided in the budget, or completion deadlines.
2. *System failure:* The system does not work properly, including not performing as expected, not being operational at a specified time, and not being used as intended.
3. *User failure:* The system is not used in the face of user resistance such as lack of training and complexity.

There are three reasons for unsuccessful information systems projects in both the public and private sectors (Whittaker, 1999):

1. *Poor project planning:* There is inadequate risk planning and a weak project plan. Risk to the organization becomes more important than planning for a successful information system.
2. *Weak business case:* The need for information systems should be justified in terms of ways that relate directly to the organization's business needs.
3. *Lack of top management support and involvement:* There needs to be buy-in from the top government officials, and a strong business case must be set up with realistic objectives.

Failure is defined differently, but a survey of executives indicated that the following were most indicative (Whittaker, 1999):

- The project budget was overrun by 30% or more.
- The project schedule was overrun by 30% or more.
- The project was canceled or deferred due to the inability to demonstrate or deliver the planned benefits.

Information Systems Success and Users

There is much research on evaluating the success of information systems in organizations (DeLone and McLean, 1992, 2003; Seddon, 1997; Petter et al., 2008). This research gives us an indication of what factors lead to successful implementation and adoption by users. Several factors define whether an information system is successful (Newcomer and Caudle, 1991). *Usefulness* is the quality and reliability of the output of an information system. An example is the completeness of the data collected, stored, and identified. The comprehensiveness of the data is also important. *Ease of use* asks if the information system design is user friendly, in that the information system provides the user with a means to interact with it easily. Some other issues identified are

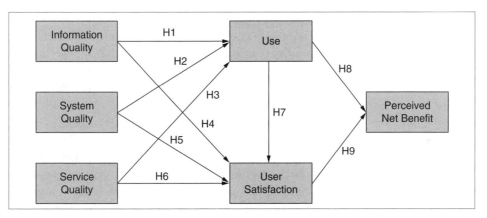

Figure 7-3 *Model of information systems success in the public sector* (Adapted from Wang and Liao, 2008)

whether the information system is *error resistant,* meaning the system has appropriate error prevention and detection procedures identified, reported, and corrected. Finally, *time savings* ensures the system provides the user with a good response time, in terms of how fast the data are retrieved, which results in greater productivity.

Figure 7-3 shows common attributes of the information systems success model that have successfully been applied to the public sector (Floropoulos et al., 2010).

- *Information quality:* This is the actual information produced by the information system and the degree that this information matches the needs of users in terms of accuracy, reliability relevance, completeness, precision of information, currency, and conciseness.
- *System quality:* This concerns how the system transfers the technical aspects such as the flexibility of the system, stability, reliability, usefulness of specific functions, user-friendly interface, ease of use, and acceptable response time.
- *Service quality:* This is the overall support delivered by the service provider and applies regardless of whether this support is delivered by the information systems department, delivered by a new organizational unit, or outsourced to a service provider.
- *Use:* This is the degree to which the stakeholders perceive a particular system enhances job performance. Users evaluate the system with respect to its usefulness, after using it to complete a certain task.
- *User satisfaction:* This is the most common success measure for information systems success. User satisfaction is the sum of the users' feelings and attitudes toward a variety of factors affecting the situation. Others have defined it as the subjective assessment of various consequences of being pleasant or unpleasant.
- *Net benefits:* This is the extent to which the e-government information system is contributing to the success of the individuals who are using the system, for example, improved decision making, improved productivity, and greater efficiency.

In Figure 7-3 each of the hypotheses represents a causal relationship between the attributes of the information systems success model. The literature shows that in the public sector information systems success is related to all five factors, impacting perceived net benefits of information systems to the organizations (Wang and Liao, 2008).

Peterson (1998) describes three actors that have a tremendous impact on the success or failure of information systems. One is the *saint*, which is the progressive senior officer in the organization who is willing to shoulder the risk of changing the organization as a result of the implementation of the information system. This individual is called the saint because he or she requires personal intervention into the organizational culture to make change happen. Because most public sector organizations are risk averse, this person must show that change is important and desirable for the organization. These saints have the ability to manage staff, to delegate tasks, and to garner resources. The *demons* can be members of the staff, project employees, and even outside contractors who undermine the development of the information system. There are two types of demons, destructive and apathetic. Destructive demons do damage in the open and get caught quickly for doing harm. But apathetic demons withhold their support of the development of the information system, and this can drastically reduce the efficiency of the project. Finally, *wizards* know how the information systems work and the process for building the information systems. Wizards can be found in the different areas of the organization such as management and information systems development, and therefore they don't have just the technical skills but are able to understand how the IT project fits into the organization. For successful information systems development in the public sector, the saints, demons, and wizards should be examined.

E-Government Projects

Seven dimensions of e-government projects can be used to understand the design-reality gap, or the difference between project design and on-the-ground reality (Heeks, 2002b, 2003): (1) information, (2) technology, (3) processes, (4) objectives and values, (5) staffing and skills, (6) management systems and structures, and (7) other resources such as time and money shows the reality and design gap. The information dimension is whether the system design was of value and is used. The issue in the design and reality of projects is that there are both hard ideas and soft factors such as people, politics, and emotions that come into play. In addition, there are public and private gaps, in which an information system is designed for the private sector and is applied to the public sector. Finally, there is a country context gap, where solutions applied in one country may or may not be applicable to another.

E-Government Project Failures

Reasons for e-government project failures include lack of internal ownership, absence of vision or strategy, poor project management, inadequate technological infrastructure, and obstacles to data interchange (Sarantis et al., 2010). In addition, there is lack of business case, over-reliance on technology as the main driver of e-government, and lack of sufficient administrative reform to accompany e-government. Without project management, projects are rarely completed on time and within acceptable costs, with this especially being the case with larger projects.

There are some reasons for project failure noted in the literature (Sarantis et al., 2010). First, the goal definition of public organizations is usually vaguer than those of the private sector, because of the political processes that impact organizational purpose. To move projects along there must be support built in from a diverse group of interests. Public sector managers face multiple goals imposed from numerous stakeholders, whereas in the private sector there is a single goal of profit. Second, the analysis of the e-government projects indicates that their structures are more complex with interactions from the technical, managerial, political, social, cultural, and legal dimensions. The private sector projects are usually described in terms of technical dimensions. Third, planning for IT projects in the public sector is much more instable largely because of the electoral process. Public sector IT projects are usually on a large scale, focusing on the whole or a regional population. As a result the planning horizon tends to be much larger given the scope of the project. Fourth, the management of government transformation projects in e-government cuts across agencies, and there are few best practices that are exclusively used for the public sector. Fifth, the legal and regulatory issues in the public sector come from legal and constitutional arrangements. Public agencies act under the authority delegated to them under the authorized statutes. Finally, politics tends to dominate the implementation of public sector e-government projects. In this situation politics drives the interests of key players by their own personal self-interest.

Challenges of E-Government Projects

E-government projects face multiple and complex challenges that are not found in IT projects in general (Gichoya, 2005). Gil-Garcia and Pardo (2005) identified five challenges important to understand for the development of e-government projects. First, information and data challenges are that e-government must capture, manipulate, use, disseminate, and share information. There could be data quality problems because of all the different stakeholders within and outside of the organization that are providing data. There is the importance of working on common data structures and definitions to make the data compatible and useable for the government. Second, there are IT challenges in which technology incompatibility is a difficult challenge for IT-intensive projects. Systems that are old or very different can increase the complexity of the IT project. The lack of relevant skills for new technology is also an issue. In addition, legacy systems are a new challenge for governments in converting mainframe systems into a client/server technology needed for e-government. Third, organizational and managerial challenges are the size, and the scope of the project can not coincide with the organizational goals of the government. There can be conflicting goals in the public sector that is an additional management challenge. Fourth, there are legal and regulatory challenges in which public managers must take into account a large number of restrictive laws and regulations. There are, for example, 1-year budget cycles and elections that can be a challenge for the implementation of e-government projects. There are also challenges in the United States with the federal system and the relationships with the different levels of government that are complex. Fifth, the institutional and environmental challenges such as privacy and security, agency autonomy, red tape, and bureaucratic constraints of organizations are all major challenges for e-government projects.

Framework in IT and Public Administration

Norris and Moon (2005) examined a framework of IT and public administration and applied this to the development of e-government at the local level. The framework derived from the IT and public administration literature examines two dimensions: (1) the inputs, internal and external organizational dimensions, and (2) impacts on internal organizational structure, outcome and outputs. The input dimension focuses on factors that explain the diffusion of innovations, and a common one examined in the literature is organizational size and other demographic variables on adoption of IT. There also is the impact of the organizational environment shown in the input studies such as demand for a service by the public. The impacts studies tend to focus on the management and organizational changes as a result of IT, such as the centralization and decentralization, organizational culture, leadership, and changing business processes. Overall, through survey evidence on e-government in local governments, Norris and Moon (2005) found more of an incremental change as a result of e-government rather than a radical transformation on these two important dimensions of inputs and impacts. These authors provide a sociotechnical framework for understanding the impact of IT on public sector organizations.

Perry and Danziger (1980), when examining the adoption of technological innovations, believed it was related to (1) the organizational domain or the organization's access to inputs and output resources; (2) integration, which refers to the ability of factors that facilitate the discovery and implementation of the innovation; (3) the level of risk, in which decision makers will calculate the expected benefits and costs of actions as a result of technology; and (4) the need of the organization requirements for the public sector to serve citizens or clients. This framework has some similarities to Norris and Moon's, but its difference is the impact of risk on technological innovations.

Examining survey evidence of local governments reveals an indication that prior adoption of computer technology is related to current computer use (Brudney and Selden, 1995). Therefore, cities with computers in the past were more likely to adopt more technology in the future. In addition, larger cities tend to be more likely to use computers because they have greater volumes of activities and can realize the benefits in terms of efficiency in operations. In addition, cities that have a city manager were more likely to adopt computer technology than ones that had the mayor–council form of government. The framework of IT and public administration provided by Brudney and Selden is one of the first to recognize the importance of having a council–manager form of government on IT adoption.

In reviewing articles on IT in public administration journals, Danziger and Andersen (2002) found both positive and negative impacts. The clearest positive impact of IT on public administration was in the areas of efficiency and productivity of government performance in its internal operations. There are also positive impacts on information access benefits. The most common negative impacts of IT in the public administration literature are citizens' and their private lives, citizens' interactions with government, and public employees' work environments.

These frameworks on the impact of IT on public administration tend to emphasize the efficiency and improved effectiveness dimension of IT adoption in public organizations.

Summary

PMIS are different from private sector MIS in structure, motives, and the environment. The most important difference noted was the environment, where public sector organizations have many interests to consider more so than the private sector. Enterprise architecture helps to align information systems holistically with the organization's mission. This approach is multidimensional and considers how the processes of the organization fit together as an integrated whole as a result of IT. Interoperability is the ability of information systems to effectively communicate with one another. In the enterprise architecture literature, interoperability is one of the most important issues to contend with. Strategic factors are important to consider in enterprise architecture, meaning the mission of the organization must be considered when constructing an enterprise architecture framework. The public administration literature has a long history of examining the impact of IT on the organization. Most of the research in this area focuses on IT's impact on improving efficiency and effectiveness of the organization.

Discussion Questions

1. How is MIS different in the public sector compared with the private sector?
2. What roles does enterprise architecture play in modern public organizations?
3. What is interoperability and how does this fit into the EAF?
4. How can enterprise architecture align with the mission of an organization?
5. What are some of the most common issues identified in the frameworks of public administration literature and IT?

Closing Case Study

Google Apps Makes Inroads in Government

Google announced, on July 26, 2010, a new version of its popular web-based e-mail productivity suite tailored to government customers that meets the federal IT security benchmarks (Williams, 2010c). This suite is called Apps for Government, which is the first to receive Federal Information Security Management Act (FISMA) accreditation. The Obama Administration has urged cloud computing to standardize services and save money. FISMA certification requires a company to review nearly 200 security controls and submit a 1,500-page documentation to the federal government.

Google has been making inroads into federal, state, and local governments with its cloud-based suite of software applications called Google Apps (Kenyon, 2010). Google Apps allows organizations to operate services such as e-mail and office productivity tools without relying on legacy hardware and software. This interest in Google Apps has especially increased since it earned the FISMA certification in July 2010. More federal agencies have shown interest in deploying Google's cloud-based applications since the FISMA certification. Google Apps right now is used more in small agencies such as the U.S. Navy's Humanitarian Branch, and University of California's Berkeley Laboratory has adopted Google Apps.

The government version of Google Apps differs from the consumer version in that it is run on a separate, Google-owned private cloud fortified with additional physical and network security. Google also maintains its FISMA certification for the life of its contracts to ensure agencies remain in compliance without additional expense.

At the state and local levels, the City of Los Angeles has migrated more than 15,000 employees to Google Apps. The move is part of a larger effort to replace the city e-mail and applications with the cloud-based collaborative suite. There were 36 of Los Angeles' city departments that had adopted Google Apps. When the project is complete there will be more than 30,000 employees using the suite for e-mail, calendaring, documents, spreadsheets, instant messaging, and video. Google Apps is viewed by the city as a way to improve collaboration and remote access to applications. Los Angeles expects to save millions of dollars by shifting IT resources currently devoted to e-mail. Google Apps will free up nearly 100 servers dedicated to e-mail, lowering the city's electricity bill by nearly $750,000 over 5 years.

Part III

Major Issues

Chapter 8

E-Procurement, E-Commerce, and Online Financial Reporting

Opening Case Study

State of Georgia's E-Procurement System

The State of Georgia's Department of Administrative Services has invested in new procurement technologies and processes to integrate statewide agencies into one comprehensive buying consortium (Anonymous, 2008). The State of Georgia is taking on a new approach to procurement within the public sector. Their approach is to aggregate spending across statewide entities such as agencies, universities, municipalities, and hospitals that typically operate independently. These entities have buying power as a single buying consortium and have the potential to drive dramatic cost savings and process efficiencies. The consolidation of buying power represents a great way to contain costs for the State of Georgia. The approach is to use technology to enable the state to free up employees from time-consuming administrative work. Georgia uses SciQuest's e-procurement solution, which provides the state with online shopping environments for supplies that are integrated with the PeopleSoft procurement system. This e-procurement system drives spending into prenegotiated contracts and eliminates much of the paperwork, reducing the administrative burden and freeing up staff.

Most state agencies have traditionally run their operations independently with different purchasing practices and systems. There has not been an e-procurement technology capable of integrating these systems and practices. It has also been common among state governments to have procurement systems that have tens of thousands of suppliers and have unlimited choices. This becomes problematic because buyers become overwhelmed by the amount of choices, making the system more complex and more difficult to find the best supplier for discounts.

Instead of recruiting thousands of suppliers to join the e-procurement network, Georgia will have a more competitive process for suppliers to join the network; with a smaller number of suppliers, the state can negotiate contracts for discounts on volume. In addition, the state will use SciQuest's open and modular architecture that can integrate with different enterprise resource planning systems of the state agencies.

As another example of e-procurement, DeKalb County, Georgia, switched from a paper-based purchasing system to an e-procurement system in the mid-2000s (Moore, 2007), enabling the county to reduce its back-office expenses while reducing the time between ordering and receiving from weeks to less than a day for some items. For many years the county used antiquated purchasing procedures: employees filled out requisition paperwork, officials issued purchase orders to vendors via fax, filled orders arrived in the county warehouse, and employees typically waited days before they received their items from the warehouse. At that time the county used a 22-year-old mainframe computer as the accounting system. Today, the county uses the Oracle E-Business Suite of financial and procurement applications. The county's procurement system is now linked with electronic catalogs and order entry systems of its major suppliers.

A major objective of e-procurement is to eliminate maverick buying, or those purchases employees make on their own, bypassing the purchasing department. With e-procurement, concentrated buying from a few preferred vendors can lead to substantial discounts and remove maverick buying.

Chapter Objectives

The five primary objectives of this chapter are as follows:

1. To provide an overview of how procurement has changed in government and what role information technology plays in this change

2. To explain the reasons government would adopt e-procurement and the technologies currently being used

3. To outline the benefits and barriers to the adoption of e-procurement

4. To provide an overview of online financial reporting and its importance to government

5. To explain the importance of public sector e-commerce and its role in public administration

Introduction

In this chapter we examine the impact of e-procurement, e-commerce, and online financial reporting on government. All three issues are critical because they deal with the use of financial resources in government operations. In the first part of this chapter we explore how traditional procurement practices have changed as a result of information technology (IT) and discuss the factors that explain e-procurement adoption in government as well as the benefits and barriers to its adoption. The most common technologies used in e-procurement are discussed as well as their frequency of use. E-commerce and its impact on public sector organizations are examined. The final part of this chapter considers the change in online financial reporting as a result of the Internet.

E-Procurement Background

E-procurement can be defined as the use of the Internet and other information and communication technologies to carry out all stages of the procurement process such as search, sourcing, negotiation, ordering, receipt, and post purchase (Vaidya et al., 2006). E-procurement can be an end-to-end system that integrates the procurement process. In the last 40 years IT has tremendously influenced the procurement process. For example, electronic data interchange, introduced in the 1960s, was an automated purchasing transaction between buyers and sellers. Enterprise resource planning (ERP) was the next technology introduced in the 1970s. Both electronic data interchange and ERP systems were very expensive and generally only accessible to large government agencies. In the 1990s the Internet, and more specifically the Web, again changed the procurement process, making it much more accessible to governments of any size. IT has greatly impacted the procurement processes of government, especially with the growth of the Internet since the late 1990s. Many facets of the procurement process, from getting electronic signatures to sourcing information on products, can now be done online.

Traditional procurement is a paper-based process characterized by fragmented purchasing, off-contract buying, and lack of control over expenditures. The paper-based procurement process has managers spending most of their time chasing paperwork rather than managing their supplier base or negotiating better prices (Reddick, 2007a). The traditional procurement process is very labor intensive, where much of the time is spent on filing reports and getting signatures, which now can be done online.

Globerman and Vining (1996) determined when to contract out to reduce costs, something essential to know in government procurement. Governments must determine when contracting out is needed to know if a good or service needs to be procured. First, task complexity is the degree of difficulty in specifying and monitoring the contract.

A high degree of task complexity makes it more difficult to justify contracting out to reduce costs, giving the information asymmetry. Second, contestability is a market that has many firms bidding for contracts. This reduces costs and is a justification for contracting out because costs are known from the competition. Third, when there is asset specificity, it becomes more difficult to contract out because there is a unique nature of the product or service being offered. IT has traditionally been a market with limited contestability because of the nature of the specific technology to meet the needs of the public sector organization. These three factors should be taken into account when considering procurement and the role of e-procurement in decisions.

MacManus (2002) outlined four purchasing principles that may be under scrutiny and e-procurement may change the debate. First, the lowest bid wins. The reason for the low bid in government purchasing is the view that efficiency is the primary goal of contracting goods and services. Competitive bidding reduces the price and lowest price wins the contract. However, the reinventing government movement in the 1990s showed that effectiveness was also an important criterion to consider when procuring. Second, there is the validity of the separation of vendor and user and its appropriateness for modern day procurement. Governments have tried to keep purchasing agencies as far apart as possible from vendors to avoid the appearance of favoritism. New IT can be used to inform vendors and government about the needs of each other. E-procurement involves tracking the movement of actual supplies to having interaction between vendor and government, which may challenge the traditional way of doing this. Too often government contracts have difficulty when there is lack of regard for the end user. Third, there is a preference for a fixed price and fixed term contract. There are benefits of this in terms of economies of scale, but the disadvantages are that they do not take into account the differences in organizations, which is often the case when purchasing IT. Fourth, open access in all situations is a challenge for procurement. There is the traditional notion that with public financing the contract is open and accessible to the public and press. Government cannot expect to maximize vendor participation in e-procurement programs without security policies in place. MacManus (2002) believed that protecting personal privacy should be given more weight than just openness to government and that there is still ongoing debate on what the impact of these initiatives will have on the procurement movement and e-procurement specifically.

E-Procurement Growth Model

The e-procurement function is located in the government-to-business relationship of e-commerce. According to Hiller and Belanger's (2001) model, this type of relationship has different stages of integration. Although businesses can receive many online services from government, a major portion of online transactions between the government and businesses involves procurement. E-procurement can use different levels of technology and different levels of sophistication in this relationship. Hiller and

Belanger (2001) described a five-stage model of e-government growth, which are particularly relevant for the public sector.

The first stage is information dissemination. This is the most basic form of e-procurement, where the procurement office simply posts information on websites for suppliers. The biggest challenge for the procurement office is to ensure the information is available, accurate, and timely. For example, posting requests for proposals online is part of the information dissemination stage. The second stage is two-way communication. In this stage e-procurement websites allow suppliers to communicate with the government and make simple requests and changes. At a simple level, procurement officers allow online requests on their website where suppliers can fill in information requests. The information is not returned immediately online but sent by regular mail in paper form or returned by email (e.g., a request for clarifications on specifications). The third stage is the transactional stage. The procurement office at this stage has a website available for actual transactions with suppliers. Suppliers interact with the procurement office and conduct transactions completely online, with web-based self-services replacing public servants in these cases (e.g., online vouchers and payment systems, digital signatures, and so forth). Hiller and Belanger (2001) described a five-stage model of e-government growth, four of the stages are particularly relevant for the public sector e-procurement. This can be accomplished with a signal portal that suppliers can use to access the department or agencies. A marketplace for vendors is prevalent in this stage of integration. For example, E-Mail in Massachusetts and GSA Advantage! used by the federal government are found in this stage. The Hiller and Belanger (2001) business-to-government relationship model can be translated into an e-procurement growth model.

The Layne and Lee (2001) model of e-government growth can be applied to e-procurement development. There are four stages of growth: (1) cataloging, (2) transactions, (3) vertical integration, and (4) horizontal integration (**Figure 8-1**). The four stages can be explained in terms of complexity involved and different levels of integration and are applied to the e-procurement growth. There is some noticeable overlap of the Layne and Lee (2001) model with the Hiller and Belanger (2001) model.

In stage one, cataloging, the efforts of state e-procurement offices are focused on establishing an online presence for the government in the procurement function (Figure 8-1). In this stage there is an online presentation of procurement information by the central procurement office. Initially, there is the presence of a website for the e-procurement function. Toward the end of this stage, governments develop more functionality with the central procurement office posting solicitations on their web page and posting contract award information online. Governments create an e-procurement website mostly due to the pressure from suppliers and other stakeholders to get on the Internet. At this stage procurement offices do not have much Internet experience, and they prefer to minimize their exposure by doing a small project. Parts of the office's nontransactional information are put on the website. One reason procurement officers establish a website is that they have become more accustomed to getting information on the Web instead of flipping through

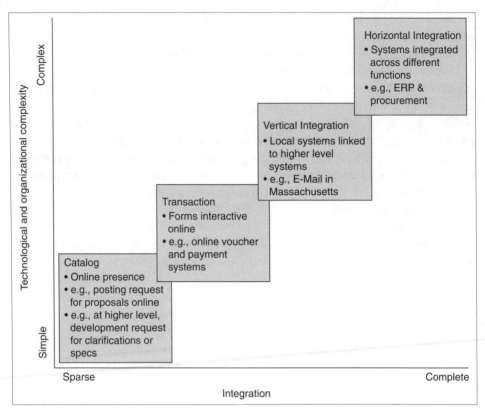

Figure 8-1 *An e-procurement growth model* (From Reddick, 2004b)

paper-based catalogs. They would no doubt be disappointed if they were unable to find information about suppliers on the Internet. The web presence is also beneficial because much government staff time is consumed in answering basic questions from suppliers about government procurement needs and procedures; the web presence would increase businesses' convenience and reduce the workload of procurement staff. In terms of functionality, the least amount of web presence occurs when the e-procurement web page has a description of the department, contact information of the procurement officer or staff, and some links to other pages. It establishes the procurement office's presence as opposed to providing service access points to the supplier. The next step is to organize by service, creating a one-stop portal with a comprehensive list of forms to be downloaded by the supplier. No transactions take place electronically, but forms can be filled out offline and sent in by fax or mail.

The second stage of the e-procurement model focuses on connecting the procurement sources to online interfaces and allowing them to transact with government electronically (Figure 8-1). This is called the transaction-based e-procurement and consists of putting live database links so that suppliers, for example, can bid for contracts over the Internet. As procurement websites evolve, officials come to realize the value of Internet as a service channel for suppliers. Electronic transactions offer improved efficiency for both the supplier and procurement office other than simply cataloging information. It also provides a more democratic process by holding interactive conversations with suppliers that are geographically disbursed. This stage empowers suppliers to deal with their governments online anytime, saving hours of paperwork, and the inconvenience of traveling to a government office. Whereas the cataloging stage helps businesses in the fact-finding process, the transactions stage of e-procurement presents government on the other side of the Internet as an active respondent. It is now a two-way communication; business transactions with the procurement office are conducted fully online by filling out forms, and the government responds by providing confirmations, receipts, and so forth. More importantly, the procurement function moves from a passive to an active role; suppliers can complete forms interactively online rather than downloading forms and mailing them to the procurement office.

The last two stages are integration of e-procurement further into the organization and can happen both vertically and horizontally (Figure 8-1). Vertical integration refers to local, state, and federal governments connecting different functions or services of government. For example, Massachusetts has actively pursued a regional procurement consortium, called E-Mail (Fountain and Osorio-Urzua, 2001; Moon 2003). A supplier of one level of government can get connected to other levels of government through a common portal.

Horizontal integration is defined as integration across different functions and services. An ERP system is an example of horizontal integration. ERP brings together the functions of an organization such as accounting, budgeting, payroll, and procurement. Therefore, a department could order supplies without the approval of the purchasing department and could simultaneously check for the availability of funds from accounting.

In defining the stages of e-procurement development, vertical integration across different levels within similar functional areas should precede horizontal integration across different functions within government because the discrepancy between different services of government is greater than the discrepancy between levels of government (Fountain, 2001). According to the Layne and Lee (2001) model, it is more difficult to integrate across different departments than with other levels of government because of the silos of bureaucracy.

The overriding theoretical reason for wanting to institute e-procurement can be found in the transaction costs literature (Williamson, 1985). Croom (2001) stated that the use of open information systems can provide greater levels of information to buyers, thereby opening up greater competitiveness between providers. In simple terms, electronic markets provide conditions approaching the economic model of perfect competition. This is primarily the result of information asymmetry between buyers and sellers (Essig & Arnold, 2001). Dealing with the problem of restricted information means contracts are unavoidably incomplete. Because contracts can never cover all possible future developments, e-procurement can be a useful instrument to gain this additional information. Transaction costs increase because information is not a free good in imperfect markets. E-procurement helps to lower these transaction costs by making a wide range of information available to buyers and saves precious resources for government.

The theoretical literature on e-procurement illustrates that (1) e-procurement can be modeled as a multistage construct, combining the government-to-business relationship with an e-government growth model, and (2) informational asymmetry between buyers and suppliers in transaction cost theory helps to explain why government would want to engage in e-procurement.

Adoption of E-Procurement

In an analysis of critical success factors that are predicted to indicate the success of e-procurement initiatives, there seems to be no single factor that stands out as being predominant in the literature (Vaidya et al., 2006). These critical success factors of e-procurement adoption can be divided into human factors and technology factors. Human issues depend on human behavior and expertise, whereas technological issues depend on technologies used. Examples of human factors are end user uptake and training, supplier adoption, project management, and top management support. Technological factors in e-procurement can involve system integration, security, and authentication. In the opening case study, the adoption of e-procurement in the State of Georgia was discussed.

Several other factors influence the adoption of e-procurement as identified by Dooley and Purchase (2006). One is supplier participation and intentions. Some suppliers apply pressure on their customers to use e-procurement to reduce costs and improve communications. Suppliers may provide encouragement, possibly through financial means, to use e-procurement systems. Second, suppliers can also exert pressure on their customers to use these systems. Powerful suppliers may stipulate that their buyers must use the e-procurement system or they will not supply them. Third, there is internal organizational support that drives organizational efficiency and lowers the cost of conducting business. Internal organizational support is vital if e-procurement is going to be implemented successfully. Fourth, in network connectivity/integration, suppliers' systems are well integrated and compatible with buyers' systems. If this is the case, a transaction is automatic and gets full benefits from e-procurement. Fifth, e-procurement is said to reduce the time spent on administrative tasks for purchasing, allowing this person to concentrate more on strategic issues. Empirical results indicate the major suppliers' willingness to transact online is a driving force that influences buyers' intentions to use e-procurement, with internal managerial support and perceived benefits having an impact on a government's willingness to adopt e-procurement.

In an examination of the U.K. public sector, some themes have surfaced from the existing literature on the impact of e-procurement (Croom and Brandon-Jones, 2007). One theme is the change in total acquisition cost as a result of e-procurement. Costs reductions noted in the literature range from a fall in cost per order on average from $140 to $30. Because e-procurement reduces the costs of search, increases access to suppliers, enables real-time control of spending, and increases information to management, this translates into reduced costs. A second theme noted in the literature is changes to organizational characteristics such as the training, education, and support of users to ensure the systems are used correctly and problems are resolved in a timely manner. End user compliance is vital for the success of e-procurement systems and will improve purchasing performance. The third theme identified was impact on supply governance of e-procurement. E-procurement typically involves a significant dependence on buyers and suppliers. E-procurement has the potential to enhance and improve the relationship between both entities in the procurement process. E-procurement should enhance the customer–supplier relationship by improving communication, increasing compliance, and increasing knowledge sharing among suppliers.

There are numerous barriers and critical success factors to e-procurement (Padhi and Mohapatra, 2010). These barriers and success factors range from technical issues, such as inadequate technology, to budget constraints and lack of leadership at the top of the organization.

To implement e-procurement successfully in government, various technical, legal, and managerial challenges must be met (Moon, 2005). Some of the suggested benefits of e-procurement to government are (1) lower transaction costs, (2) faster ordering, (3) wider vendor choice, (4) standardized and more efficient payment process, (5) greater control over procurement spending and less maverick buying, (6) more accessible Internet alternatives for buyers, (7) less paperwork and fewer administrative procedures (which can be automated), and (8) reengineering procurement workflows. The proponents of e-procurement in government believe it will overcome many problems associated with paper-based procurement, leading to better and more efficient and effective procurement management. In a survey of state governments and e-procurement, it appears they are still in the experimental stages, as using the system has not yet delivered the significant cost and time savings. In addition, larger and more managerially savvy state governments are more likely to adopt e-procurement tools. Therefore, establishing an e-procurement system requires strong managerial leadership and willingness to be innovative.

Governance Structures and Technologies Used for E-Procurement

Several e-procurement governance structures should be elaborated on to give the reader the scope of e-procurement. The most common e-procurement exchange types, as noted by Croom and Brandon-Jones (2005), are as follows:

- *Public website:* In the public website buyers have the opportunity to use the Web to search for opportunities to purchase with potential suppliers. Buyers can use standard search engines such as Yahoo.com and Google.com or specialist trading search engines. Orders may be placed online, or other methods may be used to work with many suppliers.

- *Exchange:* eBay is the most common e-commerce auction site for consumers, whereas sites like Synerdeal are most common for business-to-business e-commerce. These websites allow buyers and suppliers to bid for contracts. Online reverse auctions are a way of reducing the purchasing price for goods.
- *Marketplace:* A marketplace is a multisupplier/multiproduct catalog often maintained and hosted by a third party who provides access to both supplier and buyer online, often through a secure connection.
- *Company hub:* A company hub is similar to a marketplace but the buyer hosts and maintains the multisupplier and multiproduct catalog.
- *Extranet:* This is a secure and security-protected Internet link between buyers and sellers. The EDI is an example of such a connection.

Table 8-1 provides information on the types of e-procurement systems, their functions, impact on direct and indirect costs, and impact on the organization

Table 8-1 *Common E-Procurement Systems*

Types of System	Main Functions	Impacts on Direct and Indirect Costs of Purchasing	Organizational Impact
E-MRO (maintenance, repair, and operations)	Acquisition of services of maintenance, repairs, and operations	Low/elevated	Extended to the entire organization
Web-based ERP	Integration of the process of purchase in ERP of the agency	Low/limited to the operative phase	Extended to the entire organization
E-sourcing	Singling out providers through Internet technologies	Low/limited tactical impact	Limited to purchasing department
E-tendering	Sending requests for information and prices to providers and the collection of offers via the Internet	Low/limited tactical impact	Limited to the purchasing department
E-reverse auctioning	Online actions	Relevant/low	Limited to the purchasing department

Adapted from Bruno et al. (2005).

(Bruno et al., 2005). This table shows that these common e-procurement systems have very limited impacts on direct and indirect costs. The greatest impact of these systems is on the public organization being able to function more efficiently and effectively. The direct costs are purchases that go into the production of the good or service. Indirect costs are those costs of supplier items that support production.

In a survey of e-procurement in the Singapore government, some common activities are reported by organizations that responded (Teo et al., 2009). The three most common e-procurement technologies used were customized e-procurement software (70.4%), electronic catalogs (29.6), and electronic auctions (27.2). The three most common goods and services procured were maintenance, repair, operational (MRO) (57.6%); production goods (43.5%); and raw materials (42.4%). The three most common e-procurement activities conducted were e-mail correspondence between buyer and seller (90.8%), sending requests for proposals and information (69.0%), and identifying new suppliers and research into suppliers' markets (67.8%).

In an empirical study of e-procurement in state governments in the United States, Reddick (2004b) found that most states are merely cataloging information online. Ninety percent of states posted solicitations for bids on the Web, and three-fourths of states posted contract award information on the Web. However, there was not much in the development of more transactions-based e-procurement such as accepting contracts online or being able to procure online. For instance, only eight states accepted digital signatures as legally binding signatures on procurement documents. Only 11 states had central procurement offices conducting bids via the Internet. The most significant evidence found was that higher management capacity of state governments is a greater indication of the development of e-procurement. Therefore, states that are well managed are more likely to adopt e-procurement systems than states with less management ability.

Table 8-2 provides information from a 2002 survey of state government procurement officers on the use of e-procurement (Reddick, 2004b). Statistics show that most state governments have a website for the central procurement office (86%). State governments are using their website to post solicitations for contracts (82%). A substantial number of state governments' central procurement offices posted contract award information on the Web (64%). Almost half of the states enacted digital signatures, but their use and complexity varied among states. More advanced functions such as conducting bids online were only done by 22% of states. Finally, reverse auctions were rarely used by only 18% of states.

In an analysis of e-procurement in U.S. state governments, most movement appears to occur in the information providing phase of e-procurement. Because all states have a website, over 90% of the states post solicitations on the Web, and three-fourths of the states post contract award information on the Web. However, when it comes to the development of transaction-based e-procurement, there seems to be much room for improvement. For instance, only 8 states have accepted digital signatures and only 11 states have the central procurement office conducting bids over the Internet. This finding is not surprising and is consistent with the incremental pace of change of IT and public administration.

Table 8-2 *E-Procurement in State Governments*

E-Procurement Functions	Percent of States
Does the central procurement office have an Internet website?	86
Is the central procurement office posting solicitations on the Web?	82
Is the central procurement office posting contract award information on the Web?	64
Has the state enacted digital signature laws?	48
Does the state have rules promulgated regarding digital signatures?	34
Does the state use digital signatures to route and approve documents internally?	14
Is the state accepting digital signatures as legally binding signatures from the vendor community on procurement documents?	16
Has the state central procurement office developed procedures or do they have statutes governing Internet bidding?	32
Has the state central procurement office conducted bids via the Internet?	22
Has the state central procurement office conducted reverse auctions?	18

Adapted from Reddick (2004b).

Shared Services

Shared services involve consolidating administrative support services across organizational units. They are used to create greater effectiveness in service delivery (Miranda and Kavanagh, 2005). ERP systems facilitate shared services through process standardization and scalability. Governments can benefit from shared services; as an example, the U.S. Postal Service reduced finance costs by about 17%. Shared services can also do more than just reduce costs, because they have the potential for transforming performance of the government. Shared services can create a platform for a more integrated government, enabling the delivery of a consolidated 311 system in New York City as an example. This single call center has been able to provide a more consistent level of customer service, allowing the city to engage citizen satisfaction and interests. Another example of shared services is CitiStat used in the City of Baltimore's Mayor's office. This technology-enabled management system provides real-time indicators of department performance. The performance results are used to reward departments based on their results shown in the performance indicators. The City of Baltimore believes this system has resulted in cost savings and revenue enhancements of $40 million over a 3-year period.

Reported benefits in the private sector are that shared services are driving significant cost, productivity, and service gains (Marshall, 2009). For example, (1) most shared services initiatives save 15% to 30% of costs, (2) productivity improvements are more than 10% for 89% of users, (3) quality improved more than 10% for 82% of customers, and (4) customer service improved by more than 10% for 79% of users.

An example of some of the issues with IT outsourcing and shared services is the experience of the State of Virginia's outsourcing efforts (Vander Veen, 2010). Virginia struck an outsourcing deal with Northrop Grumman; this was a 10-year, $2.3 billion contract in which Northrop Grumman would provide the state's IT services. This was the largest project of its kind in the state governments and has been plagued by delays, cost overruns, and poor services. This partnership created in 2003 by then Governor Mark Warner launched a major initiative to centralize and overhaul how the state invested in and managed its technology and networks. There was poor planning, ineffective governance, lackluster service delivery, and unrealistic service expectations, nearly causing the contract to collapse. The move by Virginia toward a shared services model was motivated by a model of cost containment and providing services that were not provided before. However, there was considerable complexity to the system, and the rate and scope of change was much broader than anyone had anticipated. One major issue was the failure to bring agencies into the discussions; essentially, state agencies had little or no input into the outsourcing arrangements that would impact their operations.

Outsourcing IT

Management is important for outsourcing of e-government projects regardless of size and complexity of projects (Chen and Perry, 2003). When IT projects are properly managed, better performance is achieved for the organization. There are some best practices of IT and outsourcing in the public sector. First, public managers need to take a long-term perspective, a strategic approach to IT outsourcing. Public agencies need to understand their service needs and the strengths and weaknesses of vendors, in which both parties understand the long-term benefits of the project. Second, public managers need to shift their focus from traditional procurement systems to use a more relationship management approach. This means that instead of looking just for the lowest bidder, public agencies should ensure quality also is included in the procurement of IT. Third, performance measure and service-level contracts are important for the management of IT outsourcing projects. Performance measures need to be specified early in the request for proposals. Service-level agreements must allow public managers to track the performance of the contact. In an empirical examination of IT outsourcing, public management and external factors impacted the final outcome. The external factors are the political-regulatory environment and public management factors, which are the capacity of management to deal with outsourcing.

IT outsourcing projects in the public sector have faced many challenges (Moon et al., 2010). There are two dimensions to this model, which are the extent of substitution dimension and the strategic impact dimension. The model categorizes these dimensions into four types: support, reliance, alignment, and alliance. The support cell has IT vendors restricted to servicing the noncore IT activities, and the size of the contract is small. The role of the vendor is limited in the support cell, and most of the work is done in house. There are low coordination and monitoring costs in the support relationship. Outsourcing in the reliance cell requires more commitment from vendors and the public sector agency. The length of the contract is longer than in the support cell. IT functions that are outsourced in these cells are noncore, and cost reduction is the major motivation for reliance. The alignment cell for outsourcing of IT enables organizations to obtain vendors' technical expertise on a project. The vendor's impact lasts longer in the alignment cell, and the vendor is more involved with the strategic functions of the IT project. The alliance cell is based on a mutual relationship; the vendor substitutes completely for in-house IT operations but is also completely responsible for strategic IT activities of the client. The term of the contract is normally longer than the other relationships. In this relationship the vendor and the public sector agency work together strategically to reach a common goal. Empirical results show the alliance type ensures the best practice of IT outsourcing in the public sector due to its higher success rate than the other relationship types. This finding is consistent with the importance of public sector IT projects to be strategic in nature because they are more likely to have larger budgets and longer time horizon. These projects, as a result, receive more attention from vendors and IT managers. Essentially, public sector IT managers should consider more of a long-term relationship with service providers rather than a simple contract for IT outsourcing.

Contracting is very popular with public sector agencies for such services as data processing, website hosting, training, and project management, in the realm of IT management (Ni and Bretschneider, 2007). Contracting helps government overcome financial difficulties in accessing expertise from professional management skills in private sector firms to develop IT applications. Some proponents of IT contracting make the claim that contracting will address problems caused by the shortage of IT skills in public organizations. Lack of technical expertise would prevent the development of e-government applications in government. Contracting of IT could also help public organizations overcome financial constraints, as when contracts are implemented with private sector firms, governments will not have these large start-up costs. Finally, contracting can transfer some of the risk of system development to vendors when technology is new and untested.

E-government services in particular have different types of contracting than traditional IT projects (Ni and Bretschneider, 2007). First, e-government services facilitate not just the internal operations of government but have an impact on citizens and other stakeholders. Second, e-government technology is rapidly changing, creating an environment that is increasingly difficult and uncertain to keep up. Third, some e-government services involve citizen rights and security issues. There are three reasons a government would choose to contract IT. The economic rationale is that it can deliver services at a lower cost by contracting with the private sector than can direct production by government. This comes from the competitive market model, in which profit motives drive innovation. The political rationale for contracting is that government agencies are heavily influenced by politics. Public decision makers need to balance efficiency with political considerations. An ideological reason for contracting is that government is too large and this prevents a threat to freedom. Therefore, market-based solutions are preferred. The third rationale for contract is that government services differ, and because of the nature of the service there may be a greater need for contracting. Empirical research of e-government contracting at the state level indicated that political logic is present in state-level contracting decisions. Therefore, politics significantly shapes contracting decisions for e-government. Fiscal stress was not as likely to impact contracting decisions for state government projects, but when this research was completed, states were not experiencing severe budget crises as they were in late 2000.

Transactions cost theory is a framework for studying how governments choose to deliver services because it models internal versus external production as a function of both financial and management costs (Brown and Potoski, 2006; Brown et al., 2006). When a government decides to contract, it has to balance production costs against the transaction costs or management costs associated with producing a service themselves versus contracting it out. In cases when the transaction costs are low, a service has an easily measurable outcome, are not prone to monopoly provision, and goals are in congruence with the government and contracting vendor, competitive contracting can minimize bureaucratic inefficiencies stemming from direct service delivery. One of the key assumptions of transaction costs theory is the principal–agent, where the principal is government and the vendors are agents who are opportunistic and pursue their own interest. Governments can monitor agents in this model because they are uncertain of their behavior and their behavior may not coincide with the principal.

With governments facing very difficult times with budget deficits, strategic outsourcing could play a role in how government purchases (Harris, 2004). Most of the innovation in procurement has been done in the private sector, with government lagging behind. Strategic outsourcing uses innovative ways to purchase for governments rather than relying on the lowest bidder for a contract. One example, Pennsylvania spends approximately $22.5 million on office supplies for state workers, but with a reverse auction the state expected to save $9.5 million a year. Strategic outsourcing is not just one approach to procurement but describes best practices that enable organizations to buy more effectively and efficiently.

Online Financial Reporting

The Internet has become a low-cost mechanism used to report online financial information to the public and businesses and an important area of IT and public administration. The emerging research on this topic examines factors that explain whether a government places financial information online. In an examination of the Internet for financial reporting for local government authorities in New Zealand, an empirical analysis showed that leverage, municipal wealth, press visibility, and type of council were associated with Internet financial reporting practices (Laswad et al., 2005). Leverage is the use of debt to finance public activities, which is an incentive to reduce costs through Internet financial reporting. Municipal wealth and the disclosure of financial information indicate that poorer local governments decrease the likelihood of disclosure. An active press provides an incentive for municipal governments to disclose financial information on the Internet. The type of council should have an impact on financial disclosure with councils in more urban areas having more interest groups and pressure to disclose financial information.

In an examination of best practices in budget presentation and financial reporting through the Web, Justice and colleagues (2006) found some interesting results. Governments that had award-winning budget documents through preparation of the traditional budget and financial reports did not necessarily have exemplary online budget reporting. Essentially, many governments have not exploited the potential of the Internet for financial reporting. Therefore, the award-winning budgets seemed more for the reporting to peers and bondholders rather than encouraging citizen participation. These findings are consistent with governments outside of the United States, where the disclosure of financial information has not been directed at citizens to any great extent (Bolivar et al., 2007). However, fiscal transparency and direct citizen involvement in the budget process is understood as necessary for ensuring accountability of the public sector resource allocation. E-government provides a means of ensuring a greater degree of transparency in financial reporting, but it is being underutilized by governments in the Internet age (Justice et al., 2006).

Empirical research shows that use of the Web for financial disclosure is rooted in a country's administrative culture (Bolivar et al., 2006). Countries that have different administrative cultures have different views on the disclosure of financial information. Countries in North America scored the highest in terms of disclosing financial information. Anglo-Saxon countries are characterized by separation of power; therefore, accountability is important for the disclosure of performance information. Therefore, more open countries lead the way in facilitating access to financial information compared with continental European and South American countries, which have more restricted views on financial disclosure. The reporting of financial information online is a growing agenda for governments as a way of providing greater transparency and outreach to citizens.

Public Sector E-Commerce

Public sector e-commerce can be defined as any process or transaction conducted by a government organization over a computer-mediated network that transfers ownership or the rights to use goods, services, or information (Reddick, 2007b). A primary reason for implementing e-commerce in public sector organizations is the reduction of transaction costs. Transaction costs are the costs that government incurs when it buys in the marketplace what it cannot make for itself. Governments incur transaction costs when they conduct business. Some common costs include search and information costs, bargaining costs, and policing and enforcement costs. The economic theory of principal and agent can be used to examine transaction costs. As discussed in this theory, the principal (department manager) employs agents (employees) to perform work on his or her behalf. IT can reduce transaction costs because the agent should more easily be able to monitor the performance and oversee a greater number of employees. As a result, e-commerce is one way to reduce transaction costs because there is less monitoring of employees as transactions are done electronically. The closing case study at the end of the chapter provides an example of public sector e-commerce using Smartphone technology.

Some common issues are associated with the implementation of public sector e-commerce (**Table 8-3**) (Reddick, 2007b). The main issues are enterprise administration, technologies, management, and policy. In the enterprise administration category, leadership and governance are important issues for e-commerce. Leadership is critical for the advancement of e-commerce projects and to successfully implement them. The second issue is privacy; there should be informed consent at the point of collection of personal information of users. The third issue in this category is that of security, where government should support open standards and use commercially accepted technologies. The fourth issue is the use of electronic payments, where governments need to explore different payment mechanisms for users.

Another important issue for the use of e-commerce in government is the technologies that are used. Portals can create a single entry to government, but the issue becomes how to fund the portal. One method is for the consumer to pay a fee for e-commerce transactions, whereas another method is to finance the project through existing budget resources. Other issues in this category of technologies are the applications used, infrastructure, and standards incorporated. All these technologies should be aligned with the e-commerce system.

Table 8-3 *Public Sector E-Commerce Issues*

Enterprise Administration	Technologies	Management	Policy
Leadership and governance	Portals	Funding	Digital divide
Privacy	Applications	Marketing	Economic development
Security	Infrastructure	Personnel and training	Taxation
Electronic payments	Standards	Economics of scale	

Adapted from Reddick (2007b).

Management is the third, and arguably the most important, category that should be considered when adopting e-commerce. Research shows that more effective management leads to greater e-commerce adoption. In the management category, funding is one of the most difficult issues that public sector managers face. Marketing is another management challenge that is often overlooked in the public sector. In addition, training staff to work with an e-commerce system can be difficult given the change in technology and processes involved. Finally, there are economies of scale in the adoption of e-commerce, where there is possible cost savings because of placing services online.

In the policy area of e-commerce in the public sector there are issues of the digital divide—those that have access and those that do not have access to the Internet can impact e-commerce transactions. The issue of economic development and the use of e-commerce may impact community development. Finally, there is the issue of taxation and e-commerce. For instance, with the sales tax in the United States, if a business does not have a physical presence in a state, they are not responsible for submitting sales tax to the state government, which is a significant drain on state treasuries.

An empirical study of whether state governments are more e-commerce enabled shows that states that have higher IT management capacity were more developed in e-commerce (Reddick, 2004c). State wealth did not explain the development of e-commerce, meaning that just because a state government has more resources does not imply they would devote these resources to the development of e-commerce. In fact, states that have fewer resources might view e-commerce as a way of controlling spending and saving money for their government.

Summary

This chapter examined the issues of e-procurement, e-commerce, and online financial reporting. E-procurement is a movement from the traditional paper-based procurement system to using IT to streamline government purchasing. Some of the barriers to the adoption of e-procurement are fear of change and lack of commitment and support from top officials in the organization. Some of the success factors noted in the literature are support from end users in the e-procurement system and support from policymakers. There are many different types of technologies used in e-procurement, ranging from simply posting procurement information on a website to having a sophisticated online marketplace where many sellers and buyers can exchange goods.

Websites are commonly used by state governments for procurement purposes to display information for suppliers. Governments tend to use less complicated technologies for the procurement process, with digital signatures not commonly being used. E-commerce is a way of moving transactions traditionally done offline to online, through digital means (e.g., renewing a driver's licenses or registering an automobile). E-commerce involves the exchange of money in a transaction with government. As a result, there are many issues to consider such as privacy and security of the transaction. Finally, online financial reporting is a method of displaying important financial information online, which increases transparency and accountability of government to its citizens.

Discussion Questions

1. What are the benefits and costs of e-procurement compared with the traditional paper-based system of procurement?
2. What are the common technologies used for e-procurement in government?
3. What factors explain the adoption of e-procurement in government?
4. E-commerce has many issues associated with its adoption. Explain some of the most important issues.
5. Different administrative cultures have differing views on the use of online financial reporting. Explain.

Closing Case Study

Bling Nation

Bling Nation is a California-based service that allows Smartphone users to pay instantly with one swipe at participating stores and other locations (McCaney, 2010a). A few municipalities, such as the City of Palo Alto, are offering Bling Nation as another method for residents to pay their utility bills and parking tickets over their Smartphone. The system works much like a debit card. A Bling sticker is put on the Smartphone, and when consumers want to make a purchase they simply bump their Bling tag on a Blinger box reader at participating merchants or municipal governments. Money is automatically deducted from the person's Bling account, which is set up through a local bank or PayPal. A real-time transaction is confirmed, and it is sent directly to the phone through a text message. In Palo Alto citizens can use at least 75 merchants and pay their utility bills or other financial obligations through this system. Lamar, Colorado, is also using the Bling system as this tap-and-pay system is attractive to government and business because the fees are typically lower than those of credit card companies.

Many believe that the future Smartphones will function as today's credit and debit cards, with some major credit card companies doing pilots of this technology. The Bling system is secured through an encrypted network. No personal data are stored on the BlingTag. Users also make a PIN that prevents transactions from being made on lost or stolen phones. The private sector use of this technology is spreading. Bank of America and Visa conducted a mobile-payment trial in New York (McCaney, 2010a).

A concern is the potential security risk when a phone is lost. With growth of this Smartphone technology in the private sector, governments should soon catch on to this new way of purchasing.

Human Resources Information Systems

Opening Case Study

Armystrongstories.com

The U.S. Army now has a new recruiting tool called www.Armystrongstories.com, a blog that has nothing to do with recruiting (Anonymous, 2010). This blog does not feature recruiters but rather cadets, soldiers, veterans, and their families who talk about their experiences in the service. This blog has been around for a while and had a limited number of bloggers, but like other social media, anyone can register and blog about the topic. The idea behind the blog is to give potential recruits a taste for what army life is actually like, in place of the traditional style of recruiting of telling a potential recruit about the army. A more personalized experience is provided than the one provided at the recruiting office.

More than 160 soldiers have signed up to participate in the Army Strong Stories program, with background ranging from medical and human resources to legal and public affairs. The Army Strong Stories is part of the Accessories Command's over-arching digital strategy that includes several online social marketing initiatives such as www.goarmy.com, www.facebook.com/goarmy, and www.myspace.com/usarmy. These websites are designed to share the soldier's story in an authentic way, using social media and other digital communications.

Early on the Army used other digital methods of recruiting through video games as a way of contacting youth to get them involved in military service. In addition, in 2009 the Army launched a Second Life virtual platform, which is a virtual world where users are able to interact with each other through avatars (Beizer, 2008). The Army Second Life islands are information hubs for interested candidates and their families. It is designed to be a relaxed way for potential recruits to learn about what it is like to be a soldier. Army recruiters are available to answer questions about career opportunities on the Second Life platform. Visitors can attend classes and have their avatar perform tasks such as skydiving and flying an Apache helicopter.

Chapter Objectives

The four primary objectives of this chapter are as follows:

1. An overview of how human resources (HR) has changed because of information technology (IT) in the public sector
2. An overview of the technologies used for HR and IT in the public sector
3. A discussion of the benefits and challenges to the adoption of IT in HR
4. An analysis of the important issue of recruitment and retention of IT workers in public sector organizations

Introduction

In the area of HR in a public sector organization, IT has influenced this function greatly (Coursey and McCreary, 2004). This chapter provides an overview of the impact of IT on HR in the public sector. Advances in IT have created a virtual HR department, which can be more strategically aligned with the organization's mission. Human resources information systems (HRIS) is the technology used in the HR department. In this chapter we provide an overview of the operational, relational, and strategic nature of HRIS in public sector organizations and examine what HR technology is commonly used in the public sector, outlining some of its benefits and drawbacks. Finally, we discuss of one of the most important challenges facing HR and IT, the recruitment and retention of IT workers in the public sector. But first we provide some important background information on IT and HR in the public sector.

Evolution of IT in HR

The use of IT in HR management has generally lagged behind IT usage in other functions of organizations (Ball, 2001). In the 1960s personnel management was automated through payroll, benefits administration, and employee record keeping because of the intensive nature of these functions. Typically, the information was held in a mainframe computer and was accessed through keyword searches. With the advent of the Windows operating system in the 1980s, this increased the use of more affordable software that could be customized to HR. The reporting capabilities of these programs were more sophisticated and flexible in their output than mainframe systems. In the 1990s, with the advent of the Internet, there was the use of websites for posting job ads online, which greatly expanded the reach of HR.

With advances in IT in the latter half of the 20th century, many reporting activities previously done by HR professionals can now be done online by managers and employees themselves. For example, managers can now do performance appraisals, evaluate employee costs, generate HR reports, and process training requests. Employees now have access to their own personnel files and financial documents. Strategic HR management is the development and implementation of policies that are aligned with the mission of the organization. HR management effectiveness is associated with defining the HR function within the overall vision of the organization (Ruel et al., 2007). Modern day HR management in public sector organizations has been impacted by the advances in IT, essentially creating virtual HR departments.

Virtual HR

A virtual HR department is a "… network based structure built on partnerships and mediated by information technologies to help the organization acquire, develop, and deploy intellectual capital" (Snell et al., 2002, p. 84). Virtual HR is a result of the increasing demands placed on HR departments in both the public and private sectors (Lepak and Snell, 1998). There are four pressures to make HR departments function better in an information age. First, HR departments are asked to be more strategic, which requires that HR departments be involved in the development, planning, formulation, and implementation of strategies instead of spending their time on lower level administrative activities. HR managers are required to be more strategic in their approach, instead of spending their time on more routine tasks. Second, HR departments are required to be more flexible, being able to change policies and procedures more rapidly. Third, HR functions must now take a hard look at costs, which can add significantly to organizational overhead. Because HR managers are being asked to reduce costs in their operations, IT may be part of the solution. Finally, HR departments are also still required to provide excellent customer service to employees. The traditional HR department is ill suited to these new challenges, and the virtual department is a possible solution. HR departments are expected to maintain their role as service providers to managers and employees with all these changes. Essentially, HR departments must be more strategic, flexible, efficient, and customer-oriented, and IT can be used to accomplish these goals. This is obviously a difficult task for public sector HR organizations given all the constraints they face such as the lack of budget resources and political pressures.

In a national survey of city managers in local governments and their use of IT for HR management, there is some evidence of the impact of virtual HR (West and

Berman, 2001b). For example, survey evidence shows that payroll and benefits administration and online recruiting are widely used in local government. However, more
advanced systems such as IT applications for training, job analysis and evaluation,
position classification, and personnel testing were not widely used in local governments. Virtual HR departments are faster at responding to information requests
because they do it through electronic means. More traditional HR would involve pa-
per-intensive processes where people and office skills dominate business processes.
An example of virtual HR is online job posting, which is much faster than the traditional paper-based version at posting advertisements. There also is user-friendly
training technology, which can eliminate the need for employees to be attending
regular classroom training sessions. Findings from this national survey indicate that
although there is widespread availability of computer hardware, Internet, and human
resource management software, few cities had widespread use of this technology to
improve HR. The opening case study provides an example of what the Army is doing
to get new recruits using the Internet in the function of virtual HR.

Some suggestions for improving the use of IT in HR are for professionals to cultivate
a more collaborative and strategic environment, working with the chief information
officer of the city to develop these systems (West and Berman, 2001b). HR managers can
educate employees and others of the promise of this technology as a worthy investment in
their HR function. City officials should provide incentives that promote the investment of
IT in HR. HR managers should also design the proper policies and procedures for implementing HR systems for them to run efficiently and effectively for their organization.

HRIS Importance for Public Managers

The HR function has responsibility for attracting, developing, and maintaining the
agency's workforce (Pynes, 2009). As a result the HR department should identify
potential employees, maintain complete records of existing employees, and create
programs to develop employees through training. Information systems play an important role in HR in public sector agencies.

IT in the HR function impacts many areas of public sector organizations, from
routine financial functions such as payroll to planning and reporting requirements
with equal employment opportunities. Some of the more process-oriented functions
for HRIS are compensation and benefits, whereas analysis functionality includes staffing projects and organizational charts.

Strategic Orientation of Information Systems and HR

HR managers can use IT to transform their organization from administrative to strategic (Haines and Lafleur, 2008). The existing literature argues for a movement from

transactional HR to a more strategic orientation. The improved information processing ability of IT in the HR function should improve the effectiveness of organizations by being able to process a vast amount of data at greater speed and accuracy. This will free up HR managers to focus more on strategic roles of the organization.

HRIS can play a strategic role in public sector organizations. In an examination of HRIS adoption in Singapore, one study noted that relative advantage, complexity, compatibility, top management support, size, and HRIS expertise to varying degrees explained adoption (Teo et al., 2007). Relative advantage is expressed in terms of economic profits and reduced costs for the organization. Essentially, does HRIS improve the efficiency of HR departments by automating tasks? Complexity is the degree in which the technology is difficult to understand. More complex information systems can function as an inhibitor to adoption. Compatibility is the degree to which the organization embraces change and encourages employees to learn. Top management support is a key factor that is found in the literature and should encourage HRIS placement in the strategic vision of the organization. Top management would ensure that adequate resources will be allocated to this innovation. The literature shows that larger organizations have the potential to more readily use HRIS because of the larger scale of their operations (Teo et al., 2007). An organization may need to reach some critical size to justify an HRIS. HRIS expertise is the competence that employees have with these systems. Essentially, employees that are well trained in the use of HRIS translate into an increased chance of successful adoption.

As noted in previous chapters, the literature on IT adoption advocates several critical success factors. IT in HR has the ability to reengineer this critical component of an organization. There are six critical success factors identified in the literature that are part of HR reengineering efforts through the use of IT (Yeung and Brockbank, 1995):

1. Senior management involvement/championship
2. Clear vision and model for change in business and HR
3. Involvement across all levels of planning and implementation
4. Early, ongoing, and candid communications
5. Changes in supporting systems
6. Empowering the reengineering teams and holding them accountable to clear and measurable targets.

Six major pitfalls of HR reengineering efforts using IT should be noted as important (Yeung and Brockbank, 1995):

1. Being unrealistic in one's expectation by not having a clear sense of the scope of the efforts required and the complexities involved
2. A lack of understanding of the new design system and an overestimation of the presumed benefits
3. Morale problems caused, in part, by an endemic fear of change

4. An underestimation of the level of psychological and political resistance existing in the various levels of the organization
5. Top management's lack of guidance, sponsorship, and willingness to shepherd the necessary efforts through the various stages
6. An underestimation of the kinds of skills and technical knowledge necessary to ask the right questions and develop the most appropriate specifications into the process

Organizations are reluctant to implement HRIS unless they are convinced it would bring in greater benefits than costs to their organization. Some of the commonly noted benefits and barriers to the implementation of HRIS can be found in **Table 9-1** (Ngai and Wat, 2006).

Much of the existing data on the implementation of HRIS is through surveys of private sector organizations. In a survey of human resource directors (HRDs) in Texas municipal governments, the following success factors were identified by these professionals as important for implementation of IT in HR (**Table 9-2**) (Reddick, 2009a). The most common success factor was improved data accuracy as a result of IT and HR (71.6%). The second highest success factor was service improvement, according to most HRDs in Texas municipal governments (64.8%). The third most common success factor identified was IT in HR enabled HRDs to serve more strategically in their operations (53.4%).

Table 9-3 identifies some of the most common barriers to the implementation of IT in the HR function in municipal government (Reddick, 2009a). The most commonly cited barrier was inadequate budget/funding according to 67% of HRDs. The second most common barrier was that technical infrastructure was not in place (48.9%). The third most commonly cited barrier was staff resistance to change, according to 28.4% of HRDs. Lack of city manager support for IT in HR was not an issue for HRDs in this survey.

Table 9-1 *Benefits and Barriers to the Adoption of HRIS*

Benefits	Barriers
Quick response and access to information	Insufficient financial support
Improved data control	Lack of expertise in IT
Reducing data reentry and data may be used immediately	Inadequate knowledge in implementing the system
Streamlining the HR process	Lack of commitment from top managers
Allowing for fewer errors	Not suitable HRIS or software

Adapted from Ngai and Wat (2006).

Table 9-2 *Success Factors of IT and HR*

Success Factors	Percent
Improved data accuracy	71.6
Service improvement	64.8
Enable HR to serve more strategically	53.4
Quality improvement	51.1
HR staff acceptance	43.2
Employee and manager acceptance	33.0
Employee and managers make better decisions	28.4
Recruit key talent	25.0
Meeting costs savings	23.9

HR Roles and Information Systems

HR roles have been transitioning from focusing on operational and administrative to being more strategic, consultative, and proactive (Gardner et al., 2003). First, using HR strategically means making it a strategic partner in the organization. A strategic

Table 9-3 *Barriers to Adoption of IT and HR*

Barriers	Percent
Inadequate budgeting/funding	67.0
Technical infrastructure not in place	48.9
Staff resistant to change	28.4
Security/privacy fears	22.7
Inadequate change management	19.3
Lack of support from elected officials	19.3
Inability to prove need, show potential payback	15.9
Lack of CAO or city manager support	10.2

partner means helping HR manage resources and aligning it with the strategic plan of the organization. Second, HR managers must be able to deliver an efficient HR system through, for example, staffing and training. The third role is being a champion of employees by increasing employee commitment through management transformation using HR as a change agent.

There are essentially three stages of use of IT and its impact on HR: operational, informational and relational, and transformation. In the operational stage IT is used primarily to reduce the need for personnel to perform routine tasks through automation. IT automation reduces the amount of routine work to be performed, providing more opportunities for individuals to think and use their skills for more important functions of HR. Examples of tasks that need to be automated are personnel reporting and record keeping. Information and relational aspects go beyond automation to focus on effectiveness and benefits for those that use the system in the organization. Information can provide a level of transparency and accountability so individuals know more about what is taking place in their organization. This allows employees to more easily access and evaluate information. For example, they can access their personal statistics and change them if need be. Third, the transformation impact of IT and HR fosters a climate of professionals trying to be innovative and change the organization. This enables HR professionals to create innovative practices to better deliver HR services to their clients. Survey evidence is shown demonstrating the impact on all three stages of IT use in public sector HR.

Table 9-4 shows the operational impact of IT in HR for municipal governments in Texas (Reddick, 2009a). This table shows that improving efficiency was a major operational goal for these governments. Another high level of agreement was for IT automating record keeping and clerical duties. Increasing the productivity of HR employees showed a high level of agreement in the operational area. There was, however, disagreement that IT will reduce the labor force. There was disagreement that IT impacted the operational area of eliminating paperwork and lowering operating costs. The results in Table 9-4 show that IT did have an impact on improving HR operations, with the greatest impact seen through increased operational efficiency, automation of routine tasks, and increasing productivity of HR workers. However, HRIS was not able to reduce the HR labor force or eliminate paperwork for the municipal government.

Table 9-5 shows relational aspects of IT and HR through survey evidence of Texas municipal governments (Reddick, 2009a). HRIS reduced the response times to serve customers and clients, improved the quality and timeliness of services to municipal employees, and achieved staff acceptance. Overall, the relational aspects of HRIS indicated that it had an impact on municipal governments and their IT function, similarly to the operational impacts.

Table 9-6 provides information on the transformation impact of IT and HR (Reddick, 2009a). There was a high level of agreement that it has improved overall quality of HR services. HRIS increased knowledge management or the creation, capture, transfer, and use of knowledge in the organization and enabled managers of HR to become more effective at their jobs. Overall, the transformational impacts show that HRIS

Table 9-4 *Operational Impacts of IT and HR*

IT in our HR function has ...	Strongly Agree	Agree	Neutral	Disagree	Strongly Disagree
	%				
Automated record keeping and other clerical duties	25.0	52.3	12.5	9.1	1.1
Alleviated administrative burdens	17.0	40.9	22.7	13.6	5.7
Improved HR operating efficiency	31.8	47.7	13.6	5.7	1.1
Increased volume of work	6.8	21.6	31.8	36.4	3.4
Shifted additional administrative burdens to line managers because of automation	3.4	27.3	38.6	25.0	5.7
Reduced HR labor force	1.1	18.2	21.6	46.6	12.5
Lowered HR operating costs	1.1	26.1	33.0	34.1	5.7
Eliminated paperwork	4.5	30.7	19.3	33.0	12.5
Improved productivity of HR employees	19.3	53.4	21.6	4.5	1.1

improved the overall quality of HR services; knowledge management has been improved, but this technology has not reduced bureaucratic red tape.

Common Technologies Used

Various technologies can be used to impact the HR function (Florkowski and Olivas-Lujan, 2006). One technology is software targeting HR staff and end users. This is done through increased software automation of responsibilities of the HR function. Some functions that can be targeted are performance management, talent management, and stakeholder management. Another package is integrated HR software suite applications. These systems provide access to large databases through a variety of modules and can automate various aspects of the HR function. There is the ability to share data with these systems. In addition, there is software targeted toward internal customers as end users. Interactive voice response can be used to replace a live person for a phone call by automatically targeting individuals to functions using touchtone buttons. For example, if an employee has a question on when benefits enrollment takes place, interactive voice response could direct the

Table 9-5 *Relational Impacts of IT in HR*

	Strongly Agree	Agree	Neutral	Disagree	Strongly Disagree
	%				
Reduced response times to serve our customers or clients	20.5	62.5	9.1	6.8	1.1
Improved working relationships with upper management	12.5	36.4	39.8	10.2	1.1
Enhanced our ability to recruit and retain top talent	5.7	31.8	48.9	12.5	1.1
Received HR staff acceptance	20.5	54.5	20.5	3.4	1.1
Empowered employees and managers to make more decisions on their own about needs	6.8	20.5	39.8	29.5	3.4
Improved employee awareness, appreciation, and use of city government HR programs	9.1	25.0	44.3	20.5	1.1
Improved line managers' ability to meet HR responsibilities	9.1	29.5	37.5	22.7	1.1
Improved quality and timeliness of service to employees	18.2	62.5	12.5	5.7	1.1
Improved relationships with citizens and businesses and HR	6.8	31.8	51.1	8.0	2.3

employee to the correct person to answer that question. HR intranet applications provide the ability for employees to update information in databases rather than through HR. Employees may also be able to download forms and view the employee handbook through the intranet. Self-service applications allow employees to update individual records such as benefit plans, conduct training, and perform evaluations. HR extranets can be used to conduct business with vendors of HR. HR portal applications allow personalized web-based access to all information sources through the Internet. Web-based employee self-service in the HR function is likely to improve the effectiveness and efficiency of the organization to focus more on its strategic roles (Haines and Lafleur, 2008).

Table 9-7 shows four possible methods of contacting HR when employees need information and/or services (Reddick, 2009a). HRDs in Texas local governments were asked to specify the percentage of each method that employees typically used to

Table 9-6 *Transformational Impacts of IT in HR*

	Strongly Agree	Agree	Neutral	Disagree	Strongly Disagree
	%				
Redefined the scope of HR to focus more on strategic issues	3.4	29.5	46.6	19.3	1.1
Reengineered HR	4.5	35.2	31.8	23.9	4.5
Increased the flexibility of HR	8.0	59.1	19.3	12.5	1.1
Improved quality of HR services	17.0	58.0	17.0	6.8	1.1
Enabled HR to focus on its mission	4.5	44.3	38.6	11.4	1.1
Made HR a strategic partner in city government	8.0	37.5	35.2	15.9	3.4
Enabled me to become a more effective manager	13.6	53.4	20.5	11.4	1.1
Increased knowledge management (i.e., creation, capture, transfer, and use of knowledge)	17.0	55.7	18.2	8.0	1.1
Reduced the levels of bureaucracy within city government	3.4	15.9	51.1	22.7	6.8

contact their HR department. The results in Table 9-7 indicated that the most common method was in person or over a phone, with each being represented by 35% of contacts. The second most common method for contacting HR was via e-mail, with 23.2% of the contacts taking place using this approach. The least common method of contacting HR was employee self-service through an intranet (a website accessible only to city government employees) or Internet, at only 5.7% of employees using this method.

Table 9-7 *Employee Contacts with HR for Information or Services*

Methods of Contacting HR	Percent
HR specialist in person or at a meeting	35.5
HR specialist over the phone	35.3
HR specialist via email	23.2
Employee self-service through an intranet or Internet	5.7

Table 9-8 *HR Web Services for Recruiting*

Web Service	Percent
Job postings	92.0
Applications	85.2
Application tracking	35.2
Automated resume intake/management	20.5
Offer/new hire processing	19.3

Therefore, the primary methods of contacting HR have not changed much as a result of the Internet. However, e-mail represents around one-fourth of contacts, which is quite substantial. One reason for the low level of contact through employee self-service may have to do with few services actually being offered over the Web.

Table 9-8 provides information from the same survey of Texas municipal government HRDs on the web services used by HR for recruiting prospective employees (Reddick, 2009a). The most pronounced web service used in HR was for job postings, with 92% of HRDs reporting this for their local government. Accepting applications was done by 85.2% of local governments in Texas, although more sophisticated functions such as application tracking was done by 35.2% of local governments. More sophisticated functions such as an automated resume intake system was not very prevalent in HR departments (20.5%).

Table 9-9 provides information on the web services used in local government HR departments for training employees (Reddick, 2009a). The Web has allowed HR to train employees in city governments virtually from home or at work. However, there is not much evidence that online training is occurring in Texas municipal governments. Only 17% of local governments used the Web for curriculum overview and course enrollment. E-learning/training was only done by 14.8% of local governments.

Table 9-9 *HR Web Services for Training*

Web Service	Percent
Curriculum overview	17.0
Course enrollment	17.0
Training/e-learning	14.8
Mentoring	1.1

Table 9-10 *HR Web Services for Employee Benefits*

Web Service	Percent
Retirement plan information	67.0
Plan/policy information	61.4
Wellness information/education	46.6
Ongoing new hire enrollments	30.7
Annual health plan and welfare enrollment	28.4
Ongoing status/life events change	23.9
Compensation statements	17.0
Modeling/financial planning tools	12.5

The benefits of online training could be substantial in resources saved, but it is underutilized in Texas municipal government.

Table 9-10 provides information on the use of the Web for employee benefits (Reddick, 2009a). For instance, retirement plan information was provided on the Web by 67% of cities in Texas. Plan and policy information for benefits was provided by 61.4% of cities. The results in Table 9-10 generally show that the Web has been used very well for providing information on employee benefits. When it comes to more transaction-oriented annual benefit enrollment, for instance, there were only 28.4% of cities using the Web.

Table 9-11 provides information on web services in HR being used for performance/career management of city government employees (Reddick, 2009a). The most common

Table 9-11 *HR Web Services for Performance/Career Management*

Web Service	Percent
Job descriptions	43.2
Performance appraisals	33.0
Information on promotion/career paths	18.2
Skill/competency tracking	6.8
Individual goal setting	6.8
Career assessment/planning	4.5

Table 9-12 *HR Web Services for Manager Self-Service Tools*

Web Service	Percent
Financials and accounting	46.6
Time and attendance	40.9
Payroll administration	37.5
Management reports	35.2
Personnel change transactions	23.9
Diversity and compliance reporting	19.3
Workforce planning	10.2

use of the Web in this area of HR was for job descriptions (43.2%). Performance appraisals were completed by 33% of cities. More specialized information systems, such as career assessments/planning, were hardly used at all, at only 4.5% of Texas cities.

Table 9-12 provides information on the HR web services for self-service (Reddick, 2009a). Manager self-service tools such as financials and accounting for HR were conducted by 46.6% of cities through a web-based system. Time and attendance were completed by 40.9% of Texas cities. More complicated workforce planning was performed by only 10.2% of cities. The results show that self-service is generally providing information rather than advanced functions such as workforce planning and compliance reporting.

Table 9-13 provides information on the use of the Web in HR for a web portal of HR functions (Reddick, 2009a). A web portal is a one-stop shop for employees and managers to get HR information/services online. For example, real-time HR information such as personnel data entry and management by employees was conducted by 29.5% of cities through a web portal. HR financial information/transactions were completed by 26.1% of cities. Only 9.1% of cities used web-based workforce performance measurement information.

Table 9-13 *HR Services Using a Web Portal*

Web Service Portal	Percent
HR information (e.g., real-time personnel data entry and management)	29.5
HR financial information/transactions	26.1
Workforce performance measurement information	9.1

An overview of the Texas municipal government survey data revealed the Web was used more as an information source for managers and employees. There were a limited number of more advanced self-service applications used in the cities surveyed.

Telework

As governments face increasing budget constraints, one solution to reducing cost is telework. Telework involves office employees working from home for a certain portion of the week and using IT to remotely connect into their home office. The organization saves office space and general operating costs. The benefits and costs of telework for federal government employees are examined in the closing case study at the end of the chapter. Briefly, the benefit to employees is spending less time commuting to work, which can help with creating a more positive feeling toward work and greater productivity. The cost to the organization is it may be more difficult to monitor employees who are at home. This poses a unique challenge for the manager in an increasingly results-oriented public sector.

IT Workers and Government

IT employees are a critical component of the ability of governments to manage complex organizations (Reid et al., 2008). With the increased demands on government, this creates unique IT staffing challenges. Public sector IT workers have the ability to move easily to the private sector because they have very transferable skills. In addition, the public sector faces the unique challenges of a greater need for accountability than the private sector, less integration of information systems, and budget constraints that prevent agencies from purchasing the latest technology. Because of these issues, government needs to understand why IT workers stay in public sector jobs.

Three common factors explain why IT workers stay with government agencies: affective organizational commitment, job involvement, and job satisfaction (Reid et al., 2008). Affective organizational commitment is the belief and acceptance of the organization's goals and values and the willingness of employees to expend effort to achieve those goals. Job involvement is the psychological identification with the job, such as the desire to do the job. Finally, job satisfaction is the individual's attitude toward the job, essentially, does the employee find the job rewarding? In an analysis of state government IT employees, research shows that affective commitment and job satisfaction are two important areas that can be used to retain employees.

Work exhaustion occurs when employees feel overextended and drained by their work and as a result distance themselves from their job both emotionally and cognitively (Kim and Wright, 2007). Work exhaustion has negative consequences for the employee, such as increased health problems. Work exhaustion also has an adverse impact on the organization as seen through lower employee job satisfaction and increased job turnover. In addition, work exhaustion can decrease the level of customer service that an organization can offer. Research shows that the organizational context (resources, participation, and feedback) and job-related stressors (workload and role ambiguity) and opportunities for promotion affect the level of work exhaustion experienced by IT government employees. An organization can lower work exhaustion by taking into account expectations of the organization and the employees themselves. Managers need to be knowledgeable about the factors of work exhaustion to address these issues and lower employee turnover.

Hiring IT professionals has been an increasing challenge, especially since the 1990s for the public sector for several reasons (Lan et al., 2005). First, IT is a relatively new profession compared with traditional professionals such as financial manager or HR manager. The demand for technology professionals exploded in the 1990s as a result of new network technology. Hiring and retaining these workers is difficult in government because of uncertain budget situations, low compensation packages, and fixed HR procedures. Second, the nature of the IT job impacts the operation of the entire organization. A failure in the IT system impacts the entire operation. Third, in the IT area skills change very rapidly depending on the conditions of the job environment. If IT professionals do not keep current with the latest technology, their skills may become obsolete.

HR management research indicates that government rules and regulations, control systems, political context, and limited autonomy and flexibility can serve as barriers to effective HR management (Kim, 2005). Research in state governments indicates that IT managers need to pay attention to work exhaustion, participatory management, and opportunities for advancement when addressing employee turnover in IT. Some strategies are conducting assessments of job characteristics, management styles, and HR practices. This will give IT employees a sense that their departments are interested in them and their work. Major findings by Kim (2005) are that work exhaustion matters for state government IT workers and employee turnover intentions. Second, the increased participation from management should reduce state government IT employee turnover intentions. Third, there is a need for intensified organizational and managerial commitment to IT employee assessment practices to enhance career advancement for these workers.

The literature on job characteristics and their impact on workers and their satisfaction with their job are related to three themes applicable to the federal government (Mastracci, 2009). First, satisfaction with the compensation package of the government has an impact on IT worker satisfaction. Federal agencies, for instance, find it necessary to increase employees' compensation packages to keep up with the private sector. One solution is to provide IT workers with signing bonuses as a means of attracting this talent and to recruit pay scales upward to attract the best workers. Second, opportunities for advancement and job security have an impact on IT worker satisfaction. Many people look to come to government because they see it as a stable workforce. Third, a perceived high level of family-friendly workplace and employment autonomy might attract IT workers to government. Having a sense of control over work could increase employee satisfaction and ultimately decrease turnover. The same could be said for increased autonomy for workers, making them believe they can shape their positions and the organization.

In summary, IT employees are unique compared with other employee groups because they have a high need for challenging work and a lower need for social interaction. IT workers tend to be more logical, conservative, and ambitious than other employee groups. They face long hours, after-hours work, the necessity of being on call, and a continued state of rushing to respond to crisis situations and adapting to rapidly changing technology where their skills can become obsolete very quickly (Reid et al., 2008). Because of these factors it is essential to understand the challenges of recruiting and retaining IT workers in the public sector.

Summary

This chapter has examined the impact of IT on the HR function of government. Essentially, IT has created a virtual HR department, where HR information and services can be available online anytime and anywhere. There is a movement from an in-person HR department to a virtual one. IT in HR has moved from being primarily an administrative cost-cutting function to being more strategically integrated within the organization.

There are operational, relational, and transformational impacts of HR and IT in public organizations, with most of the evidence shown for IT in HR impacting the operational and relational but not as much evidence for the transformational currently taking place.

One of the most pressing issues for public sector organizations is the recruitment and retention of IT workers in public administration. The public sector has a particularly difficult time doing this because the skills of IT workers are easily translated to other sectors, making it increasingly difficult to keep these valuable workers.

Discussion Questions

1. How has IT transformed the HR department from the 1960s to the present?
2. What are the benefits and barriers to the adoption of IT in modern public organizations?
3. What are the most common technologies used in HR? Can you comment on the effectiveness of these technologies?
4. Why is recruiting and retention of IT workers in government so difficult? What are some solutions to this dilemma?

Closing Case Study

Federal Government Telework

Some federal government managers have great issue with telework, or essentially working at home and using IT to communicate with their home office and clients (Monroe, 2010). Agencies that allow employees to work at home several days a week might have an easier time attracting and retaining talent. They might also be able to more effectively continue operations in the case of an emergency, such as disaster at the federal agency. In addition, there would be less traffic in the Washington, DC, area. These arguments have generally not convinced federal managers, with some believing telework, creates new problems with employees.

Performance management is essential to telework. Managers may believe they are losing control if they are not able to see their employees working. In a survey of federal employees and telework, some broad issues of concern to management were addressed.

Technology Disconnects

When working from home, the issue of security in the equipment used is challenging. A virtual private network may have a slower connection, which in turn may slow down performance. Government-provided portable devices are needed, which can add significantly to an existing budget.

Disconnected Employees

One issue with remote workers is that they may be difficult to reach. Employees can use e-mail, instant messaging, and chat rooms to keep in touch with each other during the day, but conversations can come up in the hallway or in the kitchen. This can be especially problematic when you have quick turnaround assignments where workers may be scrambling to respond. Telework can also put extra pressures on bosses when there are impromptu meetings taking place.

Management Matters

Lack of face-to-face meetings may hinder communication. Telephones and e-mail are good for communication of facts, but nuances are often lost. It is often the things that are not said that are equally important.

Problem Employees

Some employees may not be suitable for telework. Managers have to trust employees that do telework, and this may be difficult with certain employees.

Some managers are concerned about employee work performance without direct supervision.

Employees benefit from reduced travel time and commuting costs, flexible hours, and better balance of work and family (McCaney, 2010b). Environmental benefits from telework are reduced pollution and traffic congestion. In a pilot program for the General Services Administration in Kansas City, Missouri, 42 employees worked at home for 90 days, resulting in increased productivity, reduced sick leave, better communication among employees, and fewer metric tons of carbon dioxide emission in the atmosphere. **Figure 9-1** shows the federal agencies that most often use telework.

AGENCY	NO. OF ELIGIBLE EMPLOYEES	% TELEWORKING	% TELEWORKING 1-2 DAYS/WEEK	% TELEWORKING 3-PLUS DAYS/WEEK
U.S. Patent and Trademark Office	5,314	82.7	46.1	36.6
General Services Administration	10,374	45.8	39.7	2.3
Securities and Exchange Commission	3,671	43.5	12.8	2.9
National Science Foundation	1,438	41	12.6	0.5
Office of Personnel Management	2,357	34.2	18.6	7.5

Figure 9-1 *Top 5 agencies by percentage of employees who telework* (Source: Weigand, 2010)

Chapter 10

Information Security and Privacy

Opening Case Study

Biometric Scanning

Technology that scans palm prints, eyes, and voices to allow access into rooms or data and to verify identities is on the rise (Nichols, 2010b). Based on biometrics, these devices recognize individuals by analyzing the unique characteristics of their body or behavior. With advances in technology there are more advanced biometric devices that do full body scans that the Department of Homeland Security has announced will be in 11 U.S. airports in 2010. As more scanning takes place, however, there is a concern by citizens and privacy advocates of the risks of personal information getting into the wrong hands. The question becomes what safeguards are in place to protect the privacy of individuals?

An example of the use of this technology comes from the Maryland Correctional Adjustment Center. A Baltimore inmate conned his way out of prison by pretending to be someone else. The inmate was released by mistake but was recaptured 24 hours later. To prevent future mishaps, the Maryland Division of Corrections will be implementing electronic fingerprint scanning as part of its inmate release policy and procedures.

Another example can be found in Bergen County, New Jersey. The Department of Human Services (DHS) needs to estimate the homeless individuals that receive services such as food, medicine, and shelter (Nichols, 2010b). But many people served by the department do not have accurate forms of identification, and without a precise tracking system a person could visit the shelter 10 times during the day and only be counted once. With biometric technology Bergen County has implemented a solution that allows DHS to keep a more accurate count of homeless people who receive support. The DHS unveiled a fingerprint identification system developed by Fulcrum Biometric. This is a web-based application that links finger image scanners at the DHS service sites and a fingerprint matching algorithm to the existing New Jersey Homeless Management Information System. This data-sharing method reduces check-in time to seconds; the DHS worker simply uses the new digital system. The homeless person comes into the shelter and places his or her finger on the scanner; the computer captures the data and communicates with the state database to verify the person's identity. This system has allowed funders to know exactly how many homeless people have been served in a given time and how much their contributions have helped to support them.

Chapter Objectives

The three objectives of this chapter are as follows:

1. To provide an overview of the issue of information privacy as it relates to public administration
2. To provide an overview of the important issues in information security for public sector organizations
3. To provide evidence on the importance of information security for policymakers and public managers

Introduction

Information security and privacy are two very important issues faced in modern public organizations. In this chapter we provide the context of these important issues as they are related to public sector organizations. Information security and privacy are especially important given the increased role of information technology (IT) in modern public organizations. The same is true of information privacy with the increased collection of personally identifiable information of citizens; this has translated into greater concern over what is being done with the collected information. To understand information security and privacy, one must have a grasp of the differences in public and private sector information systems as they relate to this issue.

Information Security and Privacy in Public and Private Sectors

Public sector information systems differ from their private sector counterparts in four ways regarding information security: availability, confidentiality, privacy, and integrity (Loukis and Spinellis, 2001). First, with regards to availability, because of the strategic nature of public sector organizations, information systems failures can lead to large-scale disruptions to social and economic development and could possibly endanger lives. This is increasingly true as a result of the interconnected world we live in because of the Internet. For example, a computer failure in a utility company could impact the delivery of electricity to millions of residents in a large metropolitan city. The opening case study provides an example of biometric scanning, which can provide an extra degree of information security, but this has privacy implications.

Second, information systems in the public sector are used for many functions that require collecting confidential data; therefore, these systems must guarantee a high level of confidentiality of the data they use. Governments must be aware of data handling procedures to keep data confidential. A large amount of trust must be placed on public agencies in the collection of confidential data, and evidence must be shown that security safeguards are in place to keep the data from getting into the wrong hands.

Third, there is the possibility of combining data that might create an invasion of an individual's privacy. Combining government data with another data set could lead to an issue of privacy, because the data are being used beyond their intended use. As we discover in this chapter, citizens and their views on privacy differ, where some citizens do not want any of their personal data to be used for other purposes, and other citizens will give up some privacy for other benefits.

Fourth, because data are extremely important to public sector information systems, the integrity of the data must be considered. Because of the issue of privacy, governments must ensure there is integrity in the data collected from individuals. The data may be used to determine the allocation of federal money, such as U.S. Census Bureau statistics. Integrity of data is crucial because many entitlement programs are initiated from data collected from public sector agencies.

As a result of these four differences, it is important to study information security and privacy in public administration. The following section discusses the role of information privacy in public sector organizations.

Information Privacy

Personal information privacy is an individual's ability to personally control information about him- or herself. Some common personal information includes a birth registration, income and expenditure patterns, and health records (Lim et al., 2009).

Individuals' expectations of information privacy may be an illusion if they don't know what is being done with their personal information. As e-government and e-commerce grow, there is more of a concern about the electronic collection of personal information (Belanger and Hiller, 2006). To maintain their online privacy, Internet users can use protection measures such as opting out, using privacy-enhancing technologies, and checking for secure websites.

There are three recent concerns for privacy and government. First, with a push toward e-government, there are increased citizen transactions being conducted online, which creates a new level of concern for the privacy of personal information. Second, there is a growing use of smart cards and other portable information collection devices. These devices have embedded in them personal information that can be vulnerable to privacy. Third, there are calls for greater surveillance of individuals since the terrorist attacks of September 11, 2001, in the United States. Essentially, individuals are being asked to give up a level of privacy for increased security. These three concerns make privacy of personal information critically important for public administration.

One of the most important pieces of federal government legislation that addressed information privacy is the 1974 Privacy Act. This act provided principles of fair information use that agencies must meet in handling personal information (Regan, 1986). This Act also addressed the rights for individuals who provide this information. The Privacy Act was designed to give individuals a means to control information collected about them. This involves the right to know what information is being collected and the right to challenge and correct this information. In addition, organizations are expected to follow principles of fair information use and to establish standards and regulations for the collection and use of personal information of individuals.

The Privacy Act is a very important piece of federal legislation and has a tremendous impact on IT and public administration (Holden and Millett, 2005). This Act outlines the administrative procedures to help ensure that federal agencies adhere to privacy principles when collecting and using individuals' personally identifiable information. The Privacy Act was enacted to establish a federal code of fair information practices for federal information systems. There also are procedures to support fair information practices and penalties for violators of the practices. The Act provides U.S. citizens and permanent residents with the right to amend records maintained by most federal agencies. The law also sets conditions for federal agencies to disclose information about individuals from agency systems and records.

Three groups of Americans and their views on privacy have been identified: the privacy fundamentalists, the privacy indifferent, and the privacy pragmatists (Smith, 2005). The privacy fundamentalists encompass one-fourth of Americans who do not like to disclose any personal information. They view their personal information as completely private and believe it should not be given up to others. The second group, the privacy indifferent/unconcerned, account for 10% of Americans who will easily disclose information and are not concerned about privacy implications. The privacy pragmatists comprise about two-thirds of Americans who will give up personal information in return for something of value to them. This group cares about privacy but will allow others to have access to their information when they understand the reasons and see the benefits and believe care is taken to prevent the misuse of information. Essentially, survey evidence shows that most Americans are concerned about privacy but would be willing to give up some of their privacy if they believe they could get something in return.

Information privacy is different from privacy in general as the former deals with how individuals, groups, and institutions determine how their information is communicated with others (Cullen, 2009). There often is the debate between the individual's right to privacy and the public interest. This balance is determined by society and differs from one culture to another. One key dimension that influences information privacy is inequality of power between individuals. Another dimension is individualist cultures versus collectivist cultures and their impact on information privacy. Research shows differences in cultural values across countries; with high power, distance cultures tend to have a greater tolerance of intrusions on their lives compared with lower power distance cultures. The same is true for more collective versus individualist cultures, where collectivist countries have less of an issue with government collecting information than more individualist cultures. Essentially, research shows that privacy is relative to a country's culture; therefore, issues of privacy concerns in America are different from privacy concerns in other countries (Cullen, 2009).

People in more individualistic cultures tend to place more value on private life, whereas collectivist societies more easily accept intrusion into their private life (Cho et al., 2009). Empirical results do show that individualist societies are more likely to have a higher level of concern for information privacy online. These countries are more likely to be concerned about potential privacy intrusion. The views of citizens from a more individualist country such as the United States compared with more collectivist countries such as Norway would have different privacy implications.

Empirical results indicate that Whites and Asians/Pacific Islanders have the lowest levels of concern with security on the Internet (O'Neil, 2001). Latinos and Hispanics have the highest percentage. Education level does not seem to affect whether an individual is concerned about online privacy. Those with higher income levels seem to be less concerned about privacy than those with lower income levels. Women seem to be more concerned about privacy than men. Overall, all demographic groups prefer privacy protection to convenience. As governments develop policies on privacy protection they should note their cultural characteristics and the demographics of the groups from which they are collecting personal information, because privacy concerns depend on both groups.

Policy Instruments to Enhance Information Security

Four principal policy instruments can be used to enhance information security in organizations (**Table 10-1**) (Bauer and van Eeten, 2009). These are laws and legal regulations, economic measures, technical measures, and information and behavioral measures.

Table 10-1 *Policy Instruments in Information Security*

Policy Issue	Information Security Policy
Legal and regulatory	• Tax credits and subsidies • Liability laws in case of information security failures • National legislation and regulation of information security
Economic	• Insurance markets • Markets to protect vulnerable businesses and citizens • Access of information payments • Legal and financial penalties for violation of regulations
Technical	• Information security standards • Security testing • Information security best practices in IT development
Information and behavioral	• Education of both workers and businesses • National and International sharing of information security issues

Adapted from Bauer and van Eeten (2009).

The legal and regulatory policy impacts information security policy because it dictates the constraints with which citizens and businesses must live. In this area legislation and regulations are passed to correct issues that have occurred in information security. Second, there is the economic impact on information security policy. For example, the issue of information security creates new economic markets for both the insurance of businesses and citizens in case their information security has been violated. Third, the technical policy is the information security standards put in place. For example, the use of virus protection software and other countermeasures come into play here. Finally, the information and behavior policies are the education and awareness of the issues of information security for citizens and businesses. Governments should be aware of these four important issues to enhance information security in their organizations.

Information security development in an organization is not just a technical component of IT and public administration; there are other important social and management dimensions as well. Information security development can be categorized into three views, technical, management, and institutional (Chang and Lin, 2007). The technical side of information security focuses on IT solutions to this problem. However, this approach cannot protect the organization without good management and policy of information security. Therefore, information security is not merely a technical solution, because it requires top management to be involved in establishing the appropriate policies and procedures and organizational structures to improve information security. Management has the responsibility of designing and implementing an information security program in an efficient and effective way. The institutional part of information security is the organizational culture, because the culture is the human side of information security, which cannot be ignored. Empirical research shows that organizations that have more flexible cultures may not have a favorable environment for information security.

A more controlling environment seems to be more conducive to enhancing information security, but there are limits to being controlling. Therefore, a culture that is supportive of information security is extremely important because the human dimension cannot be solved by technical and management solutions alone.

Environmental Factors and Preparedness

A survey of Texas state government information resource managers (IRMs) in 2008 demonstrated some of the environmental factors that influence information security (**Table 10-2**) (Reddick, 2009b). Some of the interesting results show that environmental factors do have a large influence on information security. For example, 26.9% of Texas state agencies strongly agreed there was an emphasis on information security in their state agency. Also, 26.9% of these agencies indicated that information security policy focused on prevention. Twenty percent of IRMs strongly agreed there was a constant evaluation of information security effectiveness in their state agency.

Table 10-2 *Environmental Factors That Influence Information Security in Texas State Agencies*

In my state agency …	Strongly Agree	Agree	Neutral	Disagree	Strongly Disagree
	%				
There is an emphasis on information security	26.9	53.8	7.7	11.5	0
There is a constant evaluation of information security effectiveness	20	52	12	16	0
There is strict enforcement of written state government information security policy	11.5	50	26.9	11.5	0
Information security policy focuses on prevention through controls (e.g., access controls, security software controls)	26.9	73.1	0	0	0
Information security policy focuses on deterrents through threat of sanctions	11.5	11.5	50	23.1	3.8
There is a high level of information security risk compared with other state agencies	3.8	19.2	23.1	42.3	11.5

However, IRMs disagreed about a high level of information security risk in their state agency compared with other state agencies, according to 53.8% of IRMs (when adding the disagree and strongly disagree responses).

The same survey of state agency IRMs also showed information security support and preparedness issues, as shown in **Table 10-3**. If you add up the strongly agree and agree responses, 57.7% of IRMs believed their state agency had a high degree of information security preparedness, 46.1% of IRMs agreed there was adequate training for employees on information security policy, and 34.6% of IRMs agreed their state agency had adequate budget resources for information security.

Because information security is multidimensional for the organization, the organization faces complex challenges. The following are some important challenges of achieving general goals of information security (Dzazali et al., 2009, p. 585):

- Safeguarding sensitive, critical, and propriety information from unauthorized access, disclosure, or modification
- Protecting information systems and supporting computer resources from loss, damage, and destruction
- Providing organizational management with reasonable assurance as to the integrity, confidentiality, and availability of information and information assets
- Recognizing and adopting all legal regulations and laws concerning the confidentiality, availability, and integrity of critical information

Information security, at a time before the Internet, was centralized and isolated in mainframe computers; the challenge today with the Internet is much greater. As information

Table 10-3 *Information Security Support and Preparedness*

In my state agency, there is ...	Strongly Agree	Agree	Neutral	Disagree	Strongly Disagree
	%				
A high level of information security preparedness	7.7	50	23.1	19.2	0
Adequate budget resources for information security	7.7	26.9	23.1	38.5	3.8
Information security taking precedence over other state IT budget priorities	0	23.1	34.6	34.6	7.7
Adequate training for employees on information security policy	3.8	42.3	38.5	15.4	0
Adequate staffing for information security	7.7	23.1	19.2	46.2	3.8

systems grew and became decentralized, more complex information security became an apparent need. Therefore, advances in technology aid in information security but also create new information security challenges in a networked world.

Management and Information Security

There are four important information technology issues public managers should be aware of in information security. Each of these information security issues is extremely important for public sector organizations.

Viruses

Viruses are a threat to any organization because they are connected externally to the Internet through digital means, which makes them vulnerable to outsiders of the organization. There is a discussion of computer viruses later in this chapter, but essentially they are an important management issue because they create an information security threat for all public organizations. Public organizations are especially vulnerable to viruses because of their public purpose. Public managers should be aware of computer viruses and what can be done to prevent them, through virus protection software, routine maintenance of machines, and employee awareness of information security policy.

Maintenance

Information systems are in constant need of maintenance. Therefore, it is essential for the public manager to be aware of issues of maintenance and to ensure computer systems are properly maintained. This ensures a greater level of information security, as threats to information systems can be especially vulnerable when a system is not properly maintained.

Perpetual Upgrades

One issue of importance to public managers is the perpetual upgrades of their information systems. Information systems technology is in constant need of upgrades as new technology becomes available. This poses a challenge financially to keep up with the latest upgrades, especially in a fiscally constrained public sector.

Top Management Support

One of the most commonly cited impacts on information security development is support from top management. Information security incidents can be highly publicized and costly to the organization; therefore, management must take them seriously (Straub and Welke, 1998; Knapp et al., 2006). Empirical research shows that top management support positively impacts information security culture and policy enforcement in an organization. Essentially, if there is no support from top management, then information security programs will fail, even if the technology used was great. With an organizational culture that embraces information security, management backing will impact information security effectiveness.

Survey evidence on the importance of information security in state government shows that management support has a positive impact on security (**Table 10-4**) (Reddick, 2009b). IRMs indicated they strongly agreed that top management supports information security policy and awareness for their state agency (35%). There was not a lot of disagreement with this statement of top management support for information security (7.7%). In regards to top management's willingness to invest in information security, 23% of IRMs strongly agreed to this statement. The results in Table 10-4 show that top management supports information security through policy and investment, according to most IRMs.

Even knowing the importance of top management support for information security, there are several reasons for low management concern about information security (Kankanhalli et al., 2003). First, managers may believe there is a low risk of information security threats; therefore, they invest little time and effort in information security. Second, managers may not see the benefit of information security protection because of the difficulty in evaluating its effectiveness. Third, managers may lack the knowledge about the possible controls that are available. Therefore, to raise the level of management involvement in information security, managers need to be convinced about the benefits of this to create a more effective organization.

An information security framework provides the organization with a clear understanding of how to minimize risks posed by employee behavior regarding the use of information assets (Veiga and Eloff, 2010). To understand information security, one must understand the organizational culture and employee behavior, which is the way things are done by employees in the organization.

Table 10-4 *Top Management Support for Information Security*

In my state agency...	Strongly Agree	Agree	Neutral	Disagree	Strongly Disagree
	%				
Top management supports information security policy and awareness	34.6	53.8	3.8	7.7	0
Top management is willing to invest in information security	23.1	42.3	23.1	11.5	0

Employees and Information Security

In addition to top management support being critical for information security development, there also is the awareness of employees of information security that is discussed in the literature. Research shows that a threat to organizations, in regards to information security, is its own employees (Vroom and Von Solms, 2004). Essentially, employee awareness is the key link to providing more effective information security in an organization. Almost half of the security breaches are caused by accidents from employees. Therefore, many security breaches are not maliciously intended but are a result of negligence or ignorance of security policies by employees. However, most organizations tend to ignore these breaches and focus more on outside breaches. They also spend the most money and time on strengthening the technical side of the organization and relatively little attention to the more human aspects of security incidents. One way to improve employee compliance with information security is to change the culture of the organization so that it values the importance of information security. An organizational culture that promotes active awareness of information security policy for employees should be effective at mitigating some of the negative consequences of employees and information security. The closing case study at the end of this chapter provides an example of information security and employee awareness of policy.

Information security success depends on the end user and their behavior and awareness (D'Arcy and Hovav, 2007). An empirical study shows that end user awareness of security policies, security-awareness programs, and preventative security software all had an effect on information security misuse by users. Each of these security measures appears to significantly reduce users' misuse intentions. Public managers often see information security as a deterrent rather than a focus on prevention. Therefore, any strategies used to impact information security are often reactive. Some more proactive approaches that can be used to prevent users from misuse are as follows (D'Arcy and Hovav, 2007, p. 117):

- Policy statements and guidelines for appropriate use of information systems resources
- Ways to inform and educate users on what constitutes legitimate use of information systems resources and the consequences of illegitimate use
- Ways to alert users to known vulnerabilities and threats to the organization's information systems assets
- Preventative security technologies that control access to information systems resources

Essentially, creating an organizational climate that encourages compliance with security policies, along with end user awareness programs, will help reduce information security breaches.

Information Security Threats and Controls

A model of computer security can be depicted with three layers of deterrents, preventatives, and detectives (Foltz, 2004). Deterrents are the policies explaining the acceptable and unacceptable uses of information systems in organizations. Deterrents can be used to reduce the amount of misuse of information security in organizations. The ability to reprimand and punish is critical to the success of deterrents. If the probability of punishment for a crime is small, deterrents will not be effective. Deterrent measures are attempts to dissuade people and criminals through fear of sanctions (Kankanhalli et al., 2003). Deterrent efforts are correlated with the amount of efforts put forth and should affect the probability of abusers getting caught. Active and visible deterrent efforts can reduce information security abuses by convincing abusers that the probability of getting caught is high.

The second layer of computer security is preventatives. Preventative measures are attempts to reduce criminal behavior through controls. These are the next line of defense in case intruders choose to ignore deterrent measures. Some examples of preventative measures are software functions that validate user passwords, access logs, and so forth. These are active measures, such as passwords and encryption technology, that are designed to block unauthorized users. Because preventative measures prevent unauthorized access, they can be used to limit access to those external to the organization and to employees that do not have authorized access. Preventatives can defend against Internet-based attacks such as virus attacks and denial of service attacks.

Detectives are the third layer of computer security and are designed to detect misuses after they occur so this problem in information security will not be repeated. Detectives do not block information security breaches; they just alert administrators of an issue that needs corrective action. Detectives are especially important to protect against the problems within the organization.

Information security controls can be classified into three categories: technical controls, operational controls, and management controls (Baker and Wallace, 2007). Technical controls include products and processes such as firewalls, antivirus software, intrusion detection software, and encryption. These controls mainly focus on protecting the organization's IT and the information stored in these systems. Operational controls are the enforcement mechanisms for correcting deficiencies that various threats could exploit, backup systems, physical access controls, and protection from environmental hazards. Management controls are usage policies, employee training, and business continuity planning, which focus on information security's nontechnical areas. Although these are important to know, technology alone cannot solve information security problems because information security is not just a technical problem, it is a social and organizational issue as well.

For management to understand information security, they must begin to comprehend the threats facing their systems (Whitman, 2004). To prevent these threats, a good security policy should outline individual responsibilities, define authorized and unauthorized uses of the system, provide venues for employees reporting suspected risks, define penalties, and provide mechanisms for updating the policy. In addition to a security policy, education prepares employees to work in a secure computing environment.

Some of the most common threats to information security and examples of these threats are shown in **Table 10-5** (Whitman, 2004). These threats range from end user error to technical failures and deliberate acts by individuals or organizations.

Table 10-6 shows common threat protection mechanisms used in organization (Sumner, 2009). These mechanisms range from employee education to more technical solutions.

In the survey of Texas state agency IRMs, there were some important causes of information security incidents, as shown in **Table 10-7** (Reddick, 2009b). IRMs indicated that employee end user error was the major cause of information security incidents, when adding up agree and strongly agree responses (57.6%). There was agreement that hackers trying to enter the state's government system were a problem (38.4%). Lack of knowledge by employees of state government acceptable use policy was reported as an issue by 34.6% of IRMs. Lack of employee training on information security policy was also viewed as a major cause of information security

Table 10-5 *Common Threats to Information Security and Example of Threats*

Common Threats	Examples
Acts of human error or failure	Accidents, employee mistakes
Compromises to intellectual property	Piracy, copyright infringement
Deliberate acts of espionage or trespass	Unauthorized access and/or data collection
Deliberate acts of information extortion	Blackmail of information disclosure
Deliberate acts of sabotage or vandalism	Destruction of systems or information
Deliberate acts of theft	Illegal confiscation of equipment or information
Deliberate software attacks	Viruses, worms, macros, denial of service
Forces of nature	Fire, flood, earthquake, lightning
Quality of service deviations from service providers	Power failure
Technical hardware failures or errors	Equipment failures
Technical software failures or errors	Bugs, code problems, unknown loopholes
Technological obsolescence	Anticipated or outdated technologies

Adapted from Whitman (2004).

Table 10-6 *Threat Protection Mechanisms for Information Security*

Use of passwords
Media backup
Virus protection software
Employee education
Audit procedures
Consistent security policy
Firewall
Encourage violations reported
Auto account logoff
Monitor computer usage
Publish formal standards
Control of workstations
Network intrusion detection
Host intrusion detection
Ethics training
No outside dialup connections
Use shrink-wrap software only
No internal internet connections
Use internally developed software only
No outside network or web connections

Adapted from Sumner (2009).

breaches (30.8%). There was disagreement by 61.5% of IRMs that a major cause of information security incidents was lack of organizational culture that values the importance of information security. There was also disagreement that technical solutions such as password protections, antivirus software, and firewalls were not working (57.7%).

The most common threats to information security in Texas state agencies are shown in **Table 10-8** (Reddick, 2009b). The most common threats are hardware and

Table 10-7 *Perceptions of Major Causes of Information Security Incidents*

Information security incidents are usually caused by ...	Strongly Agree	Agree	Neutral	Disagree	Strongly Disagree
	%				
Employee end user error	3.8	53.8	19.2	11.5	11.5
Lack of knowledge by employees of the state government's acceptable use policy	3.8	30.8	19.2	38.5	7.7
Lack of employee training on information security policy	0	30.8	26.9	26.9	15.4
Hackers trying to enter agency system	3.8	34.6	42.3	15.4	3.8
Computer crime	0	19.2	30.8	30.8	19.2
Inability of firewalls, intrusion detection software, and antivirus software to stop unauthorized access	3.8	11.5	26.9	38.5	19.2
Lack of organizational culture that values the importance of information security	0	26.9	11.5	50.0	11.5
Lack of access controls in place such as passwords	0	15.4	15.4	46.2	23.1
Suppliers and vendors	0	7.7	26.9	50	15.4

software failures according to Texas State IRMs. Acts of human error were the fourth most common threat to information security (58.6%). At the bottom of the list of threats to information security were deliberate acts of espionage or trespass (17.2%) and deliberate acts of sabotage or vandalism (6.9%). It was especially interesting that 37.9% of IRMs believed technological obsolescence was a common threat to information security.

The effectiveness of threat protection mechanisms are shown in **Table 10-9** (Reddick, 2009b). IRMs overall believed that all common threat-protection mechanisms for information security were effective. Some technologies viewed as being especially effective were media backup, virus protection software, and firewall protection.

The following section of this chapter discusses two of the most important and emerging threats to information security: cybercrime and cybersecurity.

Table 10-8 *Common Threats to Information Security*

	Percent
Technical hardware failures or errors	69
Technical software failures or errors	65.5
Deliberate software attacks	65.5
Acts of human error or failure	58.6
Technological obsolescence	37.9
Deliberate acts of theft	31
Forces of nature	20.7
Deliberate acts of espionage or trespass	17.2
Deliberate acts of sabotage or vandalism	6.9

Table 10-9 *Effectiveness of Common Threat Protection Mechanisms*

The following threat protection mechanisms for information security are very effective	Strongly Agree	Agree	Neutral	Disagree	Strongly Disagree
	%				
Media backup	57.7	26.9	11.5	3.8	0
Virus protection software	53.8	46.2	0	0	0
Firewall protection	57.7	38.5	3.8	0	0
Use of passwords	50	34.6	11.5	3.8	0
Employee education	26.9	34.6	30.8	7.7	0
Security policy	26.9	57.7	11.5	3.8	0
Information security audits	28	48	12	8	4
Reporting of information security violations	26.9	42.3	23.1	7.7	0
Automatic account logoff	24	28	36	12	0

Cybercrime and Cybersecurity

Cybercrime is a criminal activity perpetuated by the use of the Internet and other digital means (Haugen, 2005). Governments need to understand the risks associated with cybercrime and take actions to mitigate these risks. The management of online fraud control depends on the deployment of technology, and organizations need strategies to prevent, detect, and investigate these cybercrimes. As cyberattacks become more sophisticated, government agencies can fall behind in the combat against this emerging threat. The primacy reason for this is the lack of awareness of this threat and lack of governance over security issues.

Federal government agencies have a number of cybersecurity threats, but the three most common are spam, phishing, and spyware (GAO, 2005b). First, spam is the delivery of unsolicited e-mail and has become an increasing nuisance for organizations. Spam essentially fills your inbox with advertisements for products, services, and inappropriate websites. Experts believe that spam makes up around 60% of all e-mail. Advances in antispam measures have caused spammers to make their techniques more sophisticated to bypass detection and filtration software.

Second, phishing uses spam or pop-up messages to deceive people into disclosing their credit card numbers, bank account information, Social Security number, passwords, or other sensitive information. The message typically says that users need to "update" or "validate" their account information and might threaten them with dire consequences if they do not respond. This message directs users to a website that looks legitimate but is not. Phishing scams use a combination of social engineering and technical methods to deceive users. Pharming is another method used by phishers to deceive users into believing they are communicating with a legitimate website when they really are on a spoofed website.

Finally, spyware can be used to deliver advertisements to users, often in exchange for free use of an application or service. It can collect information such as the user's Internet protocol address, web-surfing history, online buying habits, e-mail address, and software and hardware specifications. It often provides end users with targeted pop-up advertisements based on their web-surfing habits.

Table 10-10 shows the sources of emerging cybersecurity threats as identified by the U.S. intelligence community and other sources (U.S. Government Accountability Office [GAO], 2005b). Governments are increasingly concerned about these threats because of the critical role that computers and networks play in our global society. There is an increased concern about the combined physical and cyber attacks, which can have a devastating impact on infrastructure and the lives of individuals and businesses.

Table 10-11 shows the types of cyber attacks, with some of the most common being computer viruses, Trojan horses, worms, and logic bombs (GAO, 2005c). Viruses and worms are commonly used to launch denial-of-service attacks, which flood targeted networks and systems by transmitting so much data that regular traffic is either

Table 10-10 *Sources of Emerging Cybersecurity Threats and Their Descriptions*

Threat	Description of Threat
Bot-network operators	Bot-network operators are hackers; however, instead of breaking into systems for the challenge or bragging rights, they take over multiple systems to coordinate attacks and to distribute phishing schemes, spam, and malware attacks. The services of these networks are sometimes made available on underground markets (e.g., purchasing a denial-of-service attack, servers to relay spam or phishing attacks, etc.).
Criminal groups	Criminal groups seek to attack systems for monetary gain. Specifically, organized crime groups use spam, phishing, and spyware/malware to commit identity theft and online fraud. International corporate spies and organized crime organizations also pose a threat to the United States through their ability to conduct industrial espionage and large-scale monetary theft and to hire or develop hacker talent.
Foreign intelligence services	Foreign intelligence services use cybertools as part of their information-gathering and espionage activities. In addition, several nations are aggressively working to develop information warfare doctrine, programs, and capabilities. Such capabilities enable a single entity to have a significant and serious impact by disrupting the supply, communications, and economic infrastructures that support military power—impacts that could affect the daily lives of U.S. citizens across the country.
Hackers	Hackers break into networks for the thrill of the challenge or for bragging rights in the hacker community. Although remote cracking once required a fair amount of skill or computer knowledge, hackers can now download attack scripts and protocols from the Internet and launch them against victim sites. Thus, whereas attack tools have become more sophisticated, they have also become easier to use. According to the Central Intelligence Agency, the large majority of hackers do not have the requisite expertise to threaten difficult targets such as critical U.S. networks. Nevertheless, the worldwide population of hackers poses a relatively high threat of an isolated or brief disruption causing serious damage.
Insiders	The disgruntled organization insider is a principal source of computer crime. Insiders may not need a great deal of knowledge about computer intrusions because their knowledge of a target system often allows them to gain unrestricted access to cause damage to the system or to steal system data. The insider threat also includes outsourcing vendors as well as employees who accidentally introduce malware into systems.
Phishers	Individuals, or small groups, execute phishing schemes in an attempt to steal identities or information for monetary gain. Phishers may also use spam and spyware/malware to accomplish their objectives.
Spammers	Individuals or organizations distribute unsolicited e-mail with hidden or false information to sell products, conduct phishing schemes, distribute spyware/malware, or attack organizations (i.e., denial of service).

(continues)

Table 10-10 *Sources of Emerging Cybersecurity Threats and Their Descriptions* (Continued)

Threat	Description of Threat
Spyware/ malware authors	Individuals or organizations with malicious intent carry out attacks against users by producing and distributing spyware and malware. Several destructive computer viruses and worms have harmed files and hard drives, including the Melissa Macro Virus, the Explore.Zip worm, the CIH (Chernobyl) Virus, Nimda, Code Red, Slammer, and Blaster.
Terrorists	Terrorists seek to destroy, incapacitate, or exploit critical infrastructures to threaten national security, cause mass casualties, weaken the U.S. economy, and damage public morale and confidence. Terrorists may use phishing schemes or spyware/malware to generate funds or gather sensitive information.

Source: U.S. Government Accountability Office (2005c).

slowed or stopped. In 2001 the Code Red worm used a denial-of-service attack to affect millions of computer users by shutting down websites, slowing Internet service, and disrupting business and government operations. Intruders quickly exploited vulnerabilities that were discovered; therefore, governments must constantly keep up with the latest security software and hardware.

Information security incidents reported by United States-Computer Emergency Readiness Team (US-CERT) are categorized by the following (GAO, 2008, pp. 20–21):

- *Unauthorized access:* In this category an individual gains logical or physical access without permission to a federal agency's network, system, application, data, or other resource.
- *Denial of service:* An attack that successfully prevents or impairs the normal authorized functionality of networks, systems, or applications by exhausting resources. This activity includes being the victim of or participating in a denial of service attack.
- *Malicious code:* Successful installation of malicious software (e.g., virus, worm, Trojan horse, or other code-based malicious entity) that infects an operating system or application. Agencies are not required to report malicious logic that has been successfully quarantined by antivirus software.
- *Improper usage:* A person violates acceptable computing use policies.
- *Scans/probes/attempted access:* This category includes any activity that seeks to access or identify a federal agency computer, open ports, protocols, service, or any combination of these for later exploit. This activity does not directly result in a compromise or denial of service.
- *Investigations:* Unconfirmed incidents that are potentially malicious or anomalous activity deemed by the reporting entity to warrant further review.

Table 10-11 *Types of Cyberattacks*

Type of Attack	Description of Attack
Denial of service	A method of attack from a single source that denies system access to legitimate users by overwhelming the target computer with messages and blocking legitimate traffic. It can prevent a system from being able to exchange data with other systems or use the Internet.
Distributed denial of service	A variant of the denial-of-service attack that uses a coordinated attack from a distributed system of computers rather than from a single source. It often makes use of worms to spread to multiple computers that can then attack the target.
Exploit tools	Publicly available and sophisticated tools that intruders of various skill levels can use to determine vulnerabilities and gain entry into targeted systems.
Logic bombs	A form of sabotage in which a programmer inserts codes that cause the program to perform a destructive action when some triggering event occurs, such as terminating the programmer's employment.
Phishing	The creation and use of e-mails and websites—designed to look like those of well-known legitimate businesses, financial institutions, and government agencies—to deceive Internet users into disclosing their personal data, such as bank and financial account information and passwords. The phishers then take that information and use it for criminal purposes, such as identity theft and fraud.
Sniffer	Synonymous with packet sniffer. A program that intercepts routed data and examines each packet in search of specified information, such as passwords transmitted in clear text.
Trojan horse	A computer program that conceals harmful code. A Trojan horse usually masquerades as a useful program a user would wish to execute.
Virus	A program that infects computer files, usually executable programs, by inserting a copy of itself into the file. These copies are usually executed when the infected file is loaded into memory, allowing the virus to infect other files. Unlike the computer worm, a virus requires human involvement (usually unwitting) to propagate.
War dialing	Simple programs that dial consecutive telephone numbers looking for modems.
War driving	A method of gaining entry into wireless computer networks using a laptop, antennas, and a wireless network adaptor that involves patrolling locations to gain unauthorized access.
Worm	An independent computer program that reproduces by copying itself from one system to another across a network. Unlike computer viruses, worms do not require human involvement to propagate.

Source: U.S. Government Accountability Office (2005c).

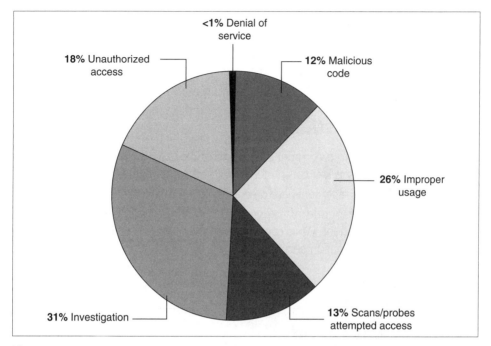

Figure 10-1 *Percentage of incidents reported by US-CERT in fiscal year 2007* (Source: GAO, 2008)

Figure 10-1 shows the percentage of these incidents reported above to US-CERT in fiscal year 2007 (GAO, 2008).

Summary

This chapter examined the impact of information security and privacy on public sector organizations. Public sector agencies must be very vigilant in information security and privacy, more so than their private sector counterparts because of the availability, confidentiality, privacy, and integrity of data they collect. Information privacy is an individual's ability to personally control his or her own information. Information privacy has become increasingly more challenging with the networked world in which we live. Cultural and demographic factors do have an influence on information privacy, where more individualistic cultures are less tolerant than more collectivist cultures of sharing information. In addition, Hispanics/Latinos and women are the most concerned about information privacy.

Information security can be classified into technical, management, and institutional dimensions. Whereas the technical dimension often gets the most attention, the management and institutional dimensions also have a substantial influence on information security in public sector organizations. For example, top management support is critical for the enhancement of information security in government. In addition, an institutional culture that supports information security is vital for information security development. Some emerging issues in information security are cybercrime and cybersecurity, and both are growing threats to governments.

Discussion Questions

1. If you were going to recommend an information security plan for a government agency, what are the key components that should be included in this plan?
2. What role does management have on enhancing information security in government?
3. Employees are often one of the greatest challenges for enhancing information security in government. What can public organizations do to increase employee awareness of information security?

Closing Case Study

IT Security Incidents in Nashville, Tennessee

In late 2007 more than 320,000 Nashville voters' personal information was breached. This was a turning point in which the incorporated Metropolitan Government of Nashville and Davidson County had to now define an IT security policy (Wilkinson, 2010). A laptop was stolen from the Davidson County Election Commission office along with other electronic equipment. There was no evidence that voters' Social Security numbers and other information was breached, but the laptop was not encrypted so the government assumed the worst case.

This was a defining moment for the municipal government because it got a lot of media attention. This incident changed many IT security policies in the municipal government, with Mayor Karl Dean setting into motion a series of executive orders that established oversight boards and training programs in the hopes of trying to prevent a security breach in the future. A comprehensive security policy was implemented, and a chief information security officer was to be hired to lead the efforts on information security. Information security training programs were also mandated under an executive order. A good information security policy, according to this municipal government, was to work to ensure the information security policy was clear and understandable to the average person in the organization. This was especially important because most information security breaches are caused internally by employees and lack of awareness of the proper policy.

The National Association of State Chief Information Officers report identified malicious employees as the number one threat to a department's data and offered ways to deal with this issue (Collins, 2008). According to the report, their activity should be monitored and audited for abnormalities and dealt with quickly through severe consequences, including criminal charges. Departments should essentially pay attention to employees under stress. They might be going through a divorce or having financial difficulties. They may have been demoted or fired and may be disgruntled. For example, employers should watch overtime use; if employees are being overworked, this can pose difficulties for information security. People too involved in their work can become overly possessive, as if they were working with personal property rather than government property. Background checks are also important to find those employees with a track record and not hiring them in the first place.

References

Allen, B.A., Juillet, L., Paquet, G., & Roy, J. (2001). E-governance and government on-line in Canada: Partnerships, people and prospects. *Government Information Quarterly*, 18, 93–104.

Alvarez, R.M., & Hall, T.E. (2004). *Point, click, and vote: The future of Internet voting*. Washington, DC: Brookings Institution Press.

Andersen, D.F., Belardo, S., & Dawes, S.S. (1994). Strategic information management: Conceptual frameworks for the public sector. *Public Productivity & Management Review*, 17(4), 335–353.

Andersen, D.F., & Dawes, S.S. (1991). *Government information management: A primer and casebook*. Englewood Cliffs, NJ: Prentice Hall.

Andersen, K.V., & Henriksen, H.Z. (2006). E-government maturity models: Extension of the Layne and Lee model. *Government Information Quarterly*, 23, 236–248.

Anderson, K.V., Henriksen, H.Z., Secher, C., & Medaglia, R. (2007). Costs of e-participation: The management challenges. *Transforming Government: People, Process, and Policy*, 1(1), 29–43.

Anonymous. (2008). Georgia Consolidates Procurement. *Government Technology*. Retrieved December 1, 2010 from http://www.govtech.com/pcio/Georgia-Consolidates-Procurement.html

Anonymous. (2009). New York City Department of Homeless Services streamlines sheltering. *Government Technology*. Retrieved December 1, 2010 from http://www.govtech.com/e-government/ New-York-City-Department-of-Homeless.html

Anonymous. (2010). Army enlists bloggers to share their stories. *Federal Computer Week*. Retrieved December 1, 2010 from http://fcw.com/articles/2010/06/07/blog-brief-army-vampire-power. aspx?sc_lang=en

Anthopoulos, L.G., Siozosa, P., & Tsoukalas, I.A. (2007). Applying participatory design and collaboration in digital public services for discovering and re-designing e-government services. *Government Information Quarterly*, 24(2), 353–376.

Anttiroiko, A.V. (2003). Building strong e-democracy: The role of technology in developing democracy for the information age. *Communications of the ACM*, 46(9), 121–128.

Anttiroiko, A.V. (2010). Innovation in democratic e-governance: Benefitting from Web 2.0 applications in the public sector. *International Journal of Electronic Government Research*, 6(2), 18–36.

Bain, B., Beizer, D., Lipowicz, A., & Weigelt, M. (2010). Obama wants nearly $80B for IT projects. Retrieved from http://fcw.com/articles/2010/02/01/fiscal–2011-obama-budget-proposal.aspx.

Bajjaly, S.T. (1998). Strategic information systems planning in the public sector. *American Review of Public Administration*, 28(1), 75–85.

Baker, W.H., & Wallace, L. (2007). Is information security under control? Investigating quality in information security management. *IEEE Security and Privacy*, 5(1), 36–44.

Ball, K.S. (2001). The use of human resource information systems: A survey. *Personnel Review*, 30(6), 677–693.

Bannister, F. (2001). Dismantling the silos: Extracting new value from IT investments in public administration. *Information Systems Journal*, 11, 65–84.

Bauer, J.M., & van Eeten, M.J. (2009). Cybersecurity: Stakeholder incentives, externalities, and policy options. *Telecommunications Policy*, 33, 706–719.

Bekkers, V., & Homburg, V. (2007). The myths of e-government: Looking beyond the assumptions of a new and better government. *The Information Society*, 23, 373–382.

Beizer, D. (2008). Army creates virtual recruiting center. *Federal Computer Week*. Retrieved December 1, 2010 from http://fcw.com/articles/2008/12/12/army-creates-virtual-recruiting-center.aspx

Beizer, D. (2009). Record numbers use IRS' e-file in 2009. *Federal Computer Week*. Retrieved December 1, 2010 from http://fcw.com/forms/emailtoauthor.aspx?AuthorItem={89BCFB27-0F13-42E2-BB16-F76FEAEA2702}&ArticleItem={F97185EB-0CC1-4226-8C91-101226C1D431}> http://fcw.com/articles/2009/11/02/irs-efile.aspx

Belanger, F., & Carter, L. (2009). The impact of the digital divide on e-government use. *Communications of the ACM*, 52(4), 132–135.

Belanger, F., & Hiller, J.S. (2006). A framework for e-government: Privacy implications. *Business Process Management*, 12(1), 48–60.

Berman, B.J., & Tettey, W.J. (2001). African states, bureaucratic culture and computer fixes. *Public Administration and Development*, 21(1), 1–13.

Bertot, J.C., Jaeger, P.T., & Grimes, J.M. (2010). Crowd-sourcing transparency: ICTs, social media, and government transparency initiatives. Retrieved from http://www.dgo2010.org/index.php?option=com_content&view=article&id=24&Itemid=36&lang=en

Biehl, M. (2007). Success factors for implementing global information systems. *Communications of the ACM*, 50(1), 53–58.

Bimber, B. (2001). Information and political engagement in America: The search for effects of information technology at the individual level. *Political Research Quarterly*, 54(1), 53–67.

Bimber, B. (2003). *Information and American democracy: Technology in the evolution of political power*. Cambridge, UK: Cambridge University Press.

Bimber, B., & Davis, R. (2003). *Campaigning online: The Internet in U.S. elections*. New York: Oxford University Press.

Bloomfield, B.P., & Coombs, R. (1992). Information technology, control and power: The centralization and decentralization debate revisited. *Journal of Management Studies*, 29(4), 459–484.

Bolivar, M.P., Perez, C.C., & Hernandez, A.M. (2006). Cultural contexts and government digital reporting. *International Review of Administrative Sciences*, 72, 269–290.

Bolivar, M.P., Perez, C.C., & Hernandez, A.M. (2007). E-government and public financial reporting: The case of Spanish regional governments. *American Review of Public Administration*, 37(2), 142–177.

Bovens, M., & Zouridis, S. (2002). From street-level to system-level bureaucracies: How information and communication technology is transforming administrative discretion and constitutional control. *Public Administration Review*, 62(2), 174–184.

Boyne, G.A. (2002). Public and private management: What's the difference? *Journal of Management Studies*, 39(1), 97–122.

Boynton, A.C., Zmud, R.W., & Jacobs, G.C. (1994). The influence of IT management practice on IT use in large organizations. *MIS Quarterly*, 18(3), 299–318.

Bozeman, B., & Bretschneider, S. (1986). Public management information systems: Theory and prescription. *Public Administration Review*, 46, 475–487.

Bozeman, B., & Kingsley, G. (1998). Risk culture in public and private organizations. *Public Administration Review*, 58(2), 109–118.

Bretschneider, S. (1990). Management information systems in public and private organizations: An empirical test. *Public Administration Review*, 50(5), 536–545.

Brown, M.M. (2007). Understanding e-government benefits: An examination of leading-edge local governments. *American Review of Public Administration*, 37(2), 178–197.

Brown, M.M., & Brudney, J.L. (1998). Public sector information technology initiatives: Implications for programs of public administration. *Administration and Society*, 30(4), 421–442.

Brown, R., & Potoski, M. (2006). Contracting for management: Assessing management capacity under alternative service delivery arrangements. *Journal of Policy Analysis and Management*, 25(2), 323–346.

Brown, T.L., Potoski, M., & Van Slyke, D.M. (2006). Managing public service contracts: Aligning values, institutions, and markets. *Public Administration Review*, 66(3), 323–331.

Brudney, J.L., & Selden, S.C. (1995). The adoption of innovation by smaller local governments: The case of computer technology. *American Review of Public Administration*, 25(1), 71–86.

Bruno, G., Esposito, E., Mastioianni, M., & Velluntino, D. (2005). Analysis of public e-procurement web site accessibility. *Journal of Public Procurement*, 5(3), 344–366.

Buehler, M. (2000). U.S. federal government CIOs: Information technology's new managers—preliminary findings. *Journal of Government Information*, 27, 29–45.

Carter, L., & Belanger, F. (2005). The utilization of e-government services: Citizen trust, innovation and acceptance factors. *Information Systems Journal*, 15, 5–25.

Cats-Baril, W., & Thompson, R. (1995). Managing information technology projects in the public sector. *Public Administration Review*, 55(6), 559–566.

Chadwick, A. (2006). *Internet politics: States, citizens, and new communication technologies*. New York: Oxford University Press.

Chadwick, A., & May, C. (2003). Interaction between states and citizens in the Age of the Internet: "e-government" in the United States, Britain, and the European Union. *Governance: An International Journal of Policy, Administration, and Institutions*, 16(2), 271–300.

Chang, S.E., & Lin, C.S. (2007). Exploring organizational culture for information security management. *Industrial Management and Data*, 107(3), 438–458.

Chen, Y.-C., & Hsieh, J.-Y. (2009). Advancing e-governance: Comparing Taiwan and the United States. *Public Administration Review*, 69(Suppl 1), S151–S158.

Chen, Y.-C., & Perry, J., (2003). Outsourcing for e-government: Managing for success. *Public Performance & Management Review*, 26(4), 404–421.

Chief Information Officers Council. (1999). Federal enterprise architecture framework. Version 1.1. Retrieved from http://www.cio.gov/documents/fedarch1.pdf

Cho, H., Rivera-Sanchez, M., & Lim, S.S. (2009). A multinational study on online privacy: Global concerns and local responses. *New Media Society*, 11(3), 395–416.

Chun, S.A., Shulman, S., Sandoval, R., & Hovy, E. (2010). Government 2.0: Making connections between citizens, data and government. *Information Polity*, 15, 1–19.

Coglianese, C. (2007). Weak democracy, strong information: The role of information technology in the rulemaking process. In V. Mayer-Schonberger & D. Lazer (Eds.), *Governance and information technology: From electronic government to information government* (pp. 101–122). Cambridge, MA: MIT Press.

Coleman, S., & Wright, S. (2008). Political blogs and representative democracy. *Information Polity*, 13, 1–5.

Collins, H. (2008). Network security: San Francisco incident raises questions for CIOs. Government technology. Retrieved from http://www.govtech.com/pcio/Network-Security-San-Francisco-Incident-Raises.html

Coursey, D., & Norris, D.F. (2008). Models of e-government: Are they correct? An empirical assessment. *Public Administration Review*, 68(3), 523–536.

Coursey, D.H., & McCreary, S.M. (2004). Using technology in the workplace. In S.E. Condrey (Ed.), *Handbook of human resource management in government* (pp. 189–214). San Francisco: Jossey-Bass.

Croom, S. (2001). Restructuring supply chains through information channel innovations. *International Journal of Operations & Production Management*, 21(4), 504–515.

Croom, S., & Brandon-Jones, A. (2007). Impact of e-procurement: Experiences from implementation in the UK public sector. *Journal of Purchasing and Supply Management*, 13, 294–303.

Croom, S.R., & Brandon-Jones, A. (2005). Key issues in e-procurement: Procurement implementation and operation in the public sector. *Journal of Public Procurement*, 5(3), 367–387.

Cullen, R. (2009). Culture, identity and information privacy in the age of digital government. *Online Information Review*, 33(3), 405–421.

Currie, W.L. (1996). Organizational structure and the use of information technology: Preliminary findings of a survey in the private and public sector. *International Journal of Information Management*, 16(1), 51–64.

D'Arcy, J., & Hovav, A. (2007). Deterring internal information systems misuse. *Communications of the ACM*, 50(10), 113–117.

Daconta, M. (2010). 10 flaws with the data on data.gov. *Government Computer News*. Retrieved from http://gcn.com/articles/2010/03/15/reality-check–10-data-gov-shortcomings.aspx

Danziger, J.N., & Anderson, K.V. (2002). The impacts of information technology on public administration: An analysis of empirical research from the "golden age" of transformation. *International Journal of Public Administration*, 25(5), 591–627.

Danziger, J.N., Dutton, W.H., Kling, R., & Kraemer, K.L. (1982). *Computers and politics: High technology in American local governments*. New York: Columbia University Press.

Davis, R., Baumgartner, J.C., Francia, P.L., & Morris, J.S. (2009). The Internet in U.S. election campaigns. In A. Chadwick & P.N. Howard (Eds.), *Routledge handbook of Internet politics* (pp. 13–24). New York: Routledge.

Dawes, S.S. (2008). The evolution and continuing challenges of e-governance. *Public Administration Review*, 68(6), S86–S102.

Dawes, S.S. (2009). Governance in the digital age: A research and action framework for an uncertain future. *Government Information Quarterly*, 26, 257–264.

Dawes, S.S. (2010). Stewardship and usefulness: Policy principles for information-based transparency. *Government Information Quarterly*, 27, 377–383.

DeLone, W.H., & McLean, E.R. (1992). Information systems success: The quest for the dependent variable. *Information Systems Research*, 3(1), 60–95.

DeLone, W.H., & McLean, E.R. (2003). The DeLone and McLean model of information systems success: A ten-year update. *Journal of Management Information Systems*, 19(4), 9–10.

Denhardt, R.B., & Denhardt, J.V. (2000). The new public service: Serving rather than steering. *Public Administration Review*, 60(6), 549–559.

Dewett, T., & Jones, G.R. (2001). The role of information technology in the organization: A review, model, and assessment. *Journal of Management*, 27, 313–346.

Dooley, K., & Purchase, S. (2006). Factors influencing e-procurement usage. *Journal of Public Procurement*, 6(1), 28–45.

Dufner, D., Holley, L.M., & Reed, B.J. (2002). Can private sector strategic information systems planning techniques work for the public sector? *Communications of the Association for Information Systems*, 8, 413–431.

Dunleavy, P., Margetts, H., Bastow, S., & Tinkler, J. (2005). New public management is dead—long live digital-era governance. *Journal of Public Administration Research and Theory*, 16(3), 467–494.

Dzazali, S., Sulaiman, A., & Zolait, A.H. (2009). Information security landscape and maturity level: Case study of Malaysian Public Service (MPS) organizations. *Government Information Quarterly*, 26, 584–593.

Ebrahim, Z., & Irani, Z. (2005). E-government and adoption: Architecture and barriers. *Business Process Management Journal*, 11(5), 589–611.

Edmiston, K.D. (2003). State and local e-government: Prospects and challenges. *American Review of Public Administration*, 33(1), 20–45.

Essig, M., & Arnold, U. (2001). Electronic Procurement in Supply Chain Management: An Information Economics-Based Analysis of Electronic Markets. *The Journal of Supply Chain Management*, 37(4), 43–49.

Fjermestad, J., & Romano, N.C. (2003). Electronic customer relationship management: Revisiting the general principles of usability and resistance—An integrative implementation framework. *Business Process Management Journal*, 9(5), 572–591.

Fleming, C. (2008). 311/CRM in-depth case studies. In C. Fleming (Ed.), *Customer service and 311/CRM technology in local governments: Lessons on connecting with citizens*. Washington, DC: International City/County Management Association. Retrieved from http://bookstore. icma.org/Customer_Service_and_311_CRM_T_P1881C141.cfm

Florkowski, G.W., & Olivars-Lujan, M.R. (2006). The diffusion of human-resource information-technology innovations in US and non-US firms. *Personnel Review*, 35(6), 684–710.

Floropoulos, J., Spathis, C., Halvatzis, D., & Tsipouridou, M. (2010). Measuring the success of the Greek Taxation Information System. *International Journal of Information Management*, 30(1), 47–56.

Foltz, C.B. (2004). Cyberterrorism, computer crime, and reality. *Information Management and Computer Security*, 12(2), 154–166.

Fountain, J., & Osorio-Urzua, C. (2001). Public sector: Early stage of a deep transformation. In R.E. Litan & A.M. Rivlin (Eds.), *The economic payoff from the Internet revolution* (pp. 235–268). Washington, DC: The Brookings Institution.

Fountain, J.E. (2001). *Building the virtual state: Information technology and institutional change.* Washington, DC: Brookings Institution Press.

Fountain, J.E. (2009). Bureaucratic reform and e-government in the United States: An institutional perspective. In A. Chadwick & P.N. Howard (Eds.), *Routledge handbook of Internet politics* (pp. 99–113). New York: Routledge.

Funilkul, S., & Chutimaskul, W. (2009). The framework for sustainable eDemocracy development. *Transforming Government: People, Process and Policy*, 3(1), 16–31.

Gardner, S.D., Lepak, D.P., & Bartol, K.M. (2003). Virtual HR: The impact of information technology on the human resource professional. *Journal of Vocational Behavior*, 63, 159–179.

Garson, G.D. (2007). *Modern public information technology systems: Issues and challenges*. Hershey, PA: IGI Publishing.

Gichoya, D. (2005). Factors affecting the successful implementation of ICT projects in government. *Electronic Journal of e-Government*, 3(4), 175–184.

Gil-García, J.R., & Pardo, T.A. (2005). E-government success factors: Mapping practical tools to theoretical foundations. *Government Information Quarterly*, 22(2), 187–216.

Globerman, S., & Vining, A.R. (1996). A framework for evaluating the government contracting-out decision with an application to information technology. *Public Administration Review*, 56(6), 577–586.

Goldfinch, S. (2007). Pessimism, computer failure, and information systems development in the public sector. *Public Administration Review*, 67(5), 917–929.

Grant, D., Hall, R., Wailes, N., & Wright, C. (2006). The false promise of technological determinism: The case of enterprise resource planning systems. *New Technology, Work and Employment*, 21(1), 2–15.

Grant, G., & Chau, D. (2005). Developing a generic framework for e-government. *Journal of Global Information Management*, 13(1), 1–10.

Greengard, S. (2009). The first Internet president. *Communications of the ACM*, 52(2), 16–18.

Grego, S., Hart, D., & Martin, N. (2007). Enterprise architectures: Enablers of business strategy and IS/IT alignment in government. *Information Technology and People*, 20(2), 96–120.

Guijarro, L. (2007). Interoperability frameworks and enterprise architectures in e-government initiatives in Europe and the United States. *Government Information Quarterly*, 24, 89–101.

Guillen, M.F., & Suarez, S.L. (2005). Explaining the global digital divide: Economic, political, and sociological drivers of cross-national Internet use. *Social Forces*, 84(2), 681–708.

Gupta, M.P., & Jana, D. (2003). E-government evaluation: A framework and case study. *Government Information Quarterly*, 20, 365–387.

Hackler, D., & Saxton, G.D. (2007). The strategic use of information technology by nonprofit organizations: Increasing capacity and untapped potential. *Public Administration Review*, 67(3), 474–487.

Haines, V.Y., & Lafleur, G. (2008). Information technology usage and human resource roles and effectiveness. *Human Resource Management*, 47(3), 525–540.

Hanson, W. (2010). Charles County, Md., wins digital counties award eight years running. Retrieved from http://www.digitalcommunities.com/articles/Charles-County-Md-Wins-Digital-Counties-Award-Eight-Years-Running.html

Haque, A. (2001). GIS, public service, and the issue of democratic governance. *Public Administration Review*, 61(3), 259–265.

Haque, A. (2003). Information technology, GIS and democratic values: Ethical implications for IT professionals in public service. *Ethics and Information Technology*, 5, 39–48.

Harris, B. (2004). Strategic sourcing. Retrieved from http://www.govtech.com/e-government/Strategic-Sourcing.html

Haugen, S. (2005). E-government, cyber-crime and cyber-terrorism: A population at risk. *Electronic Government*, 2(4), 403–412.

Heeks, R. (2002a). Information systems and developing countries: Failure, success, and local improvisations. *The Information Society*, 18, 101–112.

Heeks, R. (2002b). E-government in Africa: Promise and practice. *Information Polity*, 7, 97–114.

Heeks, R. (2003). Most e-government-for-development projects fail: How can risks be reduced? Retrieved from http://unpan1.un.org/intradoc/groups/public/documents/NISPAcee/UNPAN015488.pdf

Heintze, T., & Bretschneider, S. (2000). Information technology and restructuring in public organizations: Does adoption of information technology affect organizational structures, communications, and decision making? *Journal of Public Administration Research and Theory*, 10(4), 801–830.

Helbig, N., Gil-Garcia, J.R., & Ferro, E. (2009). Understanding the complexity of electronic government: Implications from the digital divide literature. *Government Information Quarterly*, 26, 89–97.

Henry, N. (2007). *Public administration and public affairs* (10th ed.). Upper Saddle River, NJ: Pearson Prentice Hall.

Herrnson, P.S., Niemi, R.G., Hanmer, M.J., Francia, P.L., Bederson, B.B., Conrad, F.G., & Traugott, M.W. (2008). Voters' evaluations of electronic voting systems: Results from a usability field study. *American Politics Research*, 36(4), 580–611.

Herrnson, P.S., Stokes-Brown, A.K., & Hindman, M. (2007). Campaign politics and the digital divide: Constituency characteristics, strategic considerations, and candidate Internet use in state legislative elections. *Political Research Quarterly*, 60(1), 31–42.

Hiller, J., & Belanger, F. (2001). Privacy strategies for electronic government. In M.A. Abramson & G.E. Means (Eds.), *EGovernment 2001* (pp. 162–198). Oxford, UK: Rowman & Littlefield.

Hjort-Madsen, K. (2007). Institutional patterns of enterprise architecture adoption in government. *Transforming Government: People, Process and Policy*, 1(4), 333–349.

Ho, A.T. (2002). Reinventing local governments and the e-government initiative. *Public Administration Review*, 62(4), 434–444.

Ho, A.T., & Ni, A.Y. (2004). Explaining the adoption of e-government features: A case study of Iowa county treasurers' offices. *American Review of Public Administration*, 34(2), 164–180.

Ho, A.T., & Smith, J.F. (2001). Information technology planning and the Y2K problem in local governments. *American Review of Public Administration*, 31(2), 158–180.

Holden, S.H., & Millett, L.I. (2005). Authentication, privacy, and the federal e-government. *The Information Society*, 21, 367–377.

Holleyman, R. (2010). Private sector lessons in modernizing government. Retrieved from http://gcn.com/articles/2010/01/22/private-sector-lessons-in-modernizing-government.aspx

Homburg, V. (2004). E-government and NPM: A perfect marriage? Retrieved from http://portal.acm.org/citation.cfm?id=1052289

Hood, C., & Peters, G. (2004). The middle aging of new public management: Into the age of paradox? *Journal of Public Administration Research & Theory*, 14(3), 267–282.

Howard, P.N. (2005). Deep democracy, thin citizenship: The impact of digital media in political campaign strategy. *Annals of the American Academy of Political and Social Science*, 597, 153–170.

Hughes, J. (2010). GIS-based interoperability system alters how Virginia Manages Emergencies. Retrieved from http://www.emergencymgmt.com/disaster/Virginia-Interoperability-Picture-Emergency-Response.html

Ingraham, P.W., Joyce, P.G., & Donahue, A.K. (2003). *Government performance: Why management matters*. Baltimore: John Hopkins University Press.

Jackson, J. (2009a). CIO council set up data.gov in two months, and third parties are putting the data to use. Retrieved from http://gcn.com/articles/2009/10/12/gcn-awards-datagov.aspx

Jackson, J. (2009b). Can government keep pace with Kundra? *Government Computer News:* The online authority for government IT professionals, Retrieved from http://gcn.com/Articles/2009/03/05/Kundra-federal-CIO.aspx

Jackson, W. (2010). SSA turns to online apps to keep up with boomer claims. Retrieved from http://gcn.com/articles/2010/04/16/ssa-boomer-service.aspx?sc_lang=en

Jaeger, P.T. (2005). Deliberative democracy and the conceptual foundations of electronic government. *Government Information Quarterly*, 22(4), 702–719.

Jaeger, P.T., & Bertot, J.C. (2010). Transparency and technological change: Ensuring equal and sustained public access to government information. *Government Information Quarterly*, 27, 371–376.

Jennings, M.K., & Zeitner, V. (2003). Internet use and civic engagement: A longitudinal analysis. *Public Opinion Quarterly*, 67(3), 311–334.

Jensen, M.J., Danziger, J.N., & Venkatesh, A. (2007). Civil society and cyber society: The role of the Internet in community associations and democratic politics. *The Information Society*, 23, 39–50.

Jones, J.M. (2009). In U.S. trust in state government sinks to new low. Retrieved from http://www.gallup.com/poll/122915/trust-state-government-sinks-new-low.aspx

Joseph, R.C., & Kitlan, D.P. (2008). Key issues in e-government and public administration. In G.D. Garson & M. Khosrow-Pour (Eds.), *Handbook of research on public information technology* (pp. 1–11). Hershey, PA: Information Science Reference.

Justice, J.B., Melitski, J., & Smith, D.L. (2006). E-government as an instrument of fiscal accountability and responsiveness: Do the best practitioners employ the best practices? *American Review of Public Administration*, 36(3), 301–322.

Kakabadse, A., Kakabadse, N.K., & Kouzmin, A. (2003). Reinventing the democratic governance project through information technology? A growing agenda for debate. *Public Administration Review*, 63(1), 44–60.

Kamal, M.M. (2009). An analysis of e-participation research: Moving from theoretical to pragmatic viewpoint. *Transforming Government: People, Process, and Policy*, 3(4), 340–354.

Kankanhalli, A., Teo, H.H., Tan, B.C.Y., & Wei, K.K. (2003). An integrative study of information systems security effectiveness. *International Journal of Information Management*, 23, 139–154.

Kannabiram, G., Xavier, M.J., & Anantharaaj, A. (2004). Enabling e-governance through citizen relationship management—concept, model and applications. *Journal of Services Research*, 4(2), 223–240.

Kenyon, H. (2010). Google apps government reach grows. Retrieved from http://fcw.com/articles/2010/09/13/google-apps-grows-fed-business.aspx

Kim, S. (2005). Factors affecting state government information technology employee turnover intentions. *American Review of Public Administration*, 35, 137–156.

Kim, S., & Wright, B.E. (2007). IT employee work exhaustion: Toward an integrated model of antecedents and consequences. *Review of Public Personnel Administration*, 27(2), 147–170.

King, S.F. (2007). Citizens as customers: Exploring the future of CRM in UK local government. *Government Information Quarterly*, 24, 47–63.

Knapp, K.J., Marshall, T.E., Rainer, R.K., & Ford, F.N. (2006). Information security: Management's effect on culture and policy. *Information Management and Computer Security*, 14(1), 24–36.

Kolsaker, A., & Lee-Kelly, L. (2008). Citizens' attitudes towards e-government and e-governance: A UK study. *International Journal of Public Sector Management*, 21(7), 723–738.

Kraemer, K., & King, J. (2008). Information technology and administrative reform. In D. Norris (Ed.), *E-government research: Policy and management* (pp. 1–20). Hershey, PA: IGI Publishing.

Kraemer, K., & King, J.L. (2006). Information technology and administrative reform: Will e-government be different? *International Journal of Electronic Government Research*, 2(1), 1–20.

Kraemer, K.L., & Dedrick, J. (1997). Computing and public organizations. *Journal of Public Administration Research and Theory*, 7(1), 89–112.

Kumar, V., Maheshwari, B., & Kumar, U. (2002). ERP systems implementation: Best practices in Canadian government organizations. *Government Information Quarterly*, 19, 147–172.

Lan, G.Z., Riley, L., & Cayer, N.J. (2005). How can local government become an employer of choice for technical professionals? Lessons and experiences from the City of Phoenix. *Review of Public Personnel Administration*, 25(3), 225–242.

Landsbergen, D., & Wolken, G. (2001). Realizing the promise: Government information systems and the fourth generation of information technology. *Public Administration Review*, 61(2), 206–220.

Laswad, F., Fisher, R., & Oyelere, P. (2005). Determinants of voluntary Internet financial reporting by local government authorities. *Journal of Accounting and Public Policy*, 24, 101–121.

Laudon, K.C., & Laudon, J.P. (2009). *Essentials of management information systems* (8th ed.). Upper Saddle River, NJ: Pearson Prentice Hall.

Layne, K., & Lee, J. (2001). Developing fully functional e-government: A four stage model. *Government Information Quarterly*, 18, 122–136.

Lean, O.K., Zailani, S., Ramayah, T., & Fernando, Y. (2009). Factors influencing intention to use e-government services among citizens in Malaysia. *International Journal of Information Management*, 29(6), 458–475.

Lee, G., & Perry, J.L. (2002). Are computers boosting productivity? A test of the paradox in state governments. *Journal of Public Administration Research and Theory*, 12(1), 77–102.

Lepak, D.P., & Snell, S.A. (1998). Virtual HR: Strategic human resource management in the 21st century. *Human Resource Management Review*, 8(3), 215–234.

Lim, E., Wee, C., & Pan, S.-L. (2007). E-government implementation: Balancing collaboration and control in stakeholder management. *International Journal of Electronic Government Research*, 3(2), 1–28.

Lim, J.H., & Tang, S.Y. (2008). Urban e-government initiatives and environmental decision performance in Korea. *Journal of Public Administration Research and Theory*, 18(1), 109–138.

Lim, S.S., Cho, H., & Sanchez, M.R. (2009). Online privacy, government surveillance and national ID cards. *Communications of the ACM*, 52(12), 116–120.

Lipowicz, A. (2009). Gov 2.0: Transparency without accessibility? Retrieved from http://fcw.com/articles/2009/11/16/pol-accessibility.aspx

Lipowicz, A. (2010). Agencies told to avoid links to political sites. Retrieved from http://fcw.com/articles/2010/08/24/federal-agencies-told-to-avoid-social-media-links-to-political-sites.aspx

Liptrott, M. (2007). e-Voting: Same pilots, same problems, different agendas. *Electronic Journal of E-Government*, 5(2), 205–212.

Loukis, E., & Spinellis, D. (2001). Information systems security in the Greek public sector. *Information Management and Computer Security*, 9(1), 21–31.

Macintosh, A. (2003). Promise and problems of e-democracy: Challenges of online citizen engagement. Retrieved June 1, 2010 from http://www.oecd.org/dataoecd/9/11/35176328.pdf

Macintosh, A. (2004). Characterizing e-participation in policy-making. Proceedings of the 37th Hawaii International Conference on System Sciences, 5, 1–10. Hilton Waikoloa Village Island of Hawaii, January 5–8, 2004.

Macintosh, A. (2008). E-democracy and e-participation research in Europe. In H. Chen, L. Brandt, V. Gregg, R. Traunmuller, S. Dawes, E. Hovy, A. Macintosh, & C.A. Larson (Eds.), *Digital government: E-government research, case studies, and implementation* (pp. 85–102). New York: Springer.

Macintosh, A., & Whyte, A. (2008). Towards an evaluation framework for eParticipation. *Transforming Government: People, Process and Policy*, 2(1), 16–10.

MacManus, S.A. (2002). Understanding the incremental nature of e-procurement implementation at the state and local levels. *Journal of Public Procurement*, 2(1), 5–28.

Marshall, J. (2009). The new administration's shared services opportunity. *Public Manager*, 38(2), 37–44.

Martin, S.P., & Robinson, J.P. (2007). The income digital divide: Threads and predictions for levels of Internet use. *Social Problems*, 54(1), 1–22.

Mastracci, S.H. (2009). Evaluating HR management strategies for recruiting and retaining IT professionals in the U.S. federal government. *Public Personnel Management*, 38(2), 19–34.

McCaney, K. (2010a). In Palo Alto, Bling is the thing for electronic payments. Retrieved from http://gcn.com/articles/2010/09/20/bling-payments-palo-alto-calif.aspx

McCaney, K. (2010b). The evidence speaks in favor of telework. Retrieved from http://gcn.com/articles/2010/11/01/editorial-telework-payoff.aspx

McClure, D., & Dorris, M. (2010). The Obama technology agenda: Open, transparent, and collaborative. Retrieved from http://www.thepublicmanager.org/pdf/TPM%20Forum%20Winter%202010.pdf

McDermott, P. (2010). Building open government. *Government Information Quarterly*, 27, 401–413.

McNeal, R.S., Tolbert, C.J., Mossberger, K., & Dotterweich, L.J. (2003). Innovating in digital government in the American states. *Social Science Quarterly*, 84(1), 52–70.

Medaglia, R. (2007). Measuring the diffusion of eParticipation: A survey on Italian local government. *Information Polity*, 12, 265–280.

Meijer, A., & Thaens, M. (2010). Aligning 2.0: Strategic use of new Internet technologies in government. *Government Information Quarterly*, 27, 113–121.

Milward, H.B., & Snyder, L.O. (1996). Electronic government: Linking citizens to public organizations through technology. *Journal of Public Administration Research and Theory*, 6(2), 261–275.

Miranda, R.A., & Kavanagh, S.C. (2005). Achieving government transformation through ERP systems. *Government Finance Review*, 21(3), 36–42.

Monroe, J. S. (2010). 4 reasons why managers resist telework—and why they might be wrong. *Federal Computer Week*. Retrieved December 1, 2010 from http://fcw.com/articles/2010/09/13/feat-telework-managers-objections.aspx

Montjoy, R.S. (2008). The public administration of elections. *Public Administration Review*, 68(5), 788–799.

Moon, J., Sawr, B., Choe, Y.C., Chung, M., & Jung, G.H. (2010). Innovation in IT outsourcing relationships: Where is the best practice of IT outsourcing in the public sector? *Innovation: Management, Policy & Practice*, 12(2), 217–226.

Moon, M.J. (2002). The evolution of e-government among municipalities: Rhetoric or reality? *Public Administration Review*, 62(4), 424–433.

Moon, M.J. (2003). State government e-procurement in the information age: Issues, practices, and trends. In M.A. Abramson & R.S. Harris III (Eds.), *The procurement revolution*. Oxford, UK: Rowman & Littlefield.

Moon, M.J. (2005). E-procurement management in state governments: Diffusion of e-procurement practices and its determinants. *Journal of Public Procurement*, 5(1), 54–72.

Moon, M.J., & Bretschneider, S. (2002). Does the perception of red tape constrain IT innovativeness in organizations? Unexpected results from a simultaneous equation model and implications. *Journal of Public Administration Research and Theory*, 12(2), 273–291.

Moon, M.J., & Norris, D.F. (2005). Does managerial orientation matter? The adoption of reinventing government and e-government at the municipal level. *Information Systems Journal*, 15, 43–60.

Moore, J. (2007). E-procurement pays its own way. Retrieved from http://fcw.com/articles/2007/04/02/eprocurement-pays-its-own-way.aspx

Morgeson, F., & Mithas, S. (2009). Does e-government measure up to e-business? Comparing end user perceptions of U.S. federal government and e-business websites. *Public Administration Review*, 69(4), 740–752.

Mosquera, M. (2008). IRS seeks ideas to boost e-filing. Retrieved from http://fcw.com/articles/2008/05/08/irs-seeks-ideas-to-boost-efiling.aspx

Mosquera, M. (2009). Kundra era signals digital shift for government. Retrieved from http://fcw.com/articles/2009/03/09/kundra-profile.aspx?s=fcwdaily_100309

Moynihan, D.P. (2004). Building secure elections: E-voting, security, and systems theory. *Public Administration Review*, 64(5), 515–528.

Mullen, P.R. (2005). US performance-based laws: Information technology and e-government reporting requirements. *International Journal of Public Administration*, 28, 581–598.

Musso, J., Weare, C., & Hale, M. (2000). Designing web technologies for local governance reform: Good management or good democracy? *Political Communication*, 17, 1–19.

National Association of State Chief Information Officers (NASCIO). (2010). Friends, followers, and feeds: A national survey of social media use in state government. Retrieved from http://www.nascio.org/publications/documents/NASCIO-SocialMedia.pdf

Newcombe, T. (2009a). New York City integrates social services to better serve citizens. Retrieved from http://www.govtech.com/pcio/New-York-City-Integrates-Social-Services.html

Newcombe, T. (2009b). Public CIO's role shifting to leader. Retrieved from http://www.govtech.com/pcio/Public-CIOs-Role-Shifting-to-Leader.html

Newcomer, K.E., & Caudle, S.L. (1991). Evaluating public sector information systems: More than meets the eye. *Public Administration Review*, 51(5), 377–384.

Ngai, E.W., & Wat, F.K. (2006). Human resource information systems: A review and empirical analysis. *Personnel Review*, 35(3), 297–314.

Ni, A.Y., & Bretschneider, S. (2007). The decision to contract out: A study of contracting for e-government services in state governments. *Public Administration Review*, 67(3), 531–544.

Nichols, R. (2010a). Portland launches annual apps competition. Retrieved from http://www.digitalcommunities.com/articles/Portland-Launches-Annual-Apps-Competition.html

Nichols, R. (2010b). Biometric devices help New Jersey county track delivery of homeless services. Retrieved from http://www.govtech.com/health/Biometric-Devices-Delivery-Homeless-Services.html

Noce, A.A., & McKeown, L. (2008). A new benchmark for Internet use: A logistic modeling of factors influencing Internet use in Canada, 2005. *Government Information Quarterly*, 25, 462–476.

Norris, D. (2008). *E-government research: Policy and management*. Hershey, PA: IGI Publishing.

Norris, D.F. (2007). Electronic democracy at the American grassroots. In D. F. Norris (Ed.), *Current issues and trends in e-government research*. Hershey, PA: CyberTech Publishing.

Norris, D.F., & Kraemer, K.L. (1996). Mainframe and PC computing in American cities: Myths and realities. *Public Administration Review*, 56(6), 568–576.

Norris, D.F., & Moon, M.J. (2005). Advancing e-government at the grassroots: Tortoise or hare? *Public Administration Review*, 65(1), 64–75.

Norris, P. (2001). *Digital divide: Civic engagement, information poverty, and the Internet worldwide.* Cambridge, UK: Cambridge University Press.

O'Neil, D. (2001). Analysis of Internet users' level of online privacy concerns. *Social Science Computer Review*, 29(1), 17–31.

Office of Management and Budget. (2009). Expanding e-government: Achieving results for the American people. Retrieved from http://www.whitehouse.gov/sites/default/files/omb/assets/egov_docs/2009_Expanding_E-Gov_Report.pdf

Opshal, A. (2010). Economy forces county IT departments to embrace practicality. Retrieved from http://www.govtech.com/e-government/Economy-Forces-County-IT-Departments-to.html

Organisation for Economic Co-Operation and Development (OECD). (2003). *Promise and problems of e-democracy: Challenges of online citizen engagement.* Paris: OECD Publications. Retrieved from http://www.oecd.org/dataoecd/9/11/35176328.pdf

Padhi, S.S., & Mohapatra, P.K. (2010). Adopting of e-procurement in the government departments. *Electronic Government, an International Journal*, 7(1), 41–59.

Pandey, S.K., & Bretschneider, S.I. (1997). The impact of red tape's administrative delay on public organizations' interest in new information technologies. *Journal of Public Administration Research and Theory*, 7(1), 113–130.

Parent, M., Vandebeek, C.A., & Gemino, A.C. (2005). Building citizen trust through e-government. *Government Information Quarterly*, 22, 720–736.

Pasek, J., More, E., & Romer, D. (2009). Realizing the social Internet? Online social networking meets offline civic engagement. *Journal of Information Technology and Politics*, 6, 197–215.

Pasmore, W.A. (1988). *Designing effective organizations: The sociotechnical systems perspective.* New York: John Wiley & Sons.

Peled, A. (2007). The electronic mountain: A tale of two tels. *American Review of Public Administration*, 37(4), 458–478.

Perez, C.C., Bolivar, M.P., & Hernandez, A.M. (2008). E-government process and incentives for online public and financial information. *Online Information Review*, 32(3), 379–400.

Perlman, E. (2009). Social media sites' handicap hurdle. Retrieved from http://www.governing.com/columns/tech-talk/Social-Media-Sites-Handicap.html

Perry, J.L., & Danziger, J.N. (1980). The adoptability of innovations: An empirical assessment of computer applications in local governments. *Administration and Society*, 11(4), 461–492.

Perry, J.L., & Rainey, H.G. (1988). The public-private distinction in organization theory: A critique and research strategy. *Academy of Management Review*, 13(2), 182–201.

Persson, A., & Goldkuhl, G. (2010). Government value paradigms—bureaucracy, new public management, and e-government. *Communications of the Association for Information Systems*, 27, 45–62.

Peters, B.G. (1996). *The future of governing: Four emerging models.* Lawrence, KS: University Press of Kansas.

Peterson, S.B. (1998). Saints, demons, wizards and systems: Why information technology reforms fail or underperform in public bureaucracies in Africa. *Public Administration and Development*, 18(1), 37–60.

Petter, S., DeLone, W., & McLean, E. (2008). Measuring information systems success: Models, dimensions, measures, and interrelationships. *European Journal of Information Systems*, 17, 236–263.

Phang, C.W., & Kankanhalli, A. (2008). A framework of ICT exploitation for e-participation initiatives. *Communications of the ACM*, 51(12), 128–132.

Pina, V., Torres, L., & Royo, S. (2010). Is e-government leading to more accountable and transparent local governments? An overall view. *Financial Accountability and Management*, 26(1), 3–20.

Piotrowski, S.J., & Van Ryzin, G.G. (2007). Citizen attitudes toward transparency in local government. *American Review of Public Administration*, 37(3), 306–323.

Pirog, M.A., & Johnson, C.L. (2008). Electronic funds and benefits transfers, e-government, and the winter commission. *Public Administration Review*, 68(Suppl 1), S103–S114.

Poister, T.H., & Streib, G. (2005). Elements of strategic planning and management in municipal government: Status after two decades. *Public Administration Review*, 65(1), 45–56.

Poister, T.H., & Streib, G.D., (1999). Strategic management in the public sector: Concepts, models, and processes. *Public Productivity & Management Review*, 22(3), 308–325.

Pole, A.J. (2005). E-mocracy: Information technology and the Vermont and New York state legislatures. *State and Local Government Review*, 37(1), 7–24.

Premkumar, G., Ho, A.T., & Chakraborty, P. (2006). E-government evolution: An evaluation of local online services. *International Journal of Electronic Business*, 4(2), 177–190.

Pynes, J. (2009). *Human resources management for public and nonprofit organizations: A strategic approach*. San Francisco: Jossey-Bass.

Rainey, H.G., & Bozeman, B. (2000). Comparing public and private organizations: Empirical research and the power of the a priori. *Journal of Public Administration Research and Theory*, 2, 447–469.

Rainey, H.G., & Steinbauer, P. (1999). Galloping elephants: Developing elements of a theory of effective government organizations. *Journal of Public Administration Research and Theory*, 9(1), 1–12.

Raymond, L., Uwizeyemungu, S., & Bergeron, F. (2006). Motivations to implement ERP in e-government: An analysis from success stories. *Electronic Government*, 3(3), 225–240.

Reddick, C.G. (2004a). A two-stage model of e-government growth: Theories and empirical evidence for U.S. cities. *Government Information Quarterly*, 21(1), 51–64.

Reddick, C.G. (2004b). The growth of e-procurement in American state governments: A model and empirical evidence. *Journal of Public Procurement*, 4(2), 151–176.

Reddick, C.G. (2004c). Public-sector e-commerce and state financial management. *Social Science Computer Review*, 22(3), 293–306.

Reddick, C.G. (2007a). Government e-procurement through the Internet. In A.V. Anttiroilo & M. Malkia (Eds.), *Encyclopedia of digital government* (Vol. 2, pp. 901–905). Hershey, PA: Idea Group Reference.

Reddick, C.G. (2007b). Public sector e-commerce. In A.V. Anttiroilo & M. Malkia (Eds.), *Encyclopedia of digital government* (Vol. 3, pp. 1383–1387). Hershey, PA: Idea Group Reference.

Reddick, C.G. (2008). Perceived effectiveness of e-government and its usage in city governments: Survey evidence from information technology directors. *International Journal of Electronic Government Research*, 4(4), 89–104.

Reddick, C.G. (2009a). Human resources information systems in Texas city governments: Scope and perception of its effectiveness. *Public Personnel Management*, 38(4), 19–34.

Reddick, C.G. (2009b). Management support and information security: An empirical study of Texas state agencies in the USA. *Electronic Government: An International Journal*, 6(4), 361–377.

Regan, P.M. (1986). Privacy, government information, and technology. *Public Administration Review*, 46(6), 629–634.

Reid, M.F., Riemenschneider, C.K., Allen, M.W., & Armstrong, D.J. (2008). Information technology employees in state government: A study of affective organizational commitment, job involvement, and job satisfaction. *American Review of Public Administration*, 38(1), 41–61.

Relly, J.E., & Sabharwal, M. (2009). Perceptions of transparency of government policymaking: A cross-national study. *Government Information Quarterly*, 26, 148–157.

Relyea, H.C. (2000). Paperwork Reduction Act reauthorization and government information management issues. *Government Information Quarterly*, 17(4), 367–393.

Ring, P.S., & Perry, J.L. (1985). Strategic management in public and private organizations: Implications of distinctive contexts and constraints. *Academy of Management Review*, 10(2), 276–286.

Rocheleau, B. (2006). *Public management information systems*. Hersey, PA: Idea Group Publishing.

Rocheleau, B., & Wu, L. (2002). Public versus private information systems: Do they differ in important ways? A review and empirical test. *American Review of Public Administration*, 32(4), 379–397.

Rogers, E.M. (2003). *Diffusion of innovations* (5th ed.). New York: Free Press.

Rohlinger, D.A., & Brown, J. (2009). Democracy, action, and the Internet after 9/11. *American Behavioral Scientist*, 53(1), 133–150.

Ruel, H.J., Bondarouk, T.V., & Van der Velde, M. (2007). The contribution of e-HRM to HRM effectiveness: Results from a quantitative study in a Dutch Ministry. *Employee Relations*, 29(3), 280–291.

Sarantis, D., Smithson, S., Charalabidis, Y., & Dimitris Askounis, D. (2010). A critical assessment of project management methods with respect to electronic government implementation challenges. *Systemic Practice and Action Research*, 23(4), 301–321.

Schellong, A. (2008a). Government 2.0: An exploratory study of social networking services in Japanese local government. *Transforming Government: People, Process, and Policy*, 2(4), 225–242.

Schellong, A. (2008b). *Citizen relationship management: A study of CRM in government*. Frankfurt am Main: Peter Lang Publishing Group.

Schellong, A., & Goethe, J.W. (2005). CRM in the public sector—towards a conceptual research framework. Retrieved from http://portal.acm.org/citation.cfm?id=1065226

Schlosberg, D., Zavestoski, S., & Shulman, S. (2009). Deliberation in e-rulemaking? The problem of mass participation. In T. Davies & S.P. Gangadharan (Eds.), *Online deliberation: Design, research and practice* (pp. 133–148). Stanford, CA: CSLI Publications.

Schwester, R.W., Carrizales, T., & Holzer, M. (2009). An examination of the municipal 311 system. *International Journal of Organization Theory and Behavior*, 12(2), 218–236.

Seddon, P.B. (1997). A respecification and extension of the Delone and McLean model of IS success. *Information Systems Research*, 8(3), 240–253.

Shane, P.M. (Ed.). (2004). *Democracy online: The prospects for political renewal through the Internet*. New York: Routledge.

Sharma, S.K. (2004). Assessing g-government implementations. *Electronic Government*, 1(2), 198–212.

Sherrod, D.R. (1971). Selective perception of political candidates. *Public Opinion Quarterly*, 35(4), 554–562.

Shulman, S.W. (2005). E-rulemaking: Issues in current research and practice. *International Journal of Public Administration*, 28(7/8), 621–641.

Singh, M., Davison, C., & Wickramasinghe, N. (2010). Organisational use of web 2.0 technologies: An Australian perspective. Retrieved http://aisel.aisnet.org/amcis2010/198/

Smith, A. (2009). The Internet's role in campaign 2008. Retrieved from http://www.pewinternet. org/Reports/2009/6--The-Internets-Role-in-Campaign–2008.aspx

Smith, A., Schlozman, K.L., Verba, S., & Brady, H. (2009). The Internet and civic engagement. Retrieved from http://www.pewinternet.org/Reports/2009/15--The-Internet-and-Civic-Engagement.aspx

Smith, A.D., & Clark, J.S. (2005). Revolutionising the voting process through online strategies. *Online Information Review*, 29(5), 513–530.

Smith, B. (2005). Privacy online: How Americans feel...the ways they are responding to new threats...and why they are changing their online behavior? Retrieved from http://www .pewinternet.org/Presentations/2005/Privacy-Online-A-status-report.aspx

Smith, M.R., & Marx, L. (Eds.). (1994). *Does technology drive history? The dilemma of technological determinism*. Cambridge, MA: The MIT Press.

Snell, S.A., Stueber, D., & Lepak, D.P. (2002). Virtual HR departments: Getting out of the middle. In R.L. Heneman & D.G. Greenberger (Eds.), *Human resources management in virtual organizations*. Greenwich, CT: Information Age Publishing.

Snellen, I. (2002). Electronic governance: Implications for citizens, politicians and public servants. *International Review of Administrative Sciences*, 68, 183–198.

Sternstein, A. (2010). White House kicks off contest website to find fixes to big problems. Retrieved from http://www.nextgov.com/nextgov/ng_20100907_8987.php?oref=search

Straub, D.W., & Welke, R.J. (1998). Coping with systems risk: Security planning models for management decision making. *MIS Quarterly*, 22(4), 441–469.

Sumner, M. (2009). Information security threats: A comparative analysis of impact, probability, and preparedness. *Information Systems Management*, 26, 2–12.

Swain, J.W., White, J.D., & Hubbert, E.D. (1995). Issues in public management information systems. *American Review of Public Administration*, 25(3), 279–296.

Tavani, H.T. (1999). Informational privacy, data mining, and the Internet. *Ethics and Information Technology*, 1, 137–145.

TechAmerica. (2009). Nineteenth annual survey of federal chief information officers: Learning from the past, transitioning to the future. Retrieved from http://www.gt.com/staticfiles/ GTCom/files/Industries/GlobalPublicSector/GT_TAA_Survey2009_.pdf

Teo, T.S., Lin, S., & Lai, K.H. (2009). Adopters and non-adopters of e-procurement in Singapore: An empirical study. *Omega*, 37, 972–987.

Teo, T.S.H., Lim, G.S., & Fedric, S.A. (2007). The adoption and diffusion of human resources information systems in Singapore. *Asia Pacific Journal of Human Resources*, 45(1), 44–62.

Thomas, J.C., & Streib, G. (2005). E-democracy, e-commerce, and e-research: Examining the electronic ties between citizens and governments. *Administration and Society*, 37(3), 259–280.

Tolbert, C.J., & Mossberger, K. (2006). The effects of e-government on trust and confidence in government. *Public Administration Review*, 66(3), 354–369.

Torres, L., Pina, V., & Royo, S. (2005). E-government and the transformation of public administrations in EU counties: Beyond NPM or just a second wave of reforms? *Online Information Review*, 29(5), 531–533.

U.S. Government Accountability Office (GAO). (2003). Information technology: A framework for assessing and improving enterprise architecture management (Version 1.1). GAO Publication No. GAO-03-584G. Retrieved from http://www.gpoaccess.gov/

U.S. Government Accountability Office (GAO). (2004). Federal chief information officers: Responsibilities, reporting relationships, tenure, and challenges. GAO Publication No. GAO 04-823. Retrieved from http://www.gpoaccess.gov/

U.S. Government Accountability Office (GAO). (2005a). Veterans affairs: The role of the chief information office in effectively managing information technology, statement of Linda D. Koontz. GAO Publication No. GAO-06-201T. Retrieved December 1, 2010 from http://www.gpoaccess.gov/

U.S. Government Accountability Office (GAO). (2005b). Critical infrastructure protection: Department of Homeland Security faces challenges in fulfilling cybersecurity responsibilities. GAO Publication No. GAO-05-434. Retrieved from http://www.gpoaccess.gov/

U.S. Government Accountability Office (GAO). (2005c). Information security: Emerging cybersecurity issues threaten federal information systems. GAO Publication No. GAO-05-231. Retrieved from http://www.gpoaccess.gov/

U.S. Government Accountability Office (GAO). (2007). Elections: All levels of government are needed to address electronic voting system challenges. GAO Publication No. GAO 07-741T. Retrieved from http://www.gpoaccess.gov/

U.S. Government Accountability Office (GAO). (2008). Information security: Although progress reported, federal agencies need to resolve significant deficiencies, statement of Gregory C. Wilshusen. GAO Publication No. GAO-08-496T. Retrieved from http://www.gpoaccess.gov/

U.S. Government Accountability Office (GAO). (2010). Information technology: OMB's dashboard has increased transparency and oversight, but improvements needed. GAO Publication No. GAO 10-701. Retrieved from http://www.gpoaccess.gov/

United Nations. (2008). United Nations e-government survey 2008: From e-government to connected governance. Retrieved from http://unpan1.un.org/intradoc/groups/public/documents/UN/UNPAN028607.pdf

Vaidya, K., Sajeev, A.S., & Callender, G. (2006). Critical factors that influence e-procurement implementation success in the public sector. *Journal of Public Procurement*, 6, 70–99.

Vander Veen, C. (2009). Honolulu cuts costs with first all-digital election in the U.S. government technology: Solutions for state and local government. Retrieved from http://www.govtech.com/e-government/Honolulu-Cuts-Costs-With-First-All-Digital.html

Vander Veen, C. (2010). CIO Sam Nixon tries to fix Virginia's IT outsourcing effort. Retrieved from http://www.govtech.com/policy-management/CIO-Sam-Nixon-Tries-to-Fix.html

Veasey, P.W. (2001). Use of enterprise architectures in managing strategic change. *Business Process Management*, 7(5), 420–436.

Veiga, A.D., & Eloff, J.H. (2010). A framework and assessment instrument for information security culture. *Computers & Security*, 29, 196–207.

Volti, R. (1992). *Society and technological change* (2nd ed.). New York: St. Martin's Press.

Vroom, C., & Von Solms, R. (2004). Towards information security behavioural compliance. *Computers and Security*, 23, 191–198.

Wang, Y.-S., & Liao, Y.-W. (2008). Assessing e-government systems success: A validation of the DeLone and McLean model of information systems success. *Government Information Quarterly*, 25, 717–733.

Ward, C.J. (2006). ERP: Integrating and extending the enterprise. *Public Manager*, 35(1), 30–33.

Ward, M.A., & Mitchell, S. (2004). A comparison of the strategic priorities of public and private sector information resource management executives. *Government Information Quarterly*, 21, 284–304.

Weber, M. (1919). Bureaucracy. In H. Gerth, C. Wright, & T. Mills (Eds.), *From Max Weber: Essays in sociology* (pp. 196–244). London: Routledge.

Weerakkody, V., Janssen, M., & Hjort-Madsen, K. (2007). Integration and enterprise architecture challenges in e-government: A European perspective. *International Journal of Cases on Electronic Commerce*, 3(2), 13–35.

Weigand, S. (2010). The state of telework in the government. Retrieved December 1, 2010 from http://fcw.com/articles/2010/11/08/data-mining-telework-government.aspx

Welch, E.W., & Pandey, S.K. (2006). E-government and bureaucracy: Toward a better understanding of intranet implementation and its effect on red tape. *Journal of Public Administration Research and Theory*, 17, 379–404.

Welch, E.W., Hinnant, C.C., & Moon, M.J. (2004). Linking government satisfaction with e-government and trust in government. *Journal of Public Administration Research and Theory*, 15(3), 371–391.

West, D.M. (2004). E-government and the transformation of service delivery and citizen attitudes. *Public Administration Review*, 64(1), 15–27.

West, D.M. (2005). *Digital government: Technology and public sector performance*. Princeton, NJ: Princeton University Press.

West, J.P., & Berman, E.M. (2001a). The impact of revitalized management practices on the adoption of information technology: A national survey of local governments. *Public Performance and Management Review*, 24(3), 233–253.

West, J.P., & Berman, E.M. (2001b). From traditional to virtual HR: Is the transition occurring in local government? *Review of Public Personnel Administration*, 21(1), 38–64.

Whitman, M.E. (2004). In defense of the realm: Understanding the threats to information security. *International Journal of Information Management*, 24, 43–57.

Whittaker, B. (1999). What went wrong? Unsuccessful information technology projects. *Information Management & Computer Security*, 7(1), 23–29.

Wilkinson, K. (2010). Maryland social media campaign rules take effect. Retrieved from http://www.govtech.com/e-government/Maryland-Social-Media-Campaign-Rules-Take.html

Williams, M. (2009). Data.gov launched by federal government. Retrieved from http://www.govtech.com/pcio/Datagov-Launched-by-Federal-Government.html

Williams, M. (2010a). Is secure web-based voting a decade away? Retrieved from http://www.govtech.com/e-government/Is-Secure-Web-Based-Voting-a-Decade-Away.html

Williams, M. (2010b). Bad economy will trigger shared services wave. Retrieved from http://www.govtech.com/pcio/Bad-Economy-Will-Trigger-Shared-Services.html

Williams, M. (2010c). Google announces apps for government and security certification. Retrieved from http://www.govtech.com/pcio/Google-Announces-Apps-for-Government-and.html

Williamson, O.E. (1985). *The economic institutions of capitalism*. New York: The Free Press.

Wong, W., & Welch, E. (2004). Does e-government promote accountability? A comparative analysis of website openness and government accountability. *Governance: An International Journal of Policy, Administration, and Institutions*, 17(2), 275–297.

Wright, S. (2008). Ready my day? Communication, campaigning and councillors' blogs. *Information Polity*, 13, 81–95.

Wyld, D.C. (2009). Moving to the cloud: An introduction to cloud computing in government. Retrieved from http://www.businessofgovernment.org/report/moving-cloud-introduction-cloud-computing-government

Yeung, A., & Brockbank, W. (1995). Reengineering HR through information technology. *Human Resource Planning*, 18, 24–37.

Zachman, J.A. (1987). A framework for information systems architecture. *IBM Systems Journal*, 38, 454–470.

Index

A

access divide, digital divide, 61
access layer, enterprise architecture, 141–142
accountability
   in e-commerce, 75
   in e-governance, 75, 81–82
   online financial reporting and, 174
acquisition cost, e-procurement and total, 166–167
adaptation model of e-government, 126
administrative discretion, e-government impact on, 131–132
administrative reform, IT and, 120–121
agenda setting stage of policymaking, 62
Aldridge, Richard, 133
all-digital elections, 42–43
analysis stage of policymaking, 62
Apps, Google, 156
Army Second Life, 179–180
Armystrongstories.com, 179–180

B

biometric scanning, 199–200
Bling Nation, 177–178
BlingTag, 177–178
blogs
   for e-democracy, 32–33
   e-participation and, 66
   textual nature of, 32
Bloomberg, Michael, 73
bookmarking. See social bookmarking and tagging
bot-network operators, 216

bureaucracy
   computing and, 117–119
   decreasing dysfunctional, 121–122
   e-government from, 119
   ICT and, 117
   NPM combined with, 121–123
   red tape and, 118
   strengthening, 122
Bush, George W., 37, 100–101

C

campaign websites, 25–26
   evolution of, 26
Canada, digital divide in, 61
cataloging, e-procurement, 163–164
Center for Digital Government, Digital Counties award, 133
centralization, 120
Challenge.gov, 45–46
chief information officer (CIO)
   challenges facing, 104–105
   federal government characteristics of, 107–108
   of public sector organization and leadership, 97–98
   in public sector organization compared to private sector organization, 106
   responsibilities of, 105–106
citizen relationship management (CiRM), 90–91
citizens, e-governance and, 81–82;
   See also e-participation
civic engagement
   of Americans, 53–54
   by demographics, 54–56